THE
QUICKENING

TODAY'S TRENDS,
TOMORROW'S WORLD

Art Bell

Editor: Jennifer L. Osborn

PAPER CHASE PRESS
New Orleans, Louisiana

THE
QUICKENING

TODAY'S TRENDS,
TOMORROW'S WORLD

Copyright © 1997 Art Bell

ISBN: 1-879706-70-9
LC: 97-065695

Photo credits: Cover photo, Frank Rossotto, The Stock
Exchange; Art Bell photo, Clint Karlson

PAPER CHASE PRESS
5721 Magazine Street, Suite 152
New Orleans, Louisiana 70115

Printed in the United States

For my son, Arthur W. Bell, IV

and

*For all the other sons and daughters
we have hopes for who will live the
future of the Quickening*

Contents

WARNING:

The following material may not be suitable for those of you not prepared to face the realities of the future. These may seem like isolated snapshots of some far-off world. In truth, they are all symptoms of the same cause:

The Quickening

Sometime in the Future

A tremendous explosion ripped through the basement parking garage of the World Trade Center in Manhattan. Windows of nearby buildings blasted shrapnel onto the streets below. Cars hurtled into each other as the debris smashed through drivers windows, and screams of terror and police sirens filled the air. The elusive terrorist leader known only as "Jacque" had expertly wired the C-14 plastic explosives to the detonation device only moments earlier before blowing himself up, believing that he would be rewarded in heaven by Allah.

In her Austin, Texas condominium, Monica stared at her HD television panel, horrified as she saw this destruction live on CNN. She remembered years ago when a bomb went off at the World Trade Center— only this looked much worse. The CNN reporter, ducking to avoid bits of glass still littering from the ruined buildings, said this was the third terrorist bombing in the past month. First there was the PanAm flight over Singapore, then the massive destruction of St. Peter's Cathedral in London,

England.   Both cases were explosions by suicide terrorists.

To Monica, the world was coming unglued.

She watched the next story, unwillingly transfixed, feeling the ball of terror spinning and growing in her guts. On the screen, in graphic detail, police shot at people barricaded in a house. They sent in SWAT commandos to break through the roof. The people were resisters, who did not want to register and receive the Global Identification Chip implant. Without the chip, you could not buy anything; you could not even go to the doctor. Monica lifted her hand up and examined it; there was no trace of the chip, but it was definitely there. She had not hesitated, but groups of people throughout the world did, and they were meeting an overwhelming and violent response to their protests.

Ω   Ω   Ω

Dr. Maurice Rolland raced to the Pasteur Hospital in Paris escorted by police. He was met by a frantic group of doctors and nurses at the emergency entrance. Several patients had been admitted in the past 24 hours. They were illegal immigrants from Algeria, just a handful of the virtual flood of Algerians entering France and Germany in recent weeks, fleeing renewed political unrest in their country.

These patients were a code red. Dr. Rolland was sweating even as he donned his germ proof suit and entered the room. Two patients must have just died. The remaining Algerians lay on the beds in the vicious grasp of something he had never thought he would see in his lifetime. Grotesque buboes and puss-filled boils covered the faces, hands and arms of these men, everything that was not hidden by the sheet—and Dr. Rolland could imagine the rest well enough. The dead stared vacantly as blood from their severely hemorrhaged organs dripped from their open mouths. The more Dr. Rolland looked, the faster his heart beat, the terror stealing his breath, the knowledge of the imminent future dawning on him. He had known that more diseases were re-emerging, but this...this was unthinkable. The very thing that had massacred huge numbers of people in Europe centuries ago had returned—the Black Death, the bubonic plague.

Ω   Ω   Ω

Introduction

Look around. Is the world you live in the same friendly, welcoming place it was when the latest craze was a television in every home? When flappers danced their troubles away? Or even when people gathered together in a small western town to celebrate the dedication of a church? Can you walk down the middle of a moonlit alley with your loved ones and not have a shadow of worry cross your mind? Can you work hard for one company, safe in the knowledge that your hard work and loyalty will be rewarded with years of security? Can you draw a breath of air or take a long drink of water without being concerned whether it is pure or whether it is carrying some new germ?

I know that if you are honest with yourself, you will acknowledge that the answer is *no*. The world is *not* the same, *not* a place to feel safe in. Events and faces whirl around us at the speed of light, passing us by on the highways, or on the nightly news. We live in an age of speed, of change. We live in the world of the Quickening. The very foundations of our society shift under our feet like sand on a troubled shore.

Our Technological Heart

One blink of the eye and the technology of today is outdated. That Pentium computer you saved for so long to buy? Old news—replaced by a smaller, pocket-sized version with a crystal instead of a flat silicon chip. Yes, technology, the backbone of our world, is on the increase: computers, electronics, fiber optics, satellites, HD television and more are becoming commonplace.

And not only do these technological advances directly affect the way we live, play, work, think, and, most significantly, interact with each other, but they have a direct influence upon the world economic base. Instead of manufacturing, our world is focusing on the accumulation, dissemination, and use of data and information. There seems to be no way to put the brakes on this rushing train. Is this something to be excited about or should we proceed with caution?

Creating Wealth

If I said to you, in the future, there will be no banks and no cash, you would probably heave a great sigh of relief at the prospect of not having to wait in any more long lines to deposit a Friday paycheck. It is not a fantasy. We are moving toward this as a reality, in our lifetimes. How? Technology again! If you have been to a US Bank recently, you may have seen that you can go online with a bank representative at any hour of the day and handle a transaction or get a question answered. You tap a key and a modem automatically connects you to a person whose face appears on the screen in real time.

The exchange of money and products between people and countries is more fluid and rapid than ever before. As a consequence, nation-state geopolitical boundaries are dissolving. They who hold the money hold the power, whether it manifests itself in global economy or global government—maybe both. Are we confident this is the direction in which we want to go?

Personal Power

Quite naturally, the increasing and undeniable influence of global commerce has and will continue to exert an effect upon the world political scene. The importance of *national* politics is clearly on the decline. Widespread dissatisfaction with major parties and leading political candidates has fostered an extremely high level of public disillusionment and cynicism toward government. And it's not limited to just America.

As local regions of nations become more economically, socially and culturally independent and participate more freely in global trade, national sovereignty wanes. Because we are moving toward a global economy, politicians will have little or no influence upon the actions of constituents, and because the money that people make is coming from all parts of the world, there is little reason to feel allegiance to a particular country.

Despite recent and ongoing global technological and economic strides, war has not become a thing of the past. If anything, wars have flared up in some areas of the world with increasing frequency and without an immediate end or resolution in sight. You are all familiar with the hot spots in Bosnia, the tension between Israel and her Middle East neighbors, eruptions between former states of the Soviet Union, continuing turbulence among nation-states in Africa and countless other similar situations. But the most frightening of all warfare, and perhaps the most difficult to combat is terrorism, particularly from religious zealots, yielding murderous strikes worldwide.

Moreover, is there really an end to the arms race and a reduced threat of nuclear war? I don't think so. We may have left our fears from the early 1980s behind, but there are just as many nuclear warheads now as during the Cold War. Surprised? There's more. Now dangerous groups and nations have access to nuclear devices who did not before. Thus, we may embrace political autonomy, but how do we address ongoing war and strife in this world? Is there a solution?

Social Turbulence

Perhaps the saddest changes in the world today are those reflected by society. Things have gotten worse and worse in a snowball effect. I believe one of the largest factors is the decline and breakdown of the family, especially the "traditional" family unit as we have always known it. We see increased drug use and violence, higher statistics of rape and murder, climbing divorce rates, an unprecedented number of gangs and many other pressing social problems.

In America, we have our own terrorism to fear as militia movements seek to reclaim the country on the basis of their own, often contorted social views. The broader things become on an economic and political front, the more people will struggle for their individual identities. Advanced forms of communication such as online chat rooms and video telephones will further isolate people.

So you can see that people will be simultaneously increasing their communication with other people from the privacy of their own homes at the same time that population growth continues to explode all over the planet. As we are forced to live closer and closer together, there will be an increased intolerance for each other, not unlike rats in a cage; we will be intolerant of people in our space, people who do not think the same way we do, people whose skin or religious belief is different from ours. Our social problems seem insurmountable, but is it possible that we could logically and carefully turn things around?

Age of Narcissism

People everywhere in the world realize that material items cannot quench the deep emptiness within them. As they search for something to make life meaningful, there is increased exploration of the paranormal, the supernatural, ufology, psychic powers, shamanism, and New Age thinking; the traditional Judeo-Christian practices and ideologies are being replaced. Worldwide, there has been an increase in reported spiritual or metaphysical experiences. Of course, the way people interpret all these events has everything to do with their very deepest beliefs about life and the nature of reality, about good and evil, about God, about morality, and about mankind's origin and destiny. Where are these trends in spirituality leading us?

17

Our Struggling Ecosystem

Remember when everyone "suddenly" realized you couldn't "throw things away" because there was no "away"? The new mentality became use and reuse. The environment has, understandably, become an increasing concern. Huge gaps have appeared in the ozone, we have ongoing befouling of fresh water with chemicals (it is easier and cheaper for a company to pay a fine than rebuild their factories to higher standards), the burning of rain forests, landfills over capacity—all this only bears tribute to the high price we exact for our use of the earth.

While we have become more efficient in the use of our natural resources and the manufacturing of the products we need, we still have not solved the nagging problem of how to get rid of our waste. We have thought of burying it, burning it, shooting it into space, dumping it into our bodies of water; none of these are effective methods of dealing with something that is more than just a short term problem. Are there solutions to this curse or is humanity destined to drown in its own mire?

Coming Plagues

With our ever growing numbers, we are encroaching on areas in the world where, until now, deadly viruses and bacteria have been existing quietly. Now the growing specter of new viruses such as Ebola, hanta, and AIDS, combined with the re-emergence of old diseases such as leukemia, malaria, and even bubonic plague, are killing people by the millions. Today's medicine, advanced though it may be, can easily fall prey to the insidious tendency of a virus to mutate into an antibiotic-resistant form. We have disturbed these microcosms; they are now fighting back, reminding us we are not the all-powerful rulers of the earth we imagine ourselves to be. Can we effectively defend ourselves?

Hunger Pangs

It is difficult for us in America to imagine what it is like to go without food. And yet, even though we have become so efficient at producing food that we are capable of feeding the world, millions are still starving. Much of Africa, India, and various parts of Russia, Bulgaria and Romania are starving because of exploding populations, ongoing political unrest, drought and plague. It is political turmoil over the course of the last ten years that has resulted in the worst famines in human history. In Africa alone, the World Bank estimates that over 100 million people are without adequate food supply. I remember when there was a cruel joke about finishing your food because there were starving people in the world. Is there anything we can really do to help?

Our Tumultuous Planet

Noticed anything unusual about the weather patterns around the world lately? Perhaps more extremes: hotter weather here, colder than ever there? More hurricanes hitting the coast near your city than in all of history, more tropical storms brewing in the island chains, more tornadoes violently tossing houses, cars and the like aside? Floods in dry areas where the ground can't soak the water in fast enough and droughts where people are accustomed to a generous rainfall? Even the earth beneath our feet is exhibiting unusual changes with an unprecedented number of earthquakes and heightened volcanic activity, often in places not used to, or prepared for such trends. Why is there this increase in natural disasters? Are there effective measures we can take to prepare ourselves?

The Quickening Defined

Nearly every aspect of life in every part of our world is accelerating, changing, *quickening.* Over the years, as I noted things blurring by at a faster and faster pace, I coined the term, "the Quickening," to describe the overall movement. To merely list the various elements involved is to oversimplify a significant and integral part of our lives in this world today. Instead, I want you to be able to relate to it personally. I want you to see how it indeed does affect *you* in a very tangible way. As we look at ourselves in terms of the path we have traveled through history and the world we live in today, every person must realize that we are rushing toward a new existence, or they are simply deluding themselves.

Earliest Signs of the Quickening

The Quickening is not something that just emerged from nowhere. Looking back through the tunnel of world history, we can see that it has a definite beginning, and has gained strength over time, becoming more and more apparent.

In a way, you might think of the Quickening as a pot of cold water on a fire. After a while, the water becomes warm and bubbles begin to form. You can actually count the bubbles. Eventually you see more and more bubbles, forming more and more quickly. As the temperature rises, the bubbles overwhelm your ability to count them. The water reaches a hot, roaring boil. I think in terms of this analogy, we may be on the verge of a roaring boil. But the temperature is still rising.

The Past on Fast Forward

Civilization had its origin about five thousand years ago. But it was not until the fifteenth century that global exploration began and murmurs of the Quickening could be heard. What made the change? The answer is technological advances, which in turn yielded economic and political advances. We take for granted all the inventions that we live with on a day to day basis, but the truth is, everything from electric lights to automobiles is an intrinsic piece of the structure. With the invention of anything significant, it is as if we were at a fork in the road and chose one direction over the other, forever changing our lives.

Since technology is essentially the driving force behind the Quickening, it naturally follows that, historically, the Industrial Revolution was a crucial turning point. This marked a place where the Quickening gained speed in leaps and bounds, advances and events whirling by us much like a hailstorm.

Europe's textile industry taught the world much about the techniques of organization and mass production, but what is even more interesting is that so many technological creations occurred in response to the textile industry. It may not surprise you to learn that the countries involved in the textile industry were the most prosperous in the world at that time, including Western Europe and later America. What will come as somewhat of a shock, though, is that by the dawn of the twentieth century, a mere twenty-five European nations controlled eighty-four percent of the world's land mass. For a relatively small group of nations, that kind of power is certainly a Quickening of world events.

The Invention Fast Track

Americans like to think of themselves as a dominant world power and, for the most part, we have been. It was the late nineteenth and early twentieth centuries that brought a shift in industry and commerce as America's participation became more pronounced. The United States patent office opened in 1860 and in less than 30 years, an astounding 440,000 patents were recorded! That phone you have at your side? That came about in 1876 along with its companion, AT&T or "Ma Bell." The light you are reading by? Thomas Edison can take credit for that in 1879. Your pride and joy out in the driveway? Henry Ford built his first in 1896, and in 1914 turned out half a million cars. Tired of the long wait at the airport? You wouldn't be if the Wrights had not flown their first airplane only three years into the twentieth century.

When Abraham Lincoln was elected in 1860, America was fourth among manufacturing nations; by 1900, we were number one. It should be obvious that these high speed technological advances shaped what America and the rest of the world is today.

Early Negative Signs

Unfortunately, as with today's world events, many past trends of the Quickening are negative. American social change is perhaps the most apparent. We had the same problems around the beginning of the twentieth century that we do as we approach the twenty-first century, only on a slightly smaller scale.

Burgeoning City Life

Ever wondered why cities have exploded into being and grown so robustly? Urban life was fostered by people seeking to live near their jobs. By 1900, about one-third of the American population lived in cities, a trend that only continues. City living probably sounded very attractive to rural people and foreigners; the prospect of electric lights, central heating, public water systems, indoor plumbing..., well, you get the picture.

The problem is an obvious one: millions wanted to enjoy these luxuries all at once. The result? Americans and immigrants alike crowded into cities, creating low wages, long hours, and the exploitation of child labor. Living conditions, as you can imagine in a densely populated city with a shortage of decent living space, were wretched. In addition, congested cities, such as the three million person New York of 1900 became the perfect breeding grounds for increased violence.

In today's world, it is becoming more and more frequent to see a single mother or father raising a family. Reported cases of domestic abuse are on the rise, whereas, until the woman's suffrage movement of the 1880s, women had remained silent. You are aware that we live in an age of divorce; looking back, we can see that the trend started around a hundred years ago. In 1890, one in seventeen marriages ended in divorce; by 1930, the rate was one in five, and of course, today it is one in two. This was the first sign of a coming breakdown in the traditional family unit.

Early Environmental Concerns

Creative minds were hard at work during the American Industrial Revolution. The one thing no one thought of was the unbelievable pollution that new industries would create. Various smokestack industries poked the skies, pouring out their chemicals and smoke into the air and into the water. Meanwhile, other industries stripped the earth of its resources, often leaving vast areas barren and wasted.

Ironically, the largest industries, with the most employees, were the biggest sources of pollution: oil refineries, steel mills, auto makers, lumber mills and more all contributed. Most still do, shamelessly disposing of their wastes without a thought of the consequences. So you see that this is not a new concept that the environmentalists have been up in arms against.

The Pinocchio Government

Until the American Industrial Revolution, the government was based upon the ideal that businesses should be allowed to build business with little interference from government regulations or taxes. After all, that was what America was supposed to be all about—work hard and make your dream come true. The large business owners established what were called "trusts" to control and protect all aspects of their industries. In other words, they were self-regulating.

The institution of the Sherman Anti-Trust Act of 1890 put an end to the self-regulation of business and was truly the beginning of increased government intervention in business. More intervention, more government—this is historically a negative trend.

Earth Changes in History

During the course of several hundred years of recorded history, there are few written accounts of dramatic earth changes. I suspect volcanoes and earthquakes were few and far between. However, it is clear, especially in recent times, that there is a definite increase in natural disasters. If we turn our gaze back through history, we see only a few major earthquakes near the beginning of the nineteenth century and the San Francisco earthquake of 1906. Other than that, the world seemed to exist peacefully without such disturbances. Today not only the quantity but the extreme nature of such earth events is apparent. Could it be that there is a connection between man's creations and earth's events?

Facing Reality

I have started with a thumbnail sketch of the rushing torrent of events surrounding us. But to understand what is going on, and perhaps draw some meaningful conclusions, you must study these events individually and collectively. You must decide what, if anything, can be done. And if nothing else, each of us must conclude for ourselves how we can come to terms with our own personal reality of the Quickening.

I can only think that people who are not open to the fact that there are blatant changes taking place want to bury their heads in the sand and hope that everything will be wonderful. This is a mistake. A common awareness could bring about change, but then, maybe not. However, I have always believed that knowing is better than not knowing. This book is intended for those who want to know—for those who want to look at what is going on and come to their own conclusions about what it all means.

1

Technology

Through infrared binoculars, Ishmael could see the movements of several thousand Lebanese Hezbollah troops crossing the Golan Heights. This only confirmed the satellite photos he observed on the high resolution monitor strapped to his wrist. Around him, his men jittered in place as they waited for their commander's decision. "So it has come to this," Ishmael whispered. His orders were to strike first. He relayed this to his men, who watched his troubled face over their personal monitors. "Launch, and may God be with us."

Within minutes, several softball-sized bombs were launched. Through his binoculars, Ishmael gasped as he saw a bright flash and a deep, grumbling roar. The same men he had been watching advance a moment before now lit up, and for a split second, he could see through them like looking through an x-ray. Their flesh evaporated with the force of the neutron bombs, so quickly that they became standing skeletons before crumbling to the ground in heaps. A pervasive silence stole over the land.

Ω   Ω   Ω

Twelve year old Scott Atwood stood fascinated as a parade of gold prospectors and their pack mules trudged through ankle deep mud in the streets of Nevada City, California. The small town was bustling with activity and noise. Suddenly, he heard gun fire from behind him. Two men were arguing and one shot the other. Scott felt his breath come more rapidly; this was getting a little too dangerous! He pointed his finger to a hulking black steam locomotive, leaving the gold rush of 1849, and instantly traveling back in time to late eighteenth century Europe. Here he learned just how the steam engine and early passenger trains had come about, a passenger for a few moments on the way to Scotland.

Scott was amazed at all that had happened in Europe and America. He came to appreciate more fully the technical innovations of the past, the courage of early American settlers, and the adventures of the miners in gold-crazy California. Sighing happily, he removed the virtual reality body suit and went out to meet his friends for a game of baseball.

Ω   Ω   Ω

What a delight it is to sit down in front of a computer screen and chat with people all over the world. What fun it is to become engrossed in a three dimensional computer game for hours and hours. How wonderful it is to be hooked up to a satellite television system that pipes in hundreds of games of your favorite sport. But technology is more than just entertainment.

In the past, advances in technology have served as the impetus for far-reaching change; we are propelled forward, and our lives are changed forever. Technology is the difference between where we are now and the path not taken. Not only is technology an important example of how aspects of the Quickening overlap and affect each other, much like a patchwork quilt, but technology is the *core* of the Quickening.

The Power of War

When did all this high-powered knowledge really start to exert itself on the world? In fact, it was the forty years encompassing World Wars I and II that marked a quantum leap in scientific and technological developments; more advances were made in this brief period of history than in all the years of history to that point.

Considering the drastic events of the time, perhaps it is not a surprise that the three most notable technologies—and arguably the most influential upon the time in which we are living—were those of the world's first rockets, computers, and atomic bombs. Without the world wars, technologies we take for granted could have taken much longer to materialize. Because of these wars, technologies came together simultaneously and complimented other concurrent technologies. In other words, things came together in a way similar to three people starting at different places in a city and arriving at a destination at the same time.

Bombs Away

A nuclear bomb is the most ominous technology in existence today. Ironic, isn't it? We created a threat which originally was intended to protect us, but because others have acquired the technology, this threat hangs over the heads of every person in the world. Nuclear weaponry really had its start with the discovery of x-rays in 1895. Quickly after that, radioactivity was found in uranium, and nuclear physics theory was well underway. All this science established the ground work for the atomic bomb.

Between the two world wars, scientists discovered excitedly that they could split atoms (which is nuclear fission). It dawned on them that such energy could be harnessed in two ways: to generate something positive like electricity and to generate something destructive like an atomic bomb.

Under the orders of President Franklin Delano Roosevelt, the best nuclear physicists of the 1940s built the first atomic bomb; it took about three years and an exhaustive effort to produce two bombs, and of course, you all know the purpose. World War II came to an abrupt end with the Hiroshima and Nagasaki bombs, the precursors to today's nuclear weapons.[1]

One of the ways in which America chose to use its nuclear energy was in submarines, driven by nuclear turbine power. By 1957, these subs carried more than just navy men; they were equipped with nuclear tipped missiles called ICBMs, or intercontinental ballistic missiles. Guided by computers, the ICBM brought rocket and nuclear technology together, creating another reason for countries all over the world to glance worriedly at their coasts that before had seemed impenetrable.

Rocketing Into Space

Rockets were not only used for propelling bombs. Pioneering space is another example of the Quickening: from the moment it was determined that rockets should exist to the time that man walked on the moon, a mere thirty-seven years elapsed. In the meantime, of course, we have put space stations into orbit which have enhanced our telecommunications abilities, as well as our capacity for weather forecasts, mineralogical and geological surveys of the earth. Thus, the science of rocketry is not an entirely negative one; we have progressed further in our goal to communicate with the world quickly and conveniently.

The Arms Wrestle: America vs. Russia

From the ashes of the world wars, two distinct superpowers emerged: America and the Soviet Union. Each of us applied our economic, geopolitical and technological dominance to create a checkmate known as the Cold War. Each country was particularly compelled to match each other in nuclear weaponry, developed quite naturally from the labors of the atomic bomb scientists.

This arms race is a strange, ironic reflection of some of humanity's most awe-inspiring achievements in technology, and yet is the very thing that could spell doom for humanity. Yes, the former Soviets promised to dismantle their nuclear weapons, but what they really did was dismantle them and replace old technology with new. The onboard guidance systems of these missiles are more precise, and the missiles are faster with a longer range; this does not bode well for anyone in the world today. Further, we no longer have just one nuclear enemy; dangerous countries with hot-headed, religiously fervent leaders such as Iran and Iraq have gleaned nuclear technology from the lowest bidder. Instead of less nuclear threat, there is more.

The human mind is virtually fail-safed. We can only worry about so much at once. Perhaps that is why we are able to go to sleep each night without giving the possibility of nuclear exchange much thought. In the 1980s, I remember a movie called "The Day After," a gripping, horrific take on what the world would be like in the aftermath of nuclear war. The fear level seemed intense then, but as humans, it is in our nature to push things down from our level of daily awareness. Now, more than ever, we need to be aware of the inherent dangers of a world that still presents a nuclear threat, as far away as it may seem.

Information Express

We live in an information age. Everywhere you go, the brightly flickering lights of televisions are seen, whether it's an airport, a sports bar, or someone plugged into a generator in the middle of the woods. Radio is another medium through which information is exchanged, and the equipment is following the trends of today and becoming more powerful in a smaller package. Information technology exists all around us: from the bar code reader at the grocery store to a greeting card maker at Hallmark to a washer and dryer to a VCR that does everything *but* wash the clothes. Undoubtedly, though, the central technological advance is the computer; in fact, a computer or computer chip is behind every one of the technologies I just mentioned.

Did you know that a man named Charles Babbage actually attempted to introduce the computer to an unwilling world about 160 years ago? It was not until 1934 and beyond that computer technology began to quicken and accelerate. First the Germans, then the British and finally the Americans developed a simple binary code computer—and as you can imagine, it took up a whole room with all its metal and cables! The late 1940s saw a move into vacuum tubes, replaced in 1953 by transistors, and the integrated circuit took its place in the 1960s. So, in less than thirty years, the basic approach to the computer was established.

A Computer in Every Home

The computer's role in the Quickening entered another significant period of change in the late 1970s and early 1980s. The Macintosh computer and IBM's PC have since been rivaled by many competitors clones, much less costly with virtually the same features. And the wonder of it is, the technology is advancing so quickly that the next generation of computers becomes half as big and twice as fast about every eighteen months. The prices also tend to drop every six months so that it is now possible for more people to either own or lease a computer.

Forecasters of trends in computer technology foresee the day, perhaps in the early twenty-first century, when computers will be so small and powerful, they will be integrated into our lives much like hearing aids or eye wear are today. It is also more than likely that the new versions will be combinations of tele-phones, computers and television, or video.

Web Crawling

Nowhere is the computer's role in the Quickening more obvious than on the Internet. As computers become an increasingly integral part of our lives, we realize that the computer is not just a tool to improve the way we do business, learn, or amuse ourselves, but is a real way to connect with the rest of the world. How is this achieved? As with the Internet, for example, a *network* is used; you basically have a "hub" and people dialing in on their computer mo-dems become "spokes" into that hub. Thus you are sitting in a virtual "city" with thousands of other peo-ple and you wander around going from building to building or room to room, each of which presents new people or new information.

The Internet, funded and created in the late 1970s by the American government, was originally intended to link colleges and universities as a means to facili-tate the exchange of ideas and research between academics and scientists. Electronic or "E" mail graduated to real time chat, enabling users to not only access remote data, but also to communicate with others all over the world.[2]

No one imagined the Internet would become what it is today. It has since evolved to span the world as the World Wide Web, and tens of millions of users ac-cess it daily. The most popular networks are com-mercial, such as America Online and Prodigy; they are well organized and make access to the informa-tion highway easier.

A Shared Interest Internet

The Internet is a major factor in the Quickening. What other "invention," we'll call it, will consistently enable people to avoid physical contact with the outside world, yet simultaneously interact with more people than you could meet or pass in a month walking down the street? Want a magazine or newspaper? Simply find the appropriate address and browse for hours, read articles, view color photos. Christmas rush got you worn out? Sit down in the comfort of your home and take care of everyone on your list in no time at all, without fighting those crowds or waiting in line.

The Internet will allow people to do library research, check government databases, read reviews, and more. Or you can chat with people who share the same interests as yours. Are you a horse person? A computer game fanatic? Like to cook or sew? There are places for you and everyone online. Academic and scientific researchers can meet and exchange ideas and plans online. If a scientist at Tulane University has a new method of studying cancer, the global scientific and medical research community will know about it immediately, making it more quickly beneficial.

Low Cost & Access For All

If you are wondering, well, that's fine if you speak English, but what about the people who only speak their native language? NEC, the Japanese firm, is one of several companies to anticipate that very question, and have introduced an instant online translator. So if you run into a Japanese person online, your English is automatically translated into

Japanese and vice versa. Similarly, there is a voice technology on the market that enables non-typing users to simply dictate messages to their computer, or even script technology that allows a written message to be converted to digital text. Advances such as these will encourage many more people from all walks of life to go online.

The number of online users is increasing exponentially. By 1999, more than 300 million users are expected to access the Internet daily. By 2001, the forecast is for in excess of one billion users. Dropping costs for computers and telephone charges have a lot to do with this unbelievable growth. In fact, having a computer will soon be as commonplace as having a VCR or toaster, and the cost of using it will be just pennies.[3]

The significance of the Internet and computers, as the Quickening continues, is the many ways in which they will affect all aspects of our lives. Imagine not sweating and swearing your way through morning traffic. Imagine the farthest you have to go is from your bed to your computer monitor in your home office. Imagine banking, investing, and shopping now online, soon within virtual reality. Imagine your child in a virtual classroom, interacting in a way he or she might never have had the opportunity to in a traditional classroom, able to literally "experience" history through the Internet. Can't get away for that weekend fishing trip? Try a new three dimensional fishing download or virtual reality fishing, getting back in time for a productive day of work, in front of your computer of course.

Nanotechnology

A fascinating example of how computers, science and technology are interconnected is nanotechnology, what can very basically be defined as "bottom-up" manufacturing. Nanotechnology is one of the most cutting edge technologies of today, with the potential to conceivably dwarf all factors of our lives. This involves molecular construction and the precise placement of each atom.

The fact that any manufactured product could be dramatically improved has everyone getting in on the research game with a bang; for instance, the Japanese have committed more than $200 million to a ten year development program for specific applications of nanotechnology. Some have speculated that nanotechnology could create a world in which there was no starvation, that a "food machine" in every house would take in any kind of organic material and push out steak or rice on command. Sound incredible? How about a world in which people need never die as every damaged cell is repaired instantly by a team of "nano craft" inside your veins and arteries?

It should be no surprise that the interest level is so high. Twentieth century science and engineering is focused on an ever-increasing understanding of the universe on a smaller and smaller scale—from electronics and computers to biotechnology and drug design; all the while we are creeping ever closer to unlocking magic at the atomic level.

How does this tie into computers? A great deal of nanoengineering has already been done on the computer; Eric Drexler, the world's first Ph.D. in nanotechnology, and others have come up with extensive designs for what are essentially molecular "replicators." Obviously, we must ask ourselves, "Do we have the wisdom to handle this?" It raises a lot of ethical concerns about creating and controlling artificial life. Clearly, crossing the potential threshold of nanotechnology would have far reaching socioeconomic implications for generations to come. Nanotechnology is one exciting and also scary example of our progression through the Quickening.

Computers—A Way of Life

You can see that everything in our lives will be affected in some way by the advances of computers and the networks upon which we are setting the new structure of society. But this is only the beginning. Our attitudes toward computers will change as we learn to accept these devices literally as extensions of ourselves, and this will prepare us for the astounding changes, positive and negative, in the near future.

Telecommunication Domination

Computers play a primary role in another important facet of The Quickening: telecommunications. Telecommunications will take us to an unprecedented level of sophistication and integration of technology in our lives. What is telecommunications? Essentially, it encompasses several fields of technology including telephones, television, computers, consumer electronics and satellites. Around the turn of the twentieth century, telecommunications began with the telephone combined with early electronics. This yielded wireless telegraphy, or the radio.

Telecommunications evolved very quickly in much the same way as computers and atomic weapons. The technology for radar and television emerged by

the late 1930s and after 1945, the Japanese minia-
turization of electronics gave birth to consumer electronics. Rocket technology combined with the
"brains" of a computer had satellites orbiting the
earth in the 1950s. Historically, we have been driven
to find ways to communicate faster and easier with
each other.

Wireless Wonders, Fiber Optic Fantasies

One of the biggest limitations of our constant companion, the telephone, is not being able to *see* the
person we are talking to. The not-too-distant future
will bring what may be called "teleputers,"
"picocomputers," and PAS (personal assistant system) devices, all equipped with video capability; you
can see by the very names that the emphasis will be
on smallness. These handy, inexpensive gizmos will
be highly powerful computer/wireless video phones
with which the user can send and receive data, voice,
image, or video in any language, to anyone, anywhere. Already many businesses have invested in
the available video phone technology and PC-based
conferencing systems. The use of satellites and the
Internet for this very thing will become commonplace.

An advantage of technological advances is that the
more there are, the less costly they become for us as
consumers. In our changing world, fiber optic cables
will replace more expensive copper wiring, not only
reducing the cost of laying the cables, but in fact
handling a hundred times the number of calls. In
addition, the significant increase in transmission
clarity provided by fiber optics has resulted in a
higher volume of usage. In turn, long distance calls
are cheaper, and they are poised for an even sharper

downward spiral. Fiber optics also make it possible for clear video images to be transmitted.[4]

Jumping In

Thus far, companies have been specialists in their given technology: AT&T in telephones and satellites, Sony with television and other electronic consumer products, Apple with computers, and so on. But now we are beginning to see a crossover. Even these mega-companies recognize that they cannot create and market products in a vacuum; they must learn to cooperate and compete at the same time in order to stay at the forefront of changing technology and its exploding market. Either that or smaller, versatile entrepreneurial companies will eagerly spring up to profit from this burgeoning market.

All the big players such as Motorola, AT&T, Sony and Apple, wisely conglomerating in many cases, realize that these products must address individual consumers rather than being directed solely toward business applications. The path of the future for these companies is directly related to the needs of the individual, as diverse and varied as we all are. Systems like these personal phone/computer devices will create a more independent, autonomous individual by eliminating much of the "spinning your wheels" syndrome. High tech companies are anticipating this need and are becoming better focused on the way life is changing in the Quickening.

For example, more and more people will do their shopping online. This has only been possible with a combination of telephone and computer technology, creating cyber malls; later you will see this evolve into virtual reality experiences complete with head or full body gear. You can access and wander through aisles filled with greeting cards, skis, books, airline destinations, and much more. As more and more people accept the ease and convenience of using time- and effort-saving personal devices, the demand for such products will increase.

Virtual Reality

I have mentioned virtual reality many times because that is the direction we are headed in. Virtual reality, sometimes called "cyber space," will make the phrase "reach out and touch someone" not just a cliché, but a daily occurrence. Virtual reality is the closest anyone can get to having a physical, three-dimensional experience without actually doing it. Sounds confusing and complicated, but it isn't.

Virtual reality, as we have come to understand it, is basically a machine simulating the experience that we as humans would have walking down a street, looking through a rack full of dresses, playing a video game; this technology lifts you from your place in real time and enables you to engage in multiple experiences without leaving your chair. How is this possible? It's all done in a three-dimensional computer graphics environment to which the user is connected with special headgear, eyepieces and sensory gloves.

On perhaps a more practical level, with virtual reality, engineers and architects are able to "construct" buildings and "walk" through them; in this way, they are able to inspect for structural weaknesses, or get an idea of what a certain architectural feature would look like before investing the time and money of their client. A more controversial use involves sensory

41

suits, which some say could create "cyber sex" and other full body experiences.[5]

For something less frivolous, surgeons could use virtual reality to see a three-dimensional image of organs and tissue to assist in more precise surgical procedures. Obviously, as with any powerful technology, virtual reality has the potential of being used for the good of humanity or to its detriment.

Go Clone Yourself!

The recent developments in genetic engineering are yet another example of the amazing and frightening technological advances of our time. For years, it was known that we could theoretically take the basic genetic components of life, DNA, and replicate that, recreating another organism, maybe even a person. In other words, scientists could take tissue cells from a few scrapings of my skin, derive the DNA from those scrapings and theoretically produce another Art Bell duplicate, or "clone." Only recently, has this reached beyond theory.

The Roslin Institute and PPL Therapeutics in Britain boast of having been the first group of scientists to have successfully cloned a sheep. In this case, the nucleus (the center of a cell) was extracted from adult cells, cultured in vitro and injected into the egg of a surrogate mother sheep. The mother sheep eventually birthed a healthy lamb genetically identical to the sheep from which the cells were derived. At this point, scientists can now apply this technology to clone people.

Not everyone in the world is pleased with the idea of cloning. Many people reject the idea of cloning as man's attempt to play God. They charge that, despite any potential positive results, it is unnatural to manipulate and control genetic material to create the desires of individual man. Richard Nicolson of the *Bulletin of Medical Ethics* commented that cloning could be the undoing of the human species, and to pursue it further could be like "sowing the seeds of our destruction." Of course, it is entirely likely that this technology could fall into the wrong hands. Thus, cloning is yet another serious issue our troubled world cannot ignore as just another curious piece of news.[6]

How Does All This Affect Me?

These are just a few examples of the Quickening technology. It may be difficult for you to imagine that any of these changes mean anything to you, but I assure you, they do exist and will continue to play a dominant role in our lifetime.

With all of the progress in telecommunications, chances are people will become more independent because much of what they do now out in the "real" world will be accomplished online. Errands that may mean packing you and your children into the car to get done will take a few keystrokes and a lot less stress! You won't spend the time and energy that you used to performing such mundane tasks as shopping, banking, paying bills, or even commuting to work.

Yes, I can see a smile on your face as you realize that you will spend more and more time in your cherished private space—your home. The fact is, many more of us will be doing our work at home. Does this mean we will be interacting less with people? No. Probably the opposite. People are still gre-

garious by nature and will want to identify themselves with other people. We will go online to find
others with similar interests in chat rooms, and seek
to group with them, "hang out," if you will. In some
cases, we will actually meet with them in person, but
more likely, we will communicate with them via video
conferences. Why? Because the friends and ac-
quaintances we make will be all over the globe. Telecommunications and technology have the odd effect
of making us closer even when we are far apart.

Of course, all this individualism can also produce
detrimental effects. I think it very likely that an irony
will exist: although humans are social by nature, we
also demand our own space; therefore, as people
isolate themselves more, hiding behind the convenience and privacy of high tech gadgets, we may become more selfish. A sort of divisiveness may occur.
People may be considerate only to those with whom
they have chosen to maintain contact and shun everyone else.

A recent article in the *New York Times* indicated
that students at Dartmouth University are constantly
increasing online time. Even roommates will sit on
their respective computers to communicate and play
networked games! You can see that there is already
evidence of a tendency for people to gather less frequently in groups in *person* and more of a tendency
to meet online.

Speaking of games, controversy is raging right now
over the recent announcement of the top ten computer games of the last year. The most popular and
best-selling games are all graphically violent and
many people are concerned that this will foster violence in the people who play them, especially children. Can we expect to raise compassionate, decent

children when they are addicted to games in which they mutilate and kill on screen enemies? Or are the effects that vicious?

Telecommunications—phones, computers, and all manner of electronics—can foster individual political autonomy which will also result in a diminishing sense of national identity. Why should you feel any allegiance to a country when you have your online friends, co-workers or business peers all over the world? In other words, it is possible that we will see a trend toward a sort of tribalism.

Technology and telecommunications also relate to politics in that terrorist operations have become more sophisticated. Take Iran, one of the wealthiest countries in the world. It is nothing for them to engineer a terrorist attack, transferring funds to the appropriate groups electronically and secretly. What about Iran's ongoing purchases of nuclear technology from scientists in Russia? And what Iran's leaders, and many other countries as well, have done is develop nuclear technology into a smaller and more convenient form that transports effortlessly over borders. How can we possibly guard against technology that is so advanced?

Advancing Technology

Indeed you can see that the boundaries of the aspects of the Quickening are blurred; here you have seen that technology affects the way we behave in society, it affects our global safety, it affects our political ties, and much more. We can look forward to astounding numbers of technological advances in the very near future. For the "Millennium Generation" and beyond, the sky will be the limit. At any rate, you should take a good look at the world around you because it won't be the same when you wake up tomorrow.

2

Economy

After displaying the latest designs for his artistic floor lamps on his web site, Franz could hardly believe the numbers of people around the world who wanted to order right away. The trouble was, the floor lamps did not even exist yet! They were only a three-dimensional graphic image designed by Lance, his brother and partner. Franz, the consummate entrepreneur and a resourceful business person in their small, two man operation, knew that he needed to jump on this opportunity and manufacture these products for shipment immediately.

Within a matter of hours, from his skyrise apartment in New York, glued to his computer monitor, Franz contacted a tooling company in Germany who could take the electronic file and produce the necessary tooling to manufacture certain parts of the lamp. The tooling was then delivered overnight by Federal Express to a company in Singapore prepared to make the parts. From there, the various components were sent to Mexico to be assembled and packed for delivery to an order fulfillment company in Denver. Electronic fund transfers were made instantly once agreements were entered with each company.

Back online, Franz could announce the availability of the lamps, the price, shipping options for customers around the world, and details for ordering online or via an international 800 number. Only four days would pass from tooling to the final product. Franz sat back in his chair and watched his brother next to him at work on another design.

$$\Omega \quad \Omega \quad \Omega$$

Harold counted the hot meal pouches on the racks in his truck. Eight game hen entrees, twelve chicken cordon bleu entrees, six lasagna entrees, and a mega order of Caesar salad for a total of six deliveries this hour! Ever since Harold had been with Gourmet Dinner Delivery in Orlando, Florida, he had seen the numbers of customer orders skyrocket. People just did not want to take the time to cook, and fighting crowds in a restaurant had lost most of its appeal. That was fine with Harold; it meant more money for him. Besides, it was actually a fairly pleasant job. Most people were always grateful to see him because he was saving them time and trouble with his deliveries.

It was during the Thanksgiving holiday that things got a little stressful—that much more to deliver per order. Naturally, people wanted the works, and who could blame them? The food was exceptional. Harold chuckled as he thought of the days when only pizza was delivered.

Ω   Ω   Ω

What does the word "economy" mean to you? Does it mean a secure, well-paying job? Or does it represent the fact that money—the exchange or distribution of it—means power? Perhaps you may think of economy as a thermometer taking a reading of the health of your country or a measure of how it can or cannot support its people. For many of you, economy may be no more than a vague idea, and it may be more simple to look at individual companies and their actions as a reflection of how strong or how unstable a country is. In any case, economy determines the condition of people's lives.

In relation to the Quickening, economic changes may seem gradual, but the truth is, they have increased and at an exponential rate, much like knowing that someone was around a corner, but having them jump out at you unexpectedly. Changes like a cashless society, an altered employment structure, and the globalization of the labor force wrap technological advances, which make these things possible, around an inevitably strong—soon to be global—economy.

Starting Out

Eighteenth century European Industrialism represented the greatest period of wealth creation the world had ever seen. Of course, America quickly became the economic powerhouse of the world, but many of the companies formed in America could not have begun without European money. Ironically, once American industry took off, Europe was literally left—without the resources, the open frontier, the labor pool available in America—in the dust.

Mr. Money Bags

J.P. Morgan, the quintessential industrialist and American banker, demonstrated that money is power. Morgan was a significant force in shaping the American economy from agricultural to industrial. We can thank him for the rating systems on Wall Street that created ways to rate companies and their potential investment risk. For instance, a rating system such as Standard & Poor's would define a large company like AT&T or Ford Motor Company as a blue chip company; they possessed lots of hard assets—buildings, equipment, inventory, etc.—and were thus thought to be a safer risk.

Basing the distribution of capital on existing success and assets, Morgan effectively closed small entrepreneurial companies out of the bond market, and gave large companies the command of a single industry. In essence, this defined the way that wealth would function because it so discouraged competition.

But, you're saying, why give money to a company that doesn't *need* money? By proliferating the existence of trusts, or monopolies, Morgan also benefited from his investments in these companies and set the standard for banking that exists to a large extent today.[1]

Milken the Miracle Man

The information age that we live in today had its start in the early 1970s with the expanded roles of the computer and telecommunications industries. But these fledgling high tech businesses needed a large influx of capital to go forward. Mired under the weight of the traditional industrial age mentality of banking and finance, individual entrepreneurs found it difficult to get their products to market.

Michael Milken, the J.P. Morgan of post-industrialism, ushered in a new method of finance in America that had repercussions throughout the world. Milken saw that small, entrepreneurial companies paid their debts and were willing to pay higher interest rates to investors who purchased their bonds. On this basis, Milken started to sell high yield, so called "junk" bonds of these companies and a dam of capital burst, opening windows of opportunity. Given the necessary funds, many of these companies, just as solvent as the larger entities around them, would likely produce useful products. By 1989, Milken had sold an astounding $180 billion of junk bonds![2]

One example of Milken's influence and the new-found ability of these small companies to challenge the dominance of the industrial dinosaurs was the development of the Macintosh by Apple. Had Apple not been given the chance, we would not have had the PC so quickly. IBM was forced to not only produce a competitive product in response to the Mac, but they began to devolve their heavily laden corporate structure. Milken was a visionary; he recognized that high tech industry was based not on money or equipment, but on thinking.[3]

Computers & Telecommunications

Today we walk into an office building and take for granted that the receptionist is busy on a computer, with a complicated looking phone bank in front of her. Fax machines, copy machines, phones, computers, digital recorders—we are surrounded by technology, particularly when it comes to business.

Telecommunications has facilitated the increasing tendency to do business with multiple parts of the world. In fact, telecommunications technology is the basis for the Quickening's trend toward a global economy. With computers and the Internet, satellites and fiber optics, national boundaries mean nothing; business of nearly any kind can be conducted at any time, to and from anywhere, with no limits. Monetary transactions are also completed more quickly, efficiently and profitably.

The only final barriers exist in the actual physical movement of products in and out of different countries. With services such as UPS, Federal Express and others, transportation is not as much of an issue as, say, a political barrier, but these, too, are falling quickly.

Automation Takes Hold

You may *not* be surprised to know that until the 1960s, when entrepreneurs began to see its potential business and consumer use, technology was applied almost solely for the military. The 1980s in America marked a period of transition into increased office automation. The people who were educated in the 1960s were able to see the technologies that were more fully developed in the 1970s. As a result, as businesses started realizing how useful technology and telecommunications could be, many typewriters went straight into the trash! Unfortunately, many jobs also went to the same place as office automation decreased the number of people necessary for certain tasks.

For the most part, America was at the forefront of increased automation. Of course, Japan proved to be a quick study of American technologies after 1945; they enhanced our technologies, particularly electronics, and were able to enrich themselves. For instance, Sony took our radios one step further by making them smaller. Meanwhile, Asia was looking over Japan's shoulder as Japan set the economic standard for the rest of Asia to follow, encouraging the first fragments of global competition.

Smaller Is Better

The onslaught of corporate raids and takeovers accelerated during the 1980s as well. Violent upheavals left thousands of people unemployed as companies "down-sized." Of course, the traditional financiers and big corporate captains managed to subdue part of the frenzy by arresting Michael Milken and sending him to prison. But by then it was too late; things had been irrevocably altered. By making the money available to these small companies, Milken paved the way for new industries like cellular phones, cable television, personal computers, health services and more to gain a foothold in the world market.[4]

Big companies had to learn a serious lesson in the 1980s about survival and profitability, consequently breaking themselves down into smaller, manageable and autonomous groups. Companies such as General Electric have changed their attitude from tottering, corpulent mega-company to small company spirit and energy. In fact, General Electric has reduced employment drastically over the last decade, cutting over 100,000 jobs. Within that time, sales have at least doubled and net income has tripled.[5]

In addition, AT&T, Coca Cola, General Electric and other mega-companies realized that going high tech was imperative. Manufacturers, such as the automobile industry, realized the need to automate with computers, electronic information systems, and robotics in order to offer their customers the highest quality and to remain competitive.

In June 1986, Motorola, exhibiting entrepreneurial "moxy" and technological vision, formed a team and gave it a task of monumental proportions. They were instructed to design a new radio-pager and a world-class, computer-integrated manufacturing facility for producing it; further, they were given eighteen months to find their solution and it would have to have a 99.9997 percent probability of perfect unit output.

Today in Boynton Beach, Florida, the plant churns out customized radio pagers, the physical work done by twenty seven robots. The project team succeeded—with seventeen days left till their deadline, proof that the integration of human mind with computer and telecommunications technology can indeed work outside of the heavily laden corporate environment.[6]

Regional Economic Alliances

As new industries grew, so did the demand for their products to be available on a worldwide basis. Countries have traditionally always engaged in trade, but factors such as nationalism, bureaucracy, the hoarding of technology, and quotas have often been restricting. The combination of telecommunications and an increased openness on the part of many governments has made global trade easier. We can see an example of this with the North American Free Trade Agreement (NAFTA), ratified in 1993; the countries who benefit from this agreement include America, Canada, and Mexico. In about the last ten years, other regional economic alliances have also been formed as the world steps up its trade with other countries.

America's Heavy Load

Many American companies are prospering because of NAFTA and global trade in general; this country has always been at the forefront of economic advances. For this reason, America has been an economic powerhouse for the majority of the twentieth century. For decades, immigrants have sought prosperity in this country; America has unquestionably been the leader, setting the standard for the material aspirations of the rest of the world. But there are now clear signs that suggest that America's economic strength is eroding in the face of mounting national and individual debt.

Whether you want to believe it or not, America's national debt is spinning completely out of control. Although many people consider Ross Perot to be at an extreme with many issues, he does make a strong argument about America's burden of debt; he asserts that the country is being crippled and that it should be the foremost concern of every citizen. Most Americans, however, are indifferent to the fact that every day America sinks deeper and deeper into the red; moreover, they remain pleasantly oblivious to their own heavy debts, the majority of which are carried on plastic, with overblown finance charges. It is a scary thought that this country functions with such a self-deluding attitude about the very thing that affects us the most.

If you add up the American government's indebtedness, including the trillion dollars borrowed from the Social Security trust fund, the non-financed government pension funds for military and civilian employees, and money spent on defense and social programs—the total comes to over seven and a half *trillion* dollars! How can anyone ignore that? Don't forget that the interest on this figure increases about seventy million dollars an *hour*.

The one thing that we can all relate to is higher taxes. This has placed the heaviest burden on the middle class, and essentially they carry the responsibility of making payments on the interest on the national debt. Increased taxes mean an inflated cost of living that the dollar at its present state of strength cannot quite cover.

Banks on Thin Ice

Some believe the credit union debacle of the 1980s was a warning of what could happen to the banking industry. We learned then that thousands of banks are not as financially strong as they pretend to be. One of the reasons that banks have become so weakened is that this country has made too many risky loans to Third World countries, which have in turn fallen behind in their repayment.

However, banks continue to boast of insuring the money of depositors like you and I up to $100,000 under the Federal Deposit Insurance Corporation

(FDIC). Most people either have not let the thought that a bank might fail cross their minds, or they feel assured by this FDIC promise. Think about this fact: the FDIC only has one billion dollars to cover more than four trillion dollars of deposits in 14,000 banks. Ironically, the FDIC came into being in 1933 after thousands of bank failures due to bad real estate loans, defaulted loans, and massive withdrawals by bank customers.

What could bankrupt banks and their depositors? A collapse in the highly volatile derivatives market in which thousands of banks have invested huge amounts of depositor money. Your money is not safe.

America Broken in Pieces

What could this mean to Americans? Quite simply, it could mean economic collapse. It could mean American people going hungry. It could mean some of the worst times that Americans have ever known, perhaps worse than the Great Depression of 1932. The reality is that this could happen sooner than you think.

Latin America

Tremendous economic growth is taking place in Latin American countries. Historically, this region has been fraught with political unrest, ruled by dictators who have produced strong, protective nationalism and fostered state intervention in trade. But something remarkable has happened to Latin America; people are more informed than ever before and thus capable of electing democratic leadership over dictators. The result has been increased trade between neighboring countries.

Brazil and Argentina, the largest of all South American countries, trade openly with each other, as do Uruguay and Paraguay. Argentina is leading the economic growth of this region at about ten percent. Various regional economic alliances have been formed, such as the Central American Common Market, that have made Latin America stronger overall.[7]

The European Union

America emerged from World War II as the most powerful nation in the world in large part because we were not as dramatically affected as Europe and Japan. Since then, the Europeans have struggled to compete with the economic prowess of both the United States and Japan. This constant struggle has led to the revolutionary Maastricht Treaty of 1992, which created a community of twelve European nation-states collectively referred to as the "European Union." The Maastricht Treaty has successfully opened up boundaries between these European countries, enhancing trade and the flow of money.

Although most European Union members have benefited to some degree from the open market, the economic growth has not been quite as strong as first expected. Germany thought to lead the way maybe three or four years ago, but this has not happened. Instead, the European Union has experienced a recession. Apparently, the cost of reunification and its welfare programs have placed a virtually unbearable economic burden upon these nations. Consequently, while individual entrepreneurs will have a good chance to prosper, it is likely that the European Union as a whole will continue to lag behind the Americas and Asia for some time.

Asia Grows Up—Fast!

The Asian Free Trade Agreement (AFTA) and the General Agreement on Tariffs and Trade (GATT) have resulted in a dramatic rise in trade between the countries of Asia, despite their language and cultural differences. The Japanese were steeped in cultural tradition and feudal society for hundreds of years. Following World War II, they sought to rebuild by imitating the West; we see this continue today as Japan has become a major economic force. By Japanese example, most of the Asian world has also prospered. Overall, Asia's growth rate is about seven percent, higher than the average growth rate of any other economy in the world![8]

China: The Giant Awakens

Of all the Asian countries, China is the one country to really keep an eye on. Under the visionary leadership of Deng Xiaoping, the Communist Party agreed to an economic reform proposal in December, 1978. This marked a turning point for the Chinese and today they are the third largest economy behind Japan and the United States. The future is tremendously promising in light of China's current growth. Many observers believe it is very likely that China will become the world's largest economy around the turn of the twenty-first century. Apparently, once given the freedom and encouragement to be entrepreneurial, the Chinese economy has blossomed.

Hong Kong will belong to China in 1997 and many people have speculated that this may create problems for Hong Kong. Uncertainty over whether China will allow Hong Kong businesses and its people to continue life as they have always known it—inclusive of free speech, free press, free trade—has caused many people to flee Hong Kong. Actually, the two countries have already become so economically integrated, especially southern China, that the transition may be virtually seamless.

The Chinese government regards this situation as something better left to its own devices; they realize that a free economy can benefit the country a great deal. Most members of the Chinese Communist Party seem to be more interested in political control than managing the market anyway.[9]

Russia—A Teetering Balance

In distinct contrast to Communist China, Russia's economic situation is very unstable. While Russia is still a military superpower, it is not hard to see the chaos still inherent as various factions struggle for control. It became clear to globally minded Communists like Mikhail Gorbachev in the early 1980s that the Soviet Union could not survive without reforming its economy. Gorbachev's *perestroika* and the breaking down of the Berlin Wall in 1989 signified an attempt by Gorbachev to encourage individual liberties and free trade. He reasoned that without one, you cannot have the other.

In principle, the idea of introducing a free economy in Russia would work much the same way as in China. Unfortunately, Russia was not ready for such a quick change. The people of Russia have been under the yoke of a command economy for so long, they have a great deal of difficulty in trying to think like entrepreneurs. Free economy has been a success in China because the Chinese had *time* to adjust. The closest thing to free trade in Russia before *perestroika* was the black market and that is now the only significant form of entrepreneurism in existence. In fact, it is believed that the Russian mafia and various black marketeers will simply take over the Russian economy.

Perhaps the biggest problem with the attempt at economic reform in Russia is that it has alienated most of the Russian people. These days, talk of the old ways is seriously debated. Hard line and often frightening Communists like Vladmir Zhirinovsky are being given credible consideration for leadership positions when Boris Yeltsin finally loses the battle with his health.

To raise desperately needed hard currency, the Russians have been known for some time to sell various military equipment and weapons technology, as well as loaning top scientists in weapons development to the Iraqis, Iranians, Libyans and others. It is also believed that in order for Russia to pay its troops, which go long periods of time without pay, some KGB officers have compromised the national security by smuggling and selling weapons grade plutonium and uranium. It should be apparent to you by now that there are quite a few threats posed by Russia, directly by its updated nuclear technology, and indirectly by its weapons business with other dangerous countries.

Oil and Wealth: The Middle East

The Arab nation-states are among the wealthiest and the most volatile in the world. Oil has been the predominant basis for the economy of these countries for decades. Although OPEC may have diminished in power since the 1980s, and a number of significant reserves have been exploited in other parts of the world with the advent of enhanced oil extraction technology, the Middle East is still the world's greatest single source of fuel.

These Middle Eastern states have a religio-geopolitical agenda that they finance with their seemingly endless supply of oil money. The most dangerous country is Iran. During the late 1980s, Ayatollah Khomeini, the late Iranian leader, essentially declared a religious war on the "infidels"—this means everyone in the world who does not uphold and practice the Islamic religion. Using the money they have accumulated from selling oil, they have purchased and stockpiled weapons and acquired nuclear capability. It would be a mistake to think that the Middle Eastern countries will ever relinquish their powerful economic base, especially since it gives them so much power politically.

The Starving Masses

I think everyone has turned to CNN only to watch as hundreds of thousands of Africans flee from one place to another, fearing for their lives in the face of some civil warfare. All of us are haunted by the images of the eyes of people who live from day to day, uncertain where their next meal is coming from. We commonly refer to these very poor countries as the Third World, including Africa, India, Pakistan, Bangladesh and others. Nothing indicates that the problems of these countries will ever disappear; tribal wars, ethnic hatred, overpopulation, disease, soil erosion and drought have cursed these countries for generations.

The one possible exception is South Africa, which receives constant infusions of money from the International Monetary Fund (IMF). In addition, South Africa can rely to some extent upon its diamond mines as an economic base. In fact, South Africa and Russia are the only two sources on earth for key minerals critical to the production of advanced technologies and missile defenses.

Given the fact that technology is the backbone for all that we see today, how will societies largely rooted in agriculture survive? Chances are, as the Quickening continues, these people will be left farther and farther behind. Tragically, these people collectively represent no less than *half* the population of the world—*billions!* But who will give these people technology? Who will give them the economic base with which to right themselves? What country will spend the time and money to ensure that children learn trades and get proper nutrition?

These billions will be an ongoing responsibility for the rest of the world with their vast numbers, hunger, and internal conflict. In truth, what hope can we offer them for the future?

The regional alliances discussed above represent the current state of affairs in individual regions. The economy of these regions can change quickly as the global economy develops, thus making it more and more difficult to predict the economic performance of any one country. Certain entrepreneurs will prosper even though they may be in a less prosperous country. Remember, physical location is virtually meaningless for a growing number of companies and countries. This will set the tone for the future.

On The Road To Globalism

Countries who relax trade restrictions and encourage entrepreneurs to develop business with the world will prosper greatly in the coming age of globalism. Those that do not will only continue their downward spiral into poverty. The world economy is strong and will gain momentum quickly. Most of the wealth is being created by the small, entrepreneurial companies of the world and not by the mega-companies.

The movement of money and people worldwide is also on the upswing, made possible by telecommunications and efficient transportation. Indeed, the largest international banking system is the Society for Worldwide Interbank Financial Transmission (SWIFT); SWIFT allows companies and individuals to transfer enormous amounts of money anywhere in the world at any time within seconds. To date, every twenty-four hours, about six *trillion* dollars is transferred throughout the world!

Say Goodbye to Cash

The use of telecommunications for business is a fact that is already changing the way we make our living and the way we shop. Now no matter where we happen to be in the world, it has and will continue to change the way we do our banking and the way we make our investments. You already know that credit cards and ATM cards would not be possible if it were not for sophisticated telecommunications systems to process your card for a purchase or a money withdrawal anywhere in the world. But this is only the beginning.

The Quickening will bring about a major change that it may take some people longer than others to become accustomed to: cashlessness. Credit cards have been convenient, but approaching fast on the horizon are both "smart cards" or a chip painlessly embedded under the skin in your wrist. When not online, each card or chip "holder" will have their wrist scanned to make the purchase of clothes, groceries, or whatever.

The World Trade Organization

Three major regions of the world have stepped into the limelight in terms of global economic development: the Americas, Asia, and the European Union. In 1993, 117 countries from these three regions, plus countries in Africa, signed an agreement that brought into being the World Trade Organization (WTO). The WTO is joined by the influential World Bank and the International Monetary Fund (IMF), both founded at the end of World War II and funded by the United States. The goal of the WTO is ostensibly to reduce tariffs imposed by countries seeking to keep out cheap foreign imports, but this triumvirate can be a little scary to contemplate because of the immense power it now possesses.

Just how much power *is* that? When Bill Clinton signed the agreement, he knowingly gave the WTO council the capability of preventing the United States from imposing trade embargoes on countries like China for human rights violations. In fact, if the United States were witness to such violations and imposed a trade embargo anyway, we would be subject to great pressure and criticism, high fines, and possibly a global embargo on America—no trade in, no trade out. In one fell swoop, Bill Clinton's signature on this agreement surrendered American economic influence and sovereignty, weakening our economic and political position in the world.

The Weak Will Fall Behind

Much of the world's population will not be able to keep up with the global economic trends of the Quickening. They will be unable to adapt and take advantage of the necessary technology. They will only know war, hunger, social strife and disease as constant companions. Many will never look at a computer monitor, much less have savings in an on-line account.

For instance, you can see that Russia, a country long known and respected for its military prowess, faces great challenges from uncertain leadership and a shaky economy. Despite the brilliance of great minds the world over and the progress in technology, despite the diplomatic advances and our ability to create wealth, we have not been able to right all the financial woes of our world.

How Does All This Affect Me?

Sitting safely in the comforts of your warm, well-lighted home with the television murmuring softly in the background and the kids playing happily in some other part of the house, maybe this seems distant and intangible to you. Actually, the trend toward a global economy affects you in many ways. The most significant impact for most people will be upon their job.

Many Americans complain that NAFTA compromises the jobs of American citizens as American companies seek cheaper labor in other countries to manufacture their products. It is true that many big companies farm out jobs to foreign countries. For instance, Nike has never had a manufacturing plant in America. But the fact is, the jobs which are supposedly "lost" are jobs which most Americans don't really want to do anyway, and which will end up being automated in the near future.

From the late nineteenth century until around the 1960s, the "blue collar" work force was predominant, particularly because of assembly line production. This was the beginning of mass labor and mass production and most things that could be done on the assembly line did not require skilled labor and theoretically not much education either. But after World War II, optimism and better overall opportunities led to more education which in turn led to a change in the labor pool, namely, a decrease in the blue collar workers.

The fact is, automation and information systems of today and the future will enable companies to create specific numbers of products instead of investing needless dollars into excess inventory. With smaller inventories, more companies "outsourcing" (using third party contractors) and breaking into little companies under a larger umbrella to produce a product, companies will not only need fewer employees, but the employees they do need will have to be *skilled.*

Where is this trend leading you as a worker? The reality is that we are progressing quickly toward a higher concentration of information and toward a data oriented techno-industry. This will demand workers who are better educated and trained to perform jobs that will require skill; the blue collar labor jobs will be almost completely phased out, to be replaced by information and service jobs. Service jobs that will be in highest demand will be things like food and package delivery services, plumbers and electricians, and other consultant types of work.

Rather than being preoccupied by unemployment, the focus will be on *redeployment* into the information age. By necessity, people will become more computer literate and learn to become more flexible in adapting to the high tech business environment. If you cannot or do not choose to adapt, you will simply be left behind.

Clearly, this world of ours is well on its way to a global economy, thanks in large part to the wonders of technology and the efficiency of telecommunications. Businesses are changing their attitudes and methods of manufacturing products, affecting us all on an individual basis, particularly in the area of how we generate our income. It is not a pretty forecast for many countries around the world, including America. For others, prosperity will abound as their people learn to integrate mind and machine, paving the way for a one world economy.

3

Government

Dr. Plimpton sat back in his ergonomic chair, perplexed as he listened to his electronic attendant read a message from the Global Trade & Taxation Bureau. It informed him that he would be required to pay an additional one and a half percent in taxes for the software he shipped out of his region, Singapore. That was ironic, especially because it was his company which developed the software used by the Bureau to keep track of tax payment and evasion.

"This is ridiculous. I already pay plenty and another one and a half percent is outrageous," Plimpton commented to his attendant. After thinking a moment, Plimpton recalled that a member of the Global Parliament owed him a favor from when he had given the government a discount on consultation charges last May. He turned to his attendant. "Dial up Emile Erlenmeyer."

The next day, Plimpton looked out his window, a smug smile on his face. After a brief video conference, Erlenmeyer had promised to work something out with the Global Parliament ruling panel. Within a week, the deal was done. The tax increase would be forgiven and Dr. Plimpton would continue to reap profits.

Ω Ω Ω

Jose had always been healthy. Now, after starting his new job at the plastic injection molding company in Rio de Janeiro, he had been suffering from rashes on his arms. Other employees who worked in the plant had similar symptoms, including one fellow whose eyesight had abruptly gone blurry. After nosing around a little one afternoon in the inventory warehouse, Jose spotted several long, complex chemical names on some drums. He suspected the company was using a cheaper, probably illegal plastic composite to manufacture products and wanted to confirm this with the Global Environmental Commission. They offered large rewards for reporting this sort of information! He called the number he got from the Global Parliament Information web site.

Two days later, a squad of GEC troopers stormed the company facilities, riot guns and batons in hand. The owner was quickly brought out and questioned. Jose and his fellow employees stood watching as a large black truck with the GEC emblem on it backed to the inventory warehouse. Moments later, the drums Jose had spotted were loaded on the truck and the owner was led away in handcuffs. When Jose arrived home that evening, his computer monitor beeped at him with an e-mail. The message was from the World Bank, notifying him that a sizable amount of money had been electronically transferred to his account. Jose sighed, shaking his head in wonder at what some people tried to get away with, and then sat down and started looking for another job.

Ω   Ω   Ω

What is government and why do we need it? Human beings are a strange lot. On the one hand, we enjoy freedom; it is in our nature. We want to express ourselves freely, we want to engage in commerce freely, we want to pursue happiness freely and much more. But despite the unrestrained nature of the freedoms we enjoy, we also want orderliness in our lives. We want a guarantee that certain things will be run in certain ways. Protect us, we say, from those who would take advantage of us in business, those who would seek to harm us physically, those who would stop us from saying exactly what was on our mind. We *want* to be governed. And government is just that—an attempt by people to bring a ruled certainty to the affairs of other people.

Actually, history has proven that effective, compassionate government is a good thing. In recent times, you might consider the government of Beirut, which lacks the power to function effectively. There are always members of society who will create chaos and fear, and much of the time, they get away with it. However, without government, our odds of controlling such people are significantly lower.

Where Did Government Start?

We take government for granted, but for centuries nation-states as we know them today did not exist. People were grouped mostly in a crazy mixture of fiefdoms, ports controlled by pirates, religious groups, and even a handful of nations here and there controlled by powerful monarchs. Political aspirants vied for power to assume the authority which we now associate with government. Overall, the governing system was highly diverse and heterogeneous. The homogeneous, centralized government that we have grown accustomed to was born during the Industrial Revolution and has continued to persist, but in the face of changes in this time of the Quickening, the old ways are crumbling.

Global Government

Economic advances are always accompanied by political changes; the greater the economic advance, the more far-reaching the political change. The European and American Industrial Revolutions ushered in an era of unprecedented wealth and nationalism. After World War II, the attitude in government changed as trade began to open up. Gradually, many governments have become less guarded and nationalism has declined as the world careens toward a global economy. In time, this global economy will bring about a global government. Countries will exist and, to some extent, people will maintain their unique cultural identities, but there will be one governing body controlling all economic and political activity worldwide.

What?! Can't believe it? At first, most Western free-thinking people will object to the idea and even the possibility of a global government. It seems impossible that Americans would allow the sovereignty of our country to decline, but in fact, it already has and will only continue to do so. The Quickening of economic and political events is hurtling our world toward global government.

With the advent of telecommunications, the computer and other high tech developments that enable us to communicate and engage in trade more efficiently worldwide, our current information age is propelling us forward and backward at the same time. We go forward in our quest to become prosperous, but are moving back to a more heterogeneous form of government, and thus coming full circle. People are becoming more knowledgeable about and aware of the world in which we live, like never before. People are becoming more independent. Nation-state borders do not mean as much anymore in terms of trade, money flow and communication. Obviously, this takes power away from the government and places it in the hands of the individual.

Everyone wants peace, prosperity and a clean environment in which to live. It is on this premise that a global government will evolve, but the strongest foundations will be built upon a global economy. Remember: money is power and power takes control. Global government will occur not by force, but by economic necessity.

Obsolete Government
One of the greatest challenges facing the leaders of democratic governments is their diminishing importance. This is not to say that they will go away completely, but let's be realistic; a president or prime

minister assumes a position of leadership mostly in name only anyway. The true power lies with the bureaucrats, and so the party representation of a given leader is not that significant. Whether Democrat or Republican, right or left, the existing bureaucracy makes it virtually impossible to achieve major changes. Instead, the leader is credited with what the bureaucrats have decided to change—for better or worse.

Now that Communism appears to be dwindling, political leaders have even less to do. They would strive to make economic or social changes, but again, their power is so limited as to render them ineffectual in these areas as well. The people they represent are aware of this and increasingly regard politics as uninteresting; people are gaining more control over their own lives, and this would explain in great part the high level of voter apathy. In America, Canada and Japan, barely half the people who can vote actually do so.

In the old days, states and countries fought for the number of representatives they could have in governing bodies. Before the age of information everywhere, anytime, it made sense to have a representative of the people participate in government; this is no longer necessary. Now we often know things at the same time or even before our representatives know, and make judgments without the events being strained through our representative first. This is a true sign that the centralized, "omniscient" government is becoming obsolete.

The increased spread of information globally has resulted in people seeking to identify with others of similar backgrounds, interests and concerns. This creates all kinds of divergent groups and, consequently, many more niches of issues erupt all the time—religious groups, environmentalists, ethnic proponents, single mothers and so on. Each group has what they perceive to be legitimate concerns, demanding attention from the government. The more diverse people become and the more they identify themselves with specific issues and groups, the less loyalty they may tend to feel toward government, and the less able government is to control them.

De-Centralized Government

Governments are slow to learn, but bureaucrats with the power buttons in their hands are beginning to realize that they need to interact more closely with business and shift power to regional or localized areas. They also realize the need to reduce the size of government and to be open to new ways of dealing with the people they represent.

As far as business is concerned, the most effective, useful way governments will participate in the economy is by establishing the best, most readily accessible information network infrastructure. Eventually, everyone will have ready access to computers and be able to go online anywhere. Theoretically, anyone rich or poor will have access if they choose—notwithstanding of course, people in countries who cannot afford food much less technology—perhaps making accessibility as commonplace as driving a car or using a public pay phone. This facilitates trade, learning and communication, and can even enhance the way in which people interact with government.

Singapore is a good example of a country very much aware of the advantage of establishing a telecommunications infrastructure. The government is actively building an infrastructure that includes a single fiber optics information grid connected to every home, business and government agency throughout the entire country; their goal is to finish by the year 2005.

The Japanese also have the right attitude; they believe that when information flows, people and goods flow, and so does money. The Japanese took a giant leap ahead of everyone else when they enhanced the function of the Japanese Ministry of Posts and Telecommunications (MPT). The new MPT demonstrates that the Japanese clearly see the advantage of establishing a telecommunications infrastructure that incorporates financial matters and business. Most governments might separate these functions, but it won't take long for governments to discover the benefits of this unique and powerful combination.

Fragmenting Governments

Just as mega-corporations have been downsizing into smaller, more manageable and profitable units, so governments are beginning to see the light. We will hear more and more about "privatization" as governments break off pieces of government and let private companies and organizations operate those pieces. We have just begun to see signs of this in a number of countries.

Japan sold off the state-owned Nippon Telephone and Telegraph when the Japanese government decided it no longer needed to be in the telephone business. Likewise, Britain sold off British Aerospace and British Telcom, Canada sold Air Canada and West Germany sold Volkswagen. In America, we see the use of special task forces and committees with the participation of private firms. This is only the beginning!

Declining Nation-State Sovereignty

People in today's world have more power. Why is this? Telecommunications, the computer, global media, ease of transportation and movement of money across all geopolitical boundaries have given people power. Governments simply do not have the control they once had over these things. In fact, it will be increasingly difficult for governments to control economies through taxation, bank regulation, and financial controls—traditionally a stronghold for government. In short, the sovereignty of all nation-states is declining.

When you have power, you have more choices, and that includes how you feel about being governed. People are asserting themselves according to what they perceive to be their identities. Historically, people in Europe, for instance, with different ethnic heritage, languages, religious ideals and economic conditions have lived together more or less peaceably as long as government applied sufficient force. However, the climate for tolerance is changing; people with distinct differences are demanding to separate themselves.

For example, after the Soviet Union was disassembled, the problem of the Hungarian minority in Romania and the Turks in Bulgaria came to the forefront. In the former Yugoslavia, the Serbs, Albanians and Croats head toward autonomy. We will see disparities widen and an increase in ethnic tensions during this time of the Quickening. There will also be an increased resentment toward those entering the new economic environment as those left behind resist change, as well as increased global fanaticism as various groups assert themselves.

To deal with these problems, governments will permit local and regional autonomy. More countries will come into existence as pieces of nation-states break off as the result of secession. The European Union will most likely allow secession in areas such as South Tyrol, Alsace, Flanders and Catalonia. Even in Canada, it is likely that the French-Canadians will break off to become their own country, as they have been rallying to do for years. In Africa, tribal areas may form dozens of independent administrative units. In America, we will probably see more and more power shifting to state and local areas as the federal government becomes less significant to individuals.

It is one of the ironies of the Quickening that while this looks like chaos, it is indeed an integral part of the impending global government. The world is breaking up into smaller pieces; this will occur both peacefully and violently in some cases. The paradox at work here is that as the world becomes more global, the smaller parts actually become stronger.

American Sovereignty in Decline

Americans are becoming more and more disgruntled with the state of affairs in our country. Clearly, a number of signs point to a decline in the national sovereignty of America. Traditionally and historically, the sovereignty and power of a nation-state was based on the strength of its economy and its military. At the turn of the twentieth century, America was unquestionably an economic powerhouse. Europe exhibited military strength, but by the end of World War II, even with the defeat of Japan and Germany, Europe was weak and war weary. America, however, had become a premier world military superpower. We built the best battle ships and aircraft, plus we had the atom bomb. The only contender to America's economic and military dominance was the Soviet Union.

Two-Faced Gorbachev

The former Soviet Union recognized early in the twentieth century that Communism could not compete economically with a capitalist democracy like the United States. With this understanding, the Soviets put their money and effort into bolstering their military and succeeded in building the most ominous war machine on earth. Ironically, this nearly resulted in their own economic collapse. Today, although the Soviet Union no longer exists as we have known it and the influence of Communism has declined, Communist Russia is not going away. Some believe the Russians allowed things to occur as they have with the express purpose of lulling America into believing they are no longer a threat.

Mikhail Gorbachev reflected the mentality of the Communist in his speech to the Soviet Politburo in 1987:

> "Comrades, do not be concerned about all you hear about *glasnost* and *perestroika* and democracy in the coming years. These are primarily for outward consumption. There will be no significant internal change within the Soviet Union other than for cosmetic purposes. Our

purpose is to disarm the Americans and let them fall asleep."[1]

It could not be much clearer than that! Gorbachev then outlines his ambition to see American conventional and nuclear forces withdrawn from Europe, and proclaims the end of the Strategic Defense Initiative. This speech was made by the very man who is given credit for bringing down the Iron Curtain and ushering in the new *glasnost* and *perestroika*. This from a man who tells the rest of the world that he believes the time has come to reform Russia and to introduce capitalism and democracy to its people.

Even more frightening is that Gorbachev is achieving his goal. President Bush began by withdrawing hundreds of thousands of troops from Europe, leaving a small, insignificant force. Following that, America withdrew all its nuclear weapons from Europe and later nuclear armed American Navy ships. Not long after, the fifty year ongoing Fail Safe system, which kept American B-52 bombers on constant alert, was halted.

Bill Clinton is no better than George Bush in this regard. His foreign policy has been characterized by weakness and indecisiveness—a representation that carries over to the whole country of America. Clinton threatens, but takes no action. Even former President Jimmy Carter has stepped in unofficially to assist in diplomatic visits to North Korea, Haiti, Bosnia and others. Pathetic!

American Military Sophistication Undermined

Americans have always slept easy at night, secure in the knowledge that our military strength, based on technology and sheer numbers, is intact. But President Clinton has actively gone about the business of scaling down all branches of the military. Base after base has been shut down permanently. Republican representative Jack Kemp observed that Clinton is cutting back on average "15,000 personnel, one ship, thirty-seven aircraft and one combat battalion each *month*."[italics mine][2]

I can see you shrugging your shoulders, figuring that at the very least we still outnumber most countries in soldiers. But listen to this: America has perhaps two million soldiers, of which only half a million are combat ready. To give you an idea of the contrast, Russia has close to five million *combat ready* soldiers. Moreover, the Russians have 350,000 secret police, interior ministry troops and Spetsnaz special forces commandos. The Russian Navy is four times larger than the US Navy. The Russians have 450 submarines versus America's 138. Russia has ten times as many tanks, 70,000 of which are battle tanks, and adds about 3,500 new tanks each year. What has America done? We have stopped tank production.[3]

Why are we losing control? America's technological dominance and sophistication has been supreme, but we have been undermined by technological theft occurring right outside your window. With the military being cut back, and because of the Pentagon's desire to profit in some way, little is being done to protect security secrets. For instance, the Pentagon will sell what are called "spare parts" of military hardware to anyone with the money to buy—even foreign agents. These spare parts are usually brand new armaments in perfect condition. You can even buy on the Internet!

So what is for sale? Oh, nothing too important. Just things like Tomahawk cruise missile guidance computers, guidance electronics for aircraft gunnery, sensitive communication and navigation gear, cryptography equipment, jamming hardware, M-79 grenade launchers, handguns, rifles, tank and aircraft parts...the list goes on and on. According to *U.S. News & World Report*, December 6, 1996 issue, "foreign countries can use these parts to re-supply their own armies, to find out how American weapons work, or to build their own weapons, avoiding years of costly development."

America Getting the Shaft

As if it were not enough that our own government is indiscriminately selling our military technology, America is giving hundreds of millions of dollars in loans to Russia to help them rebuild their economy. The idea is that this would prevent Russia from selling nuclear technology or armaments to volatile countries like Iran or Syria. But guess what—too late! They already sell to those countries and more. With no other readily available commodity, in the last five years, Russia has sold over twenty billion dollars worth of weaponry to the Iranians alone.

In 1995, Newt Gingrich warned the Russians that aid from the United States of over $200 million would be denied should they continue to assist the Iranians in the development of a nuclear weapons program; this threat has been largely ignored. The rogue nation-states of the world will gladly out-bid America to gain whatever technology they demand. Russia and other dangerous countries strengthen as America deliberately weakens herself.

The Government's Slippery Fingers

Ever wondered why it is so difficult lately to set interest rates and control the value of the American dollar? The government has a distinct lack of control over the flow of money. Global trade and the competition which trade encourages is out of the reach of governmental talons. In part, this fact keeps the minimum wage down and limits the availability of social programs.

The American government is also finding it harder and harder to control the activities of global megacorporations that do whatever it takes to be profitable, with or without governmental approval. Don't forget to add these challenges to the mixture: the growing national debt, the burden of paying for existing social programs, a social security system without any money, an unprecedented increase in illegal immigration, international drug trade flowing through this country's borders as though there are no restrictions, and so on.

What Flag?

With the government unable to get a handle on these and so many other problems, it may come as no surprise that patriotism is not taken very seriously anymore. In many cases, the sense of allegiance many people previously had toward America has been reduced to about the same emotional attachment to a county or parish you live in. Saluting the flag and singing the national anthem are no longer done out of pride, but a grudging formality at a baseball game. What else are Americans interested in besides what is in it for them or how high the entertainment value is?

From First to Worst

It would be amusing if it were not so pathetic that Clinton has of late identified himself with Teddy Roosevelt, even going so far as to compare himself with Roosevelt. Clinton has apparently never visited the Roosevelt Memorial and read the quote inscribed there that reflects Roosevelt's philosophy: "Alike for the nation and the individual, the one indispensable requisite is character." And yet Clinton was elected to another term. Makes you wonder, doesn't it?

I remember a time in America when you had respect for the President, when agencies like the CIA or FBI were something to trust in and rely upon. But those days are over. The Presidency is held by self-serving, dishonest, egocentric bureaucrats, and federal agencies are regarded warily. American government has become corrupt, bloated, superfluous and less powerful than ever.

While the rest of the world looks at America in bewilderment, wondering what has happened to us, the Quickening is taking our world to a much different political future. The sovereignty of once great nation-states diminishes as the individual takes precedence. People are becoming interconnected globally because of telecommunications, and new leadership will have to address world differences in new ways. The trend is from local thinking to global, from power in a hierarchy to power everywhere.

First Attempts At Globalism

After World War I, in 1919, Woodrow Wilson suggested that wars could be avoided. So it was agreed by the major players at the time to establish a world body to ensure that peace would be maintained and it was called the League of Nations. There was great optimism over this. Men like Henry Ford commented that people were too intelligent to allow world war to occur, that there was no need for war. Guess no one counted on Adolf Hitler. The League of Nations was powerless to prevent Nazi Germany from evolving into a significant threat to the world.

A second attempt to create a global governing body was made after World War II when the United Nations (UN) was formed. Fifty plus years later, we are still waiting to see if the United Nations will have any impact around the world. Of late, it is weak, disorganized and ineffectual, and I am skeptical as to whether it will ever truly assert itself with any real influence, much less take a role as world governing body.

One thing that the existence of the United Nations has brought about is the continuing decline of American sovereignty. Historically, America has taken the lead in maintaining peace and engaging in humanitarian aid throughout the world. After the Gulf War in 1991, George Bush proclaimed a New World Order, encouraging the power and influence of the United Nations.

Clinton, in turn, has sought to encourage the United Nations' intervention in global hot spots like Yugoslavia, Haiti, Somalia and Rwanda. He has also implored American soldiers to serve under foreign UN commanders and to be prepared to give their lives in the service of the UN. Although America still has the best military intelligence, spy satellites and the largest transport planes, there is an increasing tendency to relinquish the American role of world leader.

Elitist Conspiracy—Hogwash!

A number of semi-secret groups were formed after World War I, including the Council on Foreign Relations, the Club of Rome, the Bilderberger Group and the Royal Institute for International Affairs. Why did these groups come into being? The premise was world peace, and their charter spells out the desire to institute a world governing body to achieve that goal. Conspiracy theorists believe the true charter of these groups is to establish a world government and in turn reward themselves with unlimited global power and wealth.

Traditionally, the members of these groups have been prominent business men, politicians, intellectuals, military leaders and world bankers. Membership is by invitation only. The ranks of today's Council on Foreign Relations encompass most past living presidents including George Bush and Bill Clinton, intellectuals such as Henry Kissinger, and military leaders such as Colin Powell.

Presumably, the first attempt by this elite to achieve world government was their behind-the-scenes support for the League of Nations. Although this failed, they also threw their support behind the United Nations. Some conspiracy theorists like to point out the fact that John D. Rockefeller, one of the founders of the Council on Foreign Relations, donated the land on which the UN was constructed.

I do not personally ascribe to the idea that the world is being affected by the influence and money of these global-minded elitist groups. Granted, it is entirely possible that those who are more knowledgeable of world events are more likely to make a better educated guess about its direction. The significance of these elitist groups lies not so much in their influ-

ence on current world events, as much as their recognition and acceptance that these global trends are
inevitable.

Preparations For Global Government

In order to ensure that the global economy works
at its most efficient level, a global governing body will
have to be created. What sort of power will this body
possess? They will undoubtedly have the power to
enforce an international law to maintain the free flow
of trade. But there is also the desire among people
throughout the world for peace and a clean environment; this means the global government must be
given the power to regulate peace and care of the environment as well.

A global government may seem like an extremely
far-fetched idea to you right now. To achieve prosperity, peace and a clean environment will, however,
require a collective effort on the part of the entire
world. Prosperity can only come about in a highly
interconnected global economic system. Peace can
only be maintained when the world makes a common
effort. A clean environment would only happen if
everyone played by the same rules and worked together. There is no other way.

European Union

The world has been watching how things have
evolved in Europe in recent years, particularly after
1992 when Europe grouped together as the twelve
nation European Union (EU). The EU represents the
first attempt ever to group nations together in spite of
distinct differences in language, culture, ethnicity,
religion and economy. In addition, it was also the

first attempt at reducing the sovereignty of participating nations in favor of free trade, money flow, educational standards, environmental control, social programs, agricultural management and a common defense policy.

Obviously, the main impetus to form the EU was economy; the participating members realized that individually they were limited in their economic growth potential. Joined together, they hoped to be a formidable economic force in the world. The EU has had its challenges—expensive social programs, high immigrant unemployment, etc.—but it has demonstrated that nations are receptive to letting down their sovereign guard in order to benefit economically.

It is also interesting to note the manner in which the European Union governs itself; the EU has an elected European Parliament which lends a sense of democracy. However, the Parliament has no real power—it cannot choose leaders, establish laws or institute taxes. The *real* power of the EU is in its twenty-one member Executive Commission. Decisions are made secretly and imparted to the people via sophisticated media and public relations campaigns. Apparently, the Europeans understand that a traditional democratic government is not very efficient or practical for governing such a variety of nation-states.

As the global economy develops, national sovereignty is giving way to global sovereignty. What may look like an experiment in Europe may very well be translated later into a global governing body.

World Trade Organization

The General Agreement on Trade and Tariffs (GATT), updated in 1994, and NAFTA have succeeded in encouraging free regional and global trade. NAFTA is significant because it has opened up trade between America, Canada and Mexico and again demonstrated the increasing willingness on the part of these countries to lower their guard. These agreements paved the way for the World Trade Organization (WTO) treaty, which replaced GATT in January 1995.

One of the biggest flaws in GATT was its inability to enforce its own regulations. For example, in 1991, America violated a GATT dispute panel ruling by ignoring a ban on tuna shipments from Mexico to the United States. However, the WTO treaty replacing GATT ensured that every nation-state member would be forced to comply with laws and rulings set forth by the WTO panel; violations of these regulations would be met with sanctions or embargoes by all other members. In fact, these requirements are so stringent that a nation-state has to acknowledge them even if it means changing their own federal, state or provincial laws. You can see that the World Trade Organization is quite a powerful global economic governing body.

Another frightening reality about the WTO is its voting structure. America is at the mercy of all the other participating nation-states. Every country has one vote; even countries as small as Monaco have the same voting power as a country as large as the United States. No one country possesses the power to veto trade decisions. And remember, the WTO has been joined with the influential World Bank as well as the International Monetary Fund (IMF).[4]

What About the World Bank and IMF?

Originally formed after World War II to assist in the reconstruction of Europe, the World Bank and IMF boasted of redirecting their efforts toward poorer nations after achieving stability in European countries. The truth is, these organizations have been involved in financing projects which have enriched already wealthy nations at the expense of the poor. For example, the Narmanda Valley dams in India submerged several hundred villages, displacing millions of impoverished people. Human services are not the true agenda here. Rather, money is invested in high tech energy and transportation endeavors and other development schemes, putting money in the pockets of contractors, heads of state and real estate developers.

These organizations are rapidly gaining global political power. For example, the World Bank often demands that potential nation-state borrowers change laws in their own countries in order to qualify for loans. The results are weakened labor protection, trade unions, communal land holdings and even reduced child benefits in these countries. It is very likely that the World Bank and the IMF will assume the role of a global banking system to ensure that the global economy will flow seamlessly.[5]

Yes, there are benefits to a triumvirate of economic power. Import taxes are slashed globally, the food and consumer goods market is opened wider, and the financial services industry is experiencing tremendous growth with increased cross-border activity. It is hard to argue with increased prosperity as the world economy quickly burgeons to an astounding $200 trillion. But is the price too high? Is it too high when countries like America must allow outside organizations to reduce the authority of their own constitutions? Indeed, nation-state sovereignty, and to some extent, independence must be forfeited in yet another step toward global government.[6]

Global Law and Order

As our world becomes more interdependent, it also becomes a more chaotic and disorderly place. Law and order is critical. The challenge for a global government is to avoid upsetting the balance of world power, to reach some middle ground that provides all nations an equal voice. A global government will require some form of checks and balances, perhaps determined partly on the basis of population, level of prosperity and even a nation's contribution to the global economy. And just when we think we have it wrapped up neatly, other issues will arise to challenge a global government.

For instance, how can one nation with a huge arsenal of nuclear warheads presume to insist that another nation with fewer warheads cease production of these weapons? Or how can one nation be prevented from exploiting certain natural resources when those nations who wish to impose such sanctions have been guilty of that very sort of exploitation? Obviously, some consensus will need to be reached.

Global laws are necessary because the traditional nation-state laws are limited to the borders of a country. Without global control, the world is vulnerable to those who can violate the laws of one nation and hide safely in another. Terrorists can continue to murder in Greece and be smugly tucked away in Libya. A manufacturer in one country can release pollutants that carry over to a neighboring country.

91

Drug lords in Columbia can continue pouring cocaine into America. You get the idea.

A global government can be given jurisdiction over
all crimes against people everywhere, whether it is
terrorism, war crimes or environmental violations. Of
course, a global government would also monitor all
global trade, and should rightly have control over nuclear, biological and chemical weapons. A judicial
system global in nature would have to be instituted
to check possible excesses in global government in
such matters as local autonomy, ethnic, individual
and religious rights. An individual could conceivably
take cases directly to the global court, bypassing
their local government.

The enforcement of global law will require a global
police or special forces, probably unusual and highly
trained. These futuristic peace keepers will need basic commando skills and knowledge of weapons, be
fluent in high tech gear as well as languages, be
trained in diplomacy, but capable of guerrilla tactics.
They must be extremely flexible, prepared to go anywhere at any time to handle everything from terrorism or riots to disease or famine.[7]

Global Taxation

Some of you were probably expecting this! After
all, how do you pay for a global government and its
global police to enforce laws and maintain peace and
order? Already there have been a number of suggestions for funding a variety of global organizations;
these could very well apply to global government as
well. For example, in 1992, former UN Secretary
General Boutros-Boutros Ghali delivered a proposal
for creating an ongoing funding system for the United
Nations. He suggested a special global tax structure

which includes any one, all or a combination of the following:

◊ a surcharge tax on all arms sales
◊ a tax on all transnational movement of currencies
◊ a tax on all global trade
◊ a tax on the production of specific material, e.g., petroleum
◊ a levy on all global sea and air travel
◊ a "one day" income tax on all people of the world every year

As you can imagine, the ideas for things to tax have been endless, from countries responsible for certain types of pollution, like a carbon dioxide tax, to taxes on atomic energy production, satellite launches and microwave bands! No one *wants* taxes. But most people agree that it is most likely a necessity if global government is to be maintained.[8]

Global Government: Finding the Foundation

In my view, the United Nations is weak and I do not believe it has much hope of growing stronger in the future, despite various infusions of money and effort. However, the UN's global operations have fostered the feeling that cooperation among different countries to achieve joint geopolitical, military and social objectives is acceptable. Added to this, the World Trade Organization has demonstrated a certain effectiveness at controlling global trade. But will these global organizations actually be transformed into a global government? Probably not.

The UN is an unlikely candidate because of its weakness and inability to enforce regulations. In addition, it has been controlled by a security council made up of the nation-state victors of World War II; this has alienated many smaller, less powerful countries, and this is not likely to change. Despite the power of the WTO, it would be difficult to accept them as the focus of a global government because of the heavy imbalance of the voting structure.

What these organizations do is set a precedent for what is to come. There is a willingness on the part of the world to establish some form of global government, perhaps adopting the best aspects of the existing systems.

The Middle East Challenge

One of the first tasks on the agenda of the global government may well be how to deal with the Middle East. Here we have the world's greatest single source of petroleum and this automatically makes this an important issue to the whole world. But it is complicated by the tensions between Israel and her neighbors.

The Middle East is predominantly Muslim. And Muslims deplore the Jews of Israel, a challenge which runs deeper than occupied territories, as most people in the Western world are led to believe. This problem is an ethnic and a religious one. The Muslims will not be satisfied until they have control of all the land now occupied by Israel, and this attitude is encouraged both by Palestinian leader Yassir Arafat and by the Iranians.

This global government will have quite the challenge on its hands as they struggle to somehow achieve some sort of lasting peace and stability. Nothing has worked so far, and problems as delicate as this one may require a special leader in this global government with a creative way of bringing peace.

Global Dictator?

Along with our inherent desire to be governed, people always seek a leader. We always want someone to assume the authority, to make the final decision. A global government will probably have its political structure comprised of a type of parliament, made up of elected officials representing each country of the world. However, the European Union's parliament and the WTO suggest that power brokering will still exist within such a framework. Tradeoffs will be made as individual nations, megacorporations and various other groups seek their own agendas. The risk in all this jockeying for issues and power is that it can easily lead to the rise of a powerful individual, perhaps even a dictator.

Some believe that global government and a dictatorial leader is prophesied in the Bible, particularly in the book of Daniel and in Revelation. It is prophesied that some day in the future, perhaps the near future, a man—called the Antichrist in the Bible—will come on the world scene and will figure out a way to set up a global government. He is said to devise a way to monitor the world economy and achieve world peace, even in the Middle East.

Although the Bible talks about the advantages of such a system and its leaders, it also reveals how this will lead to the destruction of the world. I believe in God, but I have not formed any conclusions about such a prophesy. At the very least, it is interesting that many current world events have been foretold by Bible prophets.

Triggering a Global Government

What will trigger the formation of a global government? Will it form suddenly or will it take a decade, two decades or more? Right now, we can only guess how a global government will take shape. It is a complex matter, but one that is definitely in our future as the Quickening takes us forward. What we do know is that the economy is becoming global. We also know that there is desire to have world peace. And we know that we want to attempt to correct environmental wrongs.

We know that organizations are now in place to make some of these things happen. Most people in the world are open to globalism, seeing it as a way to improve their lives economically, socially and environmentally. Yes, even in America the recognition is dawning on many of us that world changes are coming, although Americans will probably be the last to let go of the notion of the strong America we have always known.

The past has proven that countries *can* change if they have to. America began as an "experiment" in democracy. Europe is now experimenting with a unified system. The Chinese and Russians are experimenting with free trade. New countries are being born as experiments in autonomy. Constitutions will change, governing bodies will change, armies and even tax systems will change. The world's attitude is changing and the way we live in connection with each other will be quite different than it is now. The

Quickening is a reflection of that acceleration of change.

What will trigger a global government? Some have suggested it could be anything from a financial crisis or increased terrorism to alien visitors finally revealing themselves openly. Who knows. Whatever it is, I suspect it is just around the corner.

4

Society

Ten year old Brent was bored like crazy. School was a waste of time, but when he went home there was nothing to look forward to either. His mom was working later and later now that she had to get a second job to support him and his sister, Marcy, so he saw even less of her. And he wouldn't have visiting time with his dad for at least another two weeks. TV was getting boring, too. And he had played Final Doom on his computer so many times it was no longer challenging. After laying around on the sofa for a while, Brent called his friend Steve Belden.

"Hey, Brent. Why don't you come over? Scott's here and we've been huffing. It's cool," Scott urged, enthusiastically.

Brent thought for a moment. Scott was in the 8th grade, a couple of years older, and always getting into stuff. A couple of weeks ago, he had some pot. Now they were huffing. "Yeah, I guess," Brent decided. "Better than sitting around this crappy place."

An hour later, Brent was in Steve Belden's house. Steve's mom also worked late, and he didn't have any siblings to pester him. So he always had other kids over doing something. When Brent arrived, the TV was on and Steve and Scott were playing a Nintendo Ninja combat game. It was a gory game in which you killed your opponent by breaking his neck or tearing out his heart. But Brent had played that so often, he was not much interested. After a while, Scott turned to the side of the chair he had been sitting in and produced a can of upholstery cleaner and a large plastic bag.

"Hey, man," Scott said, looking at Brent. "You should try this. You really get an amazing buzz—and it's free!" They all laughed at this. Scott put the can of cleaner into the bag, and dispensed cleaner fumes into it, promptly putting the bag over his nose and mouth. He inhaled deeply and sat back in his chair, watching as Steve repeated his actions.

Brent had been smoking pot for several months now, and that was pretty cool, so why not this, too? He reached for the cleaner and bag. Spraying the cleaner into the bag and inhaling, Brent felt a weird sensation. In about a minute, it was as though he was slipping away into darkness. His thoughts were muddled and unclear, but he could hear his friend Steve shout to Scott. "Call 9-1-1!! I think he's losing it!"

Ω   Ω   Ω

Heinrich waited at the Frankfurt train station as instructed until 10:30pm. It was January, the weather had grown bitterly cold, and although he was wearing a full length coat, standing there got on his nerves. Minutes later, he watched three men come toward him, all their heads cleanly shaven and wearing the same coats as he did. He recognized his friend, Jurgen, the leader of the group.

"These fellows are going to tag along," Jurgen announced as he came within earshot of Heinrich. Heinrich only nodded grimly, as cigarettes were lit and passed all around. "Did you bring it?" Jurgen inquired of Heinrich, looking him up and down. "Yes," Heinrich replied, motioning to the inside of his coat. "Good. Let's go then."

Now all four men hastened down several streets wordlessly. At length, they reached a run down apartment building. Three flights up, a window was lit and rock music slid out into the frigid night. Stopping in front of the apartment holding the music, Jurgen knocked heavily on the door.

"Go away!" An agitated voice shouted from inside.

"It is the landlord," Jurgen said, steadily.

"Go away! I already paid rent!"

"Naturally you would be difficult, you Turkish bastard," Jurgen said, the patience in his voice belying his intentions.

Two of the men broke open the door, finding the inhabitant of the apartment standing in the middle of the bare room, wearing only undershorts and a dirty shirt. He gasped in fear as the two men grabbed him and pasted duct tape across his mouth. They then placed him forcibly into a chair and tied his hands and feet with telephone cord. Heinrich stepped forward, removing a small canister of gasoline from under his coat. A cap was removed and the young Turkish man who had only recently arrived in Germany was doused. Heinrich stood back from the man and lit a long wooden match, as the other skinheads left the apartment.

"Today, you will burn in hell," Heinrich said softly. "Heil, Hitler." He tossed the match at the man in the chair.

Ω   Ω   Ω

Webster's dictionary describes "civilization" as people who have reached a high level of social development, and have transcended a condition of savagery or barbarism. To a large extent, we *are* that civilized society in most parts of the world. Technological developments have thrust most of the world forward. People everywhere are becoming more cosmopolitan, sampling clothes, food, art, sports, other cultures. But something is wrong with this picture. Everything is smooth on the surface of the world's lake, but churning undercurrents swirl below.

Many of us might have a hard time seeing that everything is *not* okay. People are starving in countries far away from us, but women are also being raped and murdered in the house next door. We complacently watch violence on television and in movies, but want our children to be protected from such horrors as drugs, alcohol and sex at a young age. Society and societal ills have progressed at such a rapid rate and along such extremely negative trends that most of the issues that need to be addressed are out of human control. And yet most of us—Americans and otherwise—plod through our daily lives without a thought for anything but the next meal.

With all our advances in so many areas, you would think that we would be able to maintain common decency implicit in the civilized society we have worked so hard to build. But I believe our priorities have been derailed, and our values have been buried in a sea of selfishness. The state of our society is a major factor in the Quickening, something we should all take a look at on an individual level instead of just believing that it is always someone else's fault.

The High Tech Socio-Cultural Vehicle

One of the most significant ways that technology affects society is in the way that people live. Television, via satellite, broadcasts programs into people's homes, facilitating worldwide awareness of current news and events. In America, we will soon have 400 to 500 channels available on our televisions! With recent improvements in satellite technology, hundreds of millions of people around the world will watch television for the first time by the year 2000.[1]

Another way that the world is getting closer and closer is through travel. More people than ever are getting on airplanes to explore other parts of the world. Close to one billion people will travel by air in 1996; by 2000, the numbers will be as high as two billion people.[2] Each day, nearly five million people fly from one part of the world to another. People find out how other people live, first hand, often indelibly changed by what they observe.

English: Language to the World

Language is bringing the world together faster than ever. As you probably guessed, English is becoming the official global language. What you might not have known is that historically, society and culture is most easily transferred by language. Therefore, those countries in which English is already native will have the greatest impact on society and culture globally; America, of course, is the most visible English speaking country in the world.

Once French was the official diplomatic language, but this is no longer the case. English is now most commonly used in diplomatic situations as well. Although not necessarily an easy language to learn, most people are able to speak English well enough to be understood. Perhaps as a result, English has become the native language for over 400 million people in twelve countries.[3]

Granted, English is not the most spoken language in the world (there are technically twice as many people who speak Chinese), but it is the most accepted. In fact, of some 800 million people who speak Chinese, half of them can speak English.[4] Most of the countries of the European Union make the study of the English language a compulsory part of education. Many mega-corporations, such as Nissan, the Japanese car maker and Philips, the Dutch electronics firm, have adopted English as their main language, even those companies with headquarters in countries that are not traditionally English-speaking.[5]

Social & Cultural Homogenization?

The paradox inherent in our society today is that of individuals struggling to achieve their own gains as the world as a whole comes together. Most of the social and cultural mix has been Western, mainly American, introduced into other countries. For instance, the Japanese have had a preoccupation with the American West for years, country music, square dancing, cowboy boots, etc. The Russians have had a weakness for American jeans and rock music for years; many Russian artists have patterned their own music after American-styled rock.

Of course, for years in America, we have been driving Japanese cars. The Japanese, in turn, have been eating McDonald's cheeseburgers. Everywhere you look you find Chinese restaurants, while the Chinese crowd into the world's largest Kentucky Fried Chicken franchise located in Beijing across from Mao's tomb. Germans listen to and sing Madonna's music, while a Russian soldier drinks a Diet Coke and smokes British Kent cigarettes. Nearly every young person under the age of thirty wears jeans and t-shirts whether it is in Asia, Australia, Latin America or Europe.

You can see that the world is integrated in many ways. The irony is that even though there is this trend toward homogenization, people are inclined to maintain their own cultural identity and language. There is a sort of cultural backlash or resistance to complete acceptance of other cultural influences.

In Canada, the people of Quebec fiercely seek to maintain French as their primary language. People in Wales try to keep their language, literature and customs alive as well. The Catalans, people of northern Spain, have reinvigorated their language and several of their customs. Iran has not only resisted English, but is determined to keep Western, and most particularly American, influence out of their culture, even denouncing American materialism as demonic.

The American Influence

There is no question about the tremendous influence that America has on the people of nearly every country in the world. This is nothing new. America has been the leader of just about everything in the world during the course of the twentieth century. America has been an economic and military powerhouse. America has been the leader in ingenuity, individual freedom, opportunity and prosperity. America has set the example for the rest of the world. Thus, in examining the accelerating societal changes, it is reasonable to look at America as an example of what is happening globally.

American Social Fabric Weakens

For a country so blessed in the past, with such promise, with such opportunity and prosperity, such a talented population, living so comfortably with so many conveniences and gadgets to make life easier, it is hard to believe that the social fabric of America is falling apart. But it is. The family, the very foundation of America, is disintegrating. Evidence of this and other accelerating problems within our country is everywhere.

The Shredding of Marriage & Family

Until the turn of the twentieth century, the American family was for the most part a tightly-sewn, nuclear unit. American men and women courted, married and raised families. Divorce was almost unheard of, and frowned upon by society. The Women's Suffrage movement, a precursor to the women's liberation movement of 1960s and 1970s, was one of the earliest signs of the breakdown of the family. Women had previously been tolerant of men, passively submitting to their place in society as wife and mother. After all, men were the predominant providers.

The onset of the Industrial Revolution brought women the opportunity to earn a living outside the home, simultaneously earning their independence. With newly acquired financial independence, women began to draw the line against negligent and abusive husbands. Greater numbers of women filed for divorce than ever before.

Despite this steady increase in divorce during the first half of the twentieth century, most people continued to strive for the ideal of a marriage and raising a family through the 1950s. Indeed, many women still maintained their role of staying home and raising the children, preferring that their husband be the breadwinner.

The 1960s Change Everything

The pivotal changes in these attitudes, and marked acceleration of many social changes as far as the Quickening is concerned, came during the 1960s. During this decade, America saw our children go to war in Vietnam. The offspring of those who sought to start families in the 1950s were coming of age. The so-called "Baby Boomer" generation invoked a social revolution that had its beginnings in anti-war protest; this generation further rejected everything that their parents had tried to achieve in terms of materialism as well, combining experimentation with drugs, sex, music and spirituality for good measure.

Yes, there was a distinct sexual revolution during the 1960s. It was a turbulent time when "the pill" became available for the first time to the general public. Obviously, the promise of such a simple form of birth control encouraged the open promiscuity of the 1960s as part of the Baby Boomer protest against the society of their parents. Love-ins, partner swapping and swinging were all in vogue. Men and women began to relate to each other differently. The traditional values held in marriage and raising a family were challenged as the act of having sex no longer necessarily meant getting married or bearing children.

Women's independence was heightened even more as they entered the job market in greater numbers. Spurred on by the feminist movement, women came to see that they were capable of bettering themselves, and that unlike their mothers and grandmothers before them, marriage was not necessary to assure financial security. Women became more educated than ever before, a college education not marriage leading them into professions traditionally dominated by men. Because women could now compete with men for the same jobs, this undermined the financial premise for marriage.

Rates of Divorce Escalate

The 1960s led to some startling changes in marriage, as well as an increase in the rate of divorce. In fact, the divorce rate nearly *tripled* from the optimistic 1950s to the not so optimistic 1970s, with one in three marriages ending in divorce. By the 1980s, half of all marriages ended in divorce, and to this day, at *least* half of marriages end in divorce. There is no reason to believe that this will ever change. Right now, America leads the world in this prestigious category, but statistics show that the divorce rate in other countries is increasing at such a pace as to be quickly narrowing the difference between America and the rest of the world.[6]

There was a time when divorce was a scandal. In 1930s and 1940s Hollywood, actors and actresses divorced and everyone heard about it, even though they divorced no more or less than the rest of the population. Divorce was perceived as scandalous, and yet famous people gave it a sort of glamour and acceptance. Today, in our enlightened age, the taboo of divorce has definitely diminished and the consequential disintegration of the family is gaining momentum.

It may come as a surprise but more people than ever are getting married, even in the face of staggering divorce rates! Many people have in fact opted not to marry at all, and many more are choosing to marry later in life, but they are nevertheless still taking the plunge, a leap which, in most cases, leads only to a hard, miserable landing later. Perhaps individuals consider themselves to be the exception to the current trends, but I believe we are all the same.

Single Parent Families

Invariably, with the increase in the divorce, there is the splitting of families into pieces. Most people have no trouble having children soon after they marry, but when a divorce occurs, these same children are sure to suffer. In America, each year since

1975, an average of one million children are involved in a divorce.[7]

In almost ninety percent of the cases, divorced mothers are given custody of their children. During the 1970s, there was a sharp increase in the number of children living in predominantly single mother households as the result of divorce. Women from many other countries in the world seem to be following suit. Then there is the curious trend in the world today of unmarried women having children. Denmark is at the top of the list with forty-five percent of births to unmarried women.

The combined effect of divorce, separation, abandonment and unmarried women who choose to have children is that approximately one-third of the world's children live in single mother households![8] I don't doubt that these mothers are doing the best they can to raise their children well, but it makes you wonder what kind of an influence the absence of a father figure has upon these subsequent generations.

Millennium Generation

Many millions of children are not raised in a traditional, healthy family environment, and this includes those who have one or two parents. The generations we now see—the "X" generation (offspring of the Baby Boomers) and the Millennium generation (offspring of the X generation)—are heading toward an uncertain and not very promising future.

For the single mother, despite the employment opportunities which have become increasingly available to women in the last thirty years, having a job and raising a family alone is a strain on both time and finances. On the financial forefront, most single mother families are barely scraping by, and thus many of these children are raised in lower income or near impoverished conditions. Women in this situation are forced to work at least one, sometimes two jobs, and subsequently forced to let school, television and the world raise their children.

Of course, married couples raising families are also faced with the challenge of constraints on their finances and their time. Children in these families are also left to their own resources to raise themselves, starting as early as pre-school. Given that husbands and wives grow apart to such an extent in a situation where both are forced to work simply to survive, it is no surprise that they don't know their children any better.

Education

Is the manner in which today's generations are raised having an impact on society? Absolutely. How are children growing up? Many of them are showing no interest in school. Many professional observers believe problems at home, such as child abuse or just neglect, have discouraged children from taking an interest in school, hobbies or any type of social activity.

Factors at home may also account for the fact that the children that do attend school reach their senior year in high school and yet are sliding through without learning the basics—reading, writing and simple math. Even more incredibly, many of these children actually go on to graduate from college.

Student Achievement Test (SAT) scores which measure the ability of a student to apply these basics, have dropped eighty points in the last thirty years.[9] And it is no longer a revelation that most children in America do poorly in math and sciences when compared with children in other countries, particularly Asian. This is only one indicator of the direction and future of America.

Television Addiction

What are kids doing when they are not in school? For many of them, nothing constructive. They begin life by spending enormous amounts of time staring at a television. On average, two to five year olds watch about twenty-nine hours of television per week! Prime time shows will draw as many as nine million child viewers per any given episode.[10] It is not uncommon for older children to watch twice as much television per week.

Why are kids watching so much TV? For one thing, with parents being so busy with work, it is often easier just to plop a child down in front of the television and before you know it, several hours have flown by. Once a pattern such as this has begun, many children will actually protest if they are prevented from watching certain shows or watching TV when they want to. In addition, parents find it hard to prevent kids from watching so much television because they themselves are guilty of watching television at an addictive level. After all, Baby Boomers were the first generation to really be directly affected by and raised on television.

Teen Sex

A parent's worst nightmare is that their son or daughter will become pregnant or make someone else's child pregnant. Most parents are fearful of their children having sex—at any age. The news for them is not good. Kids today are experimenting with sex earlier than ever before. A record number of teenage girls have gotten pregnant in the last decade, many of them between the ages of thirteen and fifteen. On average, about one million teenage girls become pregnant at least once every year, and forty percent of teenage girls will become pregnant before they are twenty.[11] America boasts the highest teen pregnancy rate of any developed country in the world.

What happens to these pregnant teenagers? About half of them will end their pregnancies with an abortion. Amazingly, an estimated fifteen percent of these girls will get pregnant again within a year! For those who choose to raise a child at that age, their own childhood has ended. Where are the parents in all this? Remember, it was the Baby Boomers who introduced promiscuity and sexual freedom to the world.

Kids, Drugs & Alcohol

Children are experimenting with illegal drugs at an earlier age more than ever before. They are trying everything from marijuana to cocaine, crack to LSD and even heroine, usually inhaling it as a powder. But the most popular drugs are not even drugs; they are paint thinner, upholstery cleaner, aerosol deodorizing spray and more. Kids under the age of twelve are "huffing," or inhaling the vapors of these products to get a quick, cheap high. About twenty percent of kids have tried inhalants at least once to get high, a scary figure when you consider that irreversible brain damage or death is not uncommon from such activity.[12]

Marijuana seems to be another drug of choice among eighth graders and younger. Marijuana accounts for sixteen percent of the drugs used regularly among kids, and the use increases with age. During 1995, twenty-nine percent of sophomores in high school smoked pot regularly, and thirty-five percent of high school seniors were regular marijuana users.[13]

Why are our kids using drugs at such alarming levels? Some experts believe that because many of the Baby Boomers were drug users they find it difficult to reprimand their children. Another reason is that drugs are being used in these kids' homes by their parents, and why would a child regard something that their parent did as wrong? Of course, the fact that figures we have formerly regarded as role models, such as the President and the current Speaker of the House, admit to having smoked pot does not help our children take the right path either.

Hard as it may be to believe, many of our children are alcoholics! During 1995, it is estimated that ninety-three percent of high school seniors consumed alcohol. Most of these kids started drinking when they were about thirteen, and for ten percent of them, drinking will stay with them to become a potentially lifelong problem. The likelihood that a child will become an alcoholic is again based upon parental influence; if a parent has a drinking problem, it is that much more likely that a child will follow in their footsteps. An estimated thirty percent of the children of alcoholics become alcoholics themselves.

And why should that be a surprise? Who else does a child have to look to for guidance? Given that alcohol is a problem in one out of every five families, the potential for children who will battle problems with alcohol is in the millions.

The sad irony also exists of teenagers drinking out of rebellion to parents who make drinking seem forbidden and mysterious. Even harder to fight is the peer pressure to "fit in," to conform by drinking. In these cases, perhaps more straightforward communication between parents and children could prevent some of these challenges to our future generations. Then again, many believe that kids will do what they do, no matter what they are told.

Kids & Crime

The rate of crime committed by children has increased dramatically in the last decade. In 1995, the number of juveniles (kids under the age of eighteen) locked up in jail was up seventeen percent. Of those juveniles sent to jail, fifty-five percent of them carried a gun most or all of the time; the reason they gave for this was self-defense. Nearly one-third of all high school students have asserted that they know how to get a gun. Apparently, possessing a gun is becoming readily accepted as normal. Perhaps this has something to do with the rising prevalence of youth gangs in America.

Not only is the ease of obtaining and acceptance of guns a frightening trend, but the attitude that accompanies the possession of a deadly weapon is even more shocking. About ten percent of inner city high school students believe that shooting someone is acceptable "if that's what it takes to get what you want from them." [14]

Often children become criminals out of serious family problems or merely out of sheer boredom. In fact, about half of juvenile crime occurs between three p.m. and dinner time.[15] The millions of children in homes with an alcoholic parent tend to be more aggressive than most children, and have the tendency to take illegal drugs, drink at a young age, and generally to be in trouble more frequently.

Youth Gangs

It used to be that kids just got beaten up by school yard bullies. Most disputes between kids were settled with fist fights resulting in a bloody nose or a black eye. While we never want to see our children hurt, even more disconcerting is that today our children are more likely to be shot than merely beaten. The murder rate for fourteen to seventeen year olds has increased 172 percent over the past decade. During that time, gun related murders of children by other children tripled, and the number of juveniles arrested for weapon possession has increased 100 percent.[16]

Youth gangs are definitely on the rise. One of the reasons for this may be that boys raised in single mother households have no father figure with which to identify, so they identify instead with an older member of a gang. Gangs provide peer support, camaraderie and even financial aid, sometimes the result of drug deals or other criminal activity. Possessing a gun is routine in a gang, and a rite of passage can frequently involve using the gun, perhaps on a rival gang member, perhaps on an innocent person.

Child Abuse

As if kids did not have enough to worry about, they are being abused in their very own homes. In the past, people have tried to account for child abuse by attributing it to mental health problems on the part of the adult; the truth is, this accounts for only about ten percent of the cases of child abuse.

The abuse is usually of a physical, emotional and/or sexual nature. Physical abuse can be characterized by beating a child until marks and bruises appear. Emotional abuse can take the form of something as basic as verbal insults to something more tangible like the neglect of a child's needs of clothing, food and shelter. Sexual abuse ranges from exhibitionism or fondling to intercourse and using a child to participate in producing pornographic materials.

It is difficult to obtain accurate figures for the incidence of child abuse, as so many cases undoubtedly go unreported to police or health professionals. Generally, child abuse is believed to have increased in the past decade with an estimated four million reported cases. Children who suffer any type of child abuse are often sad, fearful and angry, have difficulty getting along with other children and are mistrustful of strangers. They also tend to be stunted intellectually, socially and emotionally, and they do not function comfortably in society as adults.[17]

Teenage Suicide

According to the National Center for Health Statistics, the rate of teenage suicide in America has increased a dismaying 200 percent in the past thirty years! Children are falling through the cracks of this chaotic world, feeling unloved and ignored. Children are wondering what the point of life is, wondering where the world is going, and why it doesn't care about them. Tragically, this can compel a child to take their own life. What kind of a world do we live in when a child has absolutely no hope for the future?

Global Social Disintegration

It is blatantly apparent that America has a strong influence in more ways than one on the societies and cultures of people in other countries. International statistics indicate that the breakdown of the family has not been limited to America. Again, as in America, this has been largely because of an increase in divorce. Accordingly, there has been an increase in single mothers struggling to raise families without a sufficient income or adequate time. In other countries, children are not just neglected, improperly fed or housed, but they are often simply abandoned altogether.

Europe

UNICEF recently published a report on overall social conditions in Eastern and Central Europe. Apparently, despite favorable economic and political changes, most of the eighteen countries in the report (including bigger countries such as Russia, Hungary, Poland, Romania, Ukraine and the Czech Republic) show signs of serious social problems, particularly a decline in the stability of the family. As of year end 1995, UNICEF reports "there is no clear and comprehensive evidence that the social crisis is approaching an end." Poverty remains at excruciating levels, especially for single mother families, unemployment is stagnant and the numbers of broken marriages continue to soar.[18]

In Ireland, the Minister of Health commented at the groundbreaking of a post-natal clinic, that "Irish society and social attitudes to the family had changed dramatically in the past twenty years.... In particular, there had been a large rise in the numbers of children born outside of marriage." He went on to add that many people were "adopting modes of family life different from that of the traditional nuclear family."[19]

Obviously, as we see that this trend of family disintegration is happening all over the world, we must ask ourselves, what will come of these generations? What kind of a world will be built by people who cannot construct stable relationships and family lives? With a crumbling social foundation and generations centered only on themselves, it is difficult to devise hope for this world.

Common Decency & Civility

Why is there this strange, ironic twist? In all our brilliance, humans are able to devise the most fantastic machines, gadgets, buildings and systems. We are able to concoct ways to generate unbelievable amounts of money. And yet we are unable to control the way we behave in this world. We are killing, raping, stealing from, cheating, uttering profanities at and destroying relationships with each other.

Like never before in human civilization, we are generally uncivilized to our fellow human beings. How is this possible? In an age when we know more than ever before, when we have more, when we can do more and we have more freedom, why do we treat each other with such a lack of regard?

Moral Relativism

As I have come to understand 'civilization,' it means that people treat each other with decency and civility. That courtesy and respect for our fellow man is something we do because we know that is the right thing to do. Now I hear people say that we live in a world of moral relativism, meaning that morality is relative to how you define it. One person exploits the environment to make a buck, another person believes it is immoral to do this and would rather spend a buck to reclaim the environment. One person thinks it is okay to kill your parents if they abused you sexually as a child, another person calls it murder. It is all "relative."

Moral relativism is moral quicksand. The deeper you get, the more quickly you sink to your own doom. But this is where the world is heading fast. Generally, sociologists, psychologists, teachers, counselors, government officials, police and others in authority agree that parents are not teaching their children the difference between right and wrong. They are not teaching their children to have respect for other people. They are not even teaching them common courtesy and decency. Or if they think they are, these children are not getting the message.

How many times have you had a door slam in your face as someone went through it, intent on where they were going, completely oblivious to the fact that other people actually do exist around them? How many times have you extended yourself to someone, perhaps even in business, providing a customer with some extra service, and had them act like they deserved it and not bothered to even say a simple 'thank you'? How many times have you been driving in a car and had someone cut you off, you beep at them indignantly and they respond by making an obscene hand gesture, as if to say, 'I didn't do anything wrong!'?

The nuclear family unit is virtually extinct, and there is no real cohesive, supportive environment anymore. Many children are growing up like weeds;

their parents don't know them, the world is indifferent, and they have no clue themselves. For many people, there is nothing on which to base a moral absolute to guide their lives. Western, Judeo-Christian thinking has gone out of vogue, ostensibly replaced in many cases with Eastern philosophy and spirituality, or plain atheistic self-determination. Without a doubt, the emphasis is placed fully on self and self-awareness, only fostering and nurturing an already increasingly selfish society.

What is most discouraging is that so many of the deleterious influences in our deteriorating society are so common that they are unnoticed or simply ignored. These days to hear of murders or rapes means nothing so long as it does not happen to you. In other words, what do I care if people are starving in Ethiopia, as long as I get to go to McDonald's for dinner? What difference does it make to me whether there is racism in the world as long as I am Caucasian? How does it affect me that a homeless person has to sleep under the highway overpass? Why should I be concerned that more and more women are being beaten by their husbands and boyfriends as long as it doesn't happen to me or someone I know?

One of the saddest aspects of the Quickening of society is our extreme selfishness and indifference. Maybe we think we will never pay a price for such thinking, but that is not reality. In truth, there are consequences for most of our actions.

The Influence Of The Media

If you have ever wondered why people, including yourself, seem so desensitized to the growing tragedies in the world today, I would say, take a look at television, movies and the media in general. It is the strangest thing. Everywhere you go today, whether it is the beauty salon, a casino, even exercise gyms, there is at least one television set. I have to laugh when I see people standing in the grocery store watching television because I can't imagine that they aren't watching plenty of television at home.

The American Lust For Violence

What are we watching? Frankly, we have had a steady diet of violence, death and murder, especially those of us in the Baby Boomer generation. We have seen thousands of killings, shootings, beatings and various forms of violent behavior on the screen, and have become accustomed to the idea. We actually go to the theater and *pay* to see it!

What are some of the most violent shows on television today? Cartoons and most police dramas are both based on some type of violence. The *Roadrunner* cartoon is about a coyote who tries to kill a roadrunner, a bird, with cannons, explosives, guns, knives, and heavy objects. Is this entertainment? Is this what we are teaching our children? I wonder if James Garner of *The Rockford Files* had been hit as many times in real life as he had been in his popular television series whether he might not have been dead long ago.

Another example of a typical, popular American favorite is *Scarface*. As much as I enjoy watching Al Pacino's acting, *Scarface* was one of the most violent movies I have ever seen; of course, I am sure there are many more out there that are even more violent.

What is amazing is that the people of America and throughout the world *hunger* for violence-filled TV shows and movies. And of course, the world enjoys plenty of the same violent movies that America does with heaps of profanity and sex thrown in for good measure.

Television & the Way We Live

Even more interesting is that TV has also changed American expectations of what they 'must' have. Possessions previously considered luxuries, such as an air conditioner, a college education, or a second car, have become necessities in many households. The irony is that "individuals are pursuing bigger dreams while living in a society they perceive as increasingly unlikely to fulfill those dreams, either materially or spiritually."[20]

Television has both a local and a global effect. As TV moved from the days of *I Spy* to *NYPD Blue*, its diet of casual sex and unabashed violence "helped lower viewers' expectations about the safety and ethical character of 'other' communities."[21] In other words, television has played a critical role in changing American attitudes about the way the rest of the world lives.

America's TV & the World

Most of the world's television programming comes from America. CNN is in nearly 100 countries worldwide. Just watch CNN World Report and you will get a glimpse of how people live on the other side of the earth. American television programs like *Dallas*, *Matlock*, *Spenser For Hire*, and *Sesame Street* are enormously popular in dozens of countries, often dubbed to accommodate the local language. MTV (Music Television) is gaining popularity throughout the world, influencing millions of young people not only with what is hot in music, but what to wear, how to dance and even what parts of their bodies to pierce.

Right now an estimated one billion people throughout the world have television. Hundreds of millions more will soon join this world commonality. In China, there are 100 million TVs, with an estimated 600 million viewers, and millions more who want televisions! India has about 400 million potential viewers. As increasing numbers of people watch television and see the materialism and freedom of more technologically advanced cultures, a desire will be instilled to adopt these things for their own countries.

Growing Fringe Groups

Political and economic groupings of people are often within the context of a given geographic location and people identify with each other on the basis of their ethnicity. This is fairly normal and predictable. Humans are, after all, a basically gregarious lot. We not only want to feel like we belong, but we want to participate in the group with which we identify ourselves. Despite our need to identify with a group, there is nevertheless a growing tendency for people to retain a certain amount of their unique ethnic, linguistic and cultural heritage, even though the world is quickly becoming globally linked.

Although history has always seen groups form within the main national group (i.e., religious, trade-oriented, academic, or social), what the world is witnessing now is an unprecedented number of divergent and violent groups. Recent evidence of violent expression by divergent groups in America includes terrorism such as the Oklahoma City bombing, the

New York World Trade Center bombing, the series of bombings by the Unabomber, and the derailing of the Amtrak train in Arizona. It is these groups, what I call fringe groups, which force America and the world to notice them using terrorist tactics.

Fringe Group Evolution

During the 1960s, America saw the anti-war movement and the civil rights movement; both were the impetus for many of the militant fringe groups that exist today in this country. In the midst of American involvement in the Vietnam War, this country was sending young American men to fight the Viet Cong, and a daily average of 100 men returned in body bags. Great consternation swept the country, as people began to see the results of the Vietnam War and became convinced that America had no clear objective to be at war in Southeast Asia.

Anti-war protests were staged throughout the country in nearly every major American city. Student protests turned into violent confrontations with heavily armed police and national guard, as in the case of Kent State University. Among the anti-war protesters were those chanting Viet Cong war slogans, running through the streets with Viet Cong flags, and generally existing in a state of confusion and anger.

American Militias On The Move

Distrust and cynicism toward the government, with a great deal of roots in the 1960s, brought about the formation of various militant groups, or militias, concerned with the way America was being run. In the 1990s, militia observers have identified militia activity in about forty states, with the highest concentration in the Western states. Hard core, gun toting, survivalist type militia membership stands at about 10,000 members and growing quickly; those who hold similar views and could potentially become members number at least five million.

The militia system is a complex one, but the majority of militia members and sympathizers with the same world view belong to the "Patriot" movement. According to Chip Berlet, a militia observer for Political Research Associates in Cambridge, Massachusetts, "on the far right flank of the Patriot movement are white supremacists and anti-Semites, who believe the world is controlled by a cabal of Jewish bankers [such as the Rothchilds of Europe]."[22] Berlet notes that this far right milieu also accommodates a number of other Patriot sub-movements, including the Identity Christians, Constitutionalists, tax protesters and the semi-secret Posse Comitatus.

On the other end of this bewildering spectrum of militias and the militia-minded are members of the John Birch Society. This group repudiates anti-Semitism and does not subscribe to the Jewish banker idea. Instead, they have contrived their own brand of paranoia. The John Birchers advocate the elitist conspiracy theory that the world is controlled by members of semi-secret institutions like the Council on Foreign Relations, the Trilateral Commission; they also look fearfully at the rise in power by the United Nations.

Several key events in recent history have invigorated the militia movement. For years, Americans of this lilt have been enthralled by the "evil empire," the Soviet Union, and its aim to rule the world. But when the Cold War ended, they were left looking for a new enemy. Attention was refocused on the American government. Further, these groups were not exempt from such economic changes as corporate downsizing, computer proliferation and automation.

Most Patriots are white males in the middle or working class sector of the economy. Many have either lost their jobs or have seen a sharp decline in their wages, and probably experienced an overall social dislocation. The result has been heightened resentment toward the establishment, the global corporations and the American government, which they believe participate in a conspiracy of either elitist groups or bankers.

Alienation is a feeling that these people, either ignored or attacked by the government, have grown accustomed to. For instance, Patriots are very sensitive to their right to form militias and to bear arms as stipulated in the Second Amendment of the US Constitution. Therefore, laws such as the Brady Bill, passed to control guns, have only incited Patriots; to them, this represents an illegal attempt on the part of the establishment to control Americans and to take one step closer to disarming Americans completely.

Oklahoma City, Waco, Montana & Ruby Ridge

The contempt, mistrust and cynicism has only continued to fester since its first strong signs in the 1960s. It was only a matter of time before something would snap. In 1992, when Randy Weaver, a Patriot tax protester and white separatist, decided to take on the Federal Bureau of Investigation (FBI), America got its first taste of raw nerves over the militia. Weaver was arrested in 1991 on gun charges. When he did not appear for the trial, the FBI went in pursuit of him. An eleven day standoff resulted in gunfire and the death of one FBI agent, Weaver's wife and his son. Patriots everywhere were incensed, and militia membership increased.

The Branch Davidians, a religious/survivalist cult led by David Koresh, was believed to be engaged in the sale and purchase of illegal firearms. In early 1993, in Waco, Texas, after a month long standoff with the FBI, the Koresh compound was stormed by Federal agents, who set it on fire and killed many of the cult members including Koresh. The Patriots were outraged by the behavior of the FBI, the ATF (Alcohol, Tobacco & Firearms) and other law enforcement authorities involved in the Waco incident.

Barely a year after Waco, the response became unbelievably clear when a truck bomb exploded outside the Federal building in downtown Oklahoma City. Dozens of people were killed and injured, and the front half of the building was blown off. Americans prayed that it was the act of some foreign terrorist group, but it was not long before Timothy McVeigh, an American Patriot, was arrested on charges of perpetrating this bombing in retaliation for the Waco incident.

Later in 1995, the world was made aware of the presence of the Freemen of Montana, another fanatic, relatively militant religious group. They believe that the Federal Reserve is illegal and that they are entitled to print their own money and establish their own economic system. The Freemen, in their own peculiar way, resist what they believe to be an overly intrusive government.

Unfortunately, the only tangible result of their resistance was that the federal government noticed when they failed to make mortgage payments to banks outside of their community, and chose not to send their children to public schools. And of course, the situation escalated when the Freemen decided to combat law enforcement authorities with guns.

The Future of the Militia

Many militia advocates warn that instances such as these are only the beginning. Threats ring through the country as militia members proclaim that it is time Americans take back their country from the government, from foreigners and from anyone else they perceive to be infringing on the American way of life.

Black American Civil Rights Movement

The civil rights movement of the 1960s challenged the white person's perception of black people in America. Historically, a homogeneous current has woven its way through American society, but this has changed in the last forty years as this country has become more of a heterogeneous mix. People— blacks in particular—want to maintain their own unique ethnic and cultural identity. From the anti-segregation laws of the 1950s to the civil rights peace marches by Martin Luther King, Jr., from Malcolm X followers to the "Black Power" movement, America was destined to emerge from the twentieth century as a changed country.

The Black & White War

Fringe groups emerged or reemerged as Americans who felt threatened by these social changes sought to resist them. One example is the white hooded, cross burning lynch mob, the Ku Klux Klan. Although the Klan was formed 100 years earlier, it gained more media attention during the 1960s as the Klan lashed out against the black civil rights movement.

Some social observers, such as Dr. William Pierce, author of the renowned book, *The Turner Diaries*, contend that there is an ongoing war between the black people and the white people in America today. It may not be blatantly obvious to us because, as Pierce says, "the race war is going on at a low level right now. The crime situation in this country has been to a large extent a war of the black underclass against the white majority. And I believe the situation will get worse."[23]

Those who agree with Dr. Pierce and others like him point to the 1992 Los Angeles riots, invoked by the Rodney King case of white police violence against an unarmed black man. The riot was about black people literally making the predominantly white police force back off out of fear for their lives. Rioters looted, burned stores and assaulted people, turning Los Angeles into a war zone worse than the Watts race riots of the 1960s. Some believe blacks were destroying anything symbolic of white materialism and superiority.

Neo-Nazis

The saying goes that some things spread like wildfire. That has certainly been the case with anti-race groups, particularly factions such as the Skin Heads or Neo-Nazis. Derivatives of the Ku Klux Klan and often Patriots, these people outwardly and violently express their hatred for non-Arian races, mostly targeting blacks and Jews.

But black people have not been waiting passively for hate groups to intimidate them. Instead, they have been going about the business of taking control of their own situation. In many cases, they are finding solutions politically and by pressuring the government to pay attention to their needs. Otherwise, new black leaders are coming to the forefront of the black community in an attempt to provide leadership and direction. For instance, Jesse Jackson has been active as an advocate for black Americans with his Rainbow Coalition. New to black leadership are other, perhaps more radical black advocates such as Louis Farrakhan.

Nation of Islam

I am sure you remember watching hundreds of thousands of black men converge on Washington, D.C. to participate in what was called the Million Man March, an event orchestrated by a charismatic, influential but frightening black leader, Louis Farrakhan. Why did so many black men elect to take planes, cars, trains and buses to participate in this historical gathering? The premise was that Farrakhan would call for black unity, promoting legitimate goals of increased responsibility, discipline and self-reliance. What the men in attendance got instead was a heavy dose of Farrakhan's interpretation of Islamic Fundamentalism and an introduction to his Nation of Islam organization.

Farrakhan does not preach the Orthodox Islam of the Middle East, but he did gain the attention of the Islamic leaders there. He was invited to speak before the people in Iran during his African and Muslim World Friendship Tour (this in itself is telling of his true motives). During a speaking engagement on this tour, he commented, "God will not give Japan and Europe the honor of bringing down the United States. This is an honor God will bestow upon Muslims." Suddenly you can see some of the path he is taking, can't you? Later during the same tour, Farrakhan was reported to say, "if we Muslims can come together all over the world, we could become the superpower of the twenty-first century."[24]

Louis Farrakhan is a black separatist, and would prefer that the American government just give his Nation of Islam a strip of land on which to build a country inhabited solely by black Muslims. Libyan leader and madman, Muammar Qaddafi was so impressed by Farrakhan that he pledged one billion dollars to the Nation of Islam. Some believe that this money could be used in the future to pay for militant measures in the name of Islam, perhaps for the purchase of nuclear or other types of armaments. Farrakhan is indeed a daunting force, growing in power and influence.

American Militants & Society

There should be little doubt in your mind by now that we are seeing a trend in America. Many people are becoming more open to the idea of arming themselves and challenging government authority and each other. This is not a good sign. It is entirely possible that we may see a civil war of some kind in the near future, blacks against whites, militant right wing extremists against the government or some other dreadful combination of violence, self-righteousness and anger.

The worst possible scenario could be that one or a few members of such groups make the choice to use the most effective weapon to make their point: terrorism. These days, given the ease with which one can obtain nuclear, biological or chemical weapons, this is well within the realm of plausibility. And not only do we have to worry about potential terrorism at the hands of our own citizens, but on a worldwide basis as well.

Global Fringe Groups: Terrorism

The world is not a safe place because terrorism is global. The most dangerous and frightening of all appear to be those groups whose objectives are based on some religious or political ideology. You cannot rationalize with people like this because so often their ideologies are precisely what justify their violence. These are the groups which the world should fear the most, as their terrorism is not contained by any geo-political boundaries. Former US Defense Secretary Casper Weinberger predicted that such factions would be the "most immediate threat to free-world security."

Religious extremism and fanaticism have existed as long as civilization. The most notorious and widely known religious extremist groups of today have roots centuries old, such as the Islamic Fundamentalists of Iran. Mohammed went on his religious Crusades throughout the Mediterranean during the eighth century, killing everyone who did not convert to Islam. Now his cause is pursued even more zealously than in centuries past.

For decades in Europe, the Catholic-based Irish Republican Army (IRA) has sought to establish a united, free Ireland. They believe this is possible with the removal of every last Protestant from the country. The IRA has tentacles that reach globally in an effort to achieve this goal. Money and weapons are made available to them by any means, and anyone who stands in their way is simply eliminated.

Elsewhere, in Greece for instance, the elusive November 17 group creates chaos. In France, it is the Corsican National Liberation Front. In Italy, it is the Red Brigades, and all throughout Europe, people fear the Neo-Nazis and their dissemination of hate.

Terrorism in an Unexpected Place

The latest entry into the foray of global terrorism is the disturbing Buddhist cult, Aum Shirin Kyo in Japan. The leader, Shoko Asahara, established roots in various parts of the world, but most of his converts are centered in Japan, South Korea (via the South Korean Unification Church), Russia and even the United States. Aum espouses the apocalyptic idea that the world will end between 1997 and the year 2000. If you think this cult sounds familiar, it is because they drew attention to themselves in early 1995 with the release of an extremely lethal chemical agent, sarin, on the Tokyo subway system.

Sarin is a nerve gas invented by the Germans during World War II. The Aum Shirin Kyo purposely released this gas during the busiest time of the day, the morning work rush. Over 600 people were affected and seven people died. The only reason more people were not killed was that the gas was not released efficiently, as it only takes one gram in contact with skin to kill a person within a few minutes. Even though the cult's leader was arrested, what is disturbing is that these activities are now occurring in countries, such as Japan, which historically have not had these problems. Clearly this is a trend of the Quickening.

Each of these groups have resorted to terror to achieve their aim of religious and political power. Each of these groups have also demonstrated how powerless the people of the world are to defend themselves from terrorism. No one—in any society in the world, no matter how 'civilized'—can ever feel completely safe.

Islamic Fundamentalism

It is not hard to see that, of the existing terrorist groups, the Islamic Fundamentalists are the most insidious and deadly. From Iran, the ideological center of Islamic Fundamentalism, Ayatollah Ruhollah Khomeini declared a holy war, the Islamic Jihad, on the rest of the world a few years ago. The late Iranian leader once spoke these words of encouragement to his people: "The governments of the world should know that Islam cannot be defeated. Islam will be victorious in all the countries of the world, and Islam and the teachings of the Koran will prevail all over the world." The Muslims mean business. Their threat to the world needs to be taken seriously.

Muslim terrorists may give themselves many different names, such as Yassir Arafat's Palestine Liberation Organization (PLO), the Algerian Islamic Armed Group (GIA), or the Lebanese Hezbollah, but the mission is the same: to spread Islam throughout the world, to drive the West (particularly America) out of the Middle East, and to destroy the Israelis. Today's Islamic leader, Iranian President Akbar Hashemi Rafsanjani is no less committed to this mission. A few incidents for which these Islamic terrorist groups can take credit are:

◊ The PanAm 103 explosion over Lockerbie, Scotland, killing 259 passengers
◊ The 1992 bombing of the Israeli Embassy in Argentina, killing twenty-eight people, injuring 200

135

◊ The 1984 truck bombing of marine barracks in Beirut, Lebanon, killing 241 marines
◊ The 1972 murder of eleven Israeli athletes at the Munich Olympic Games

And these only account for some of the most *remembered* terrorist incidents. Overall, it is estimated that in the last twenty to twenty-five years, Islam influenced and funded over 600 acts of terrorism, responsible for the deaths of over 500 people, and the injury of more than 2,000. These terrorist acts have been perpetrated in over seventy countries throughout the world.[25]

Can't the Islamic Fundamentalists Be Stopped?

The most popular theory is that the Muslims simply want land, but the exchange of land for peace will not work. Islam is committed in every way to the achievement of their mission. They will use natural resources, including their huge oil reserves, money, political and religious influence, terrorism or whatever it takes.

Iran and its Muslim neighbors have a vast source of wealth in their oil, giving them power and the ability to take advantage of such cash-strapped countries as Russia as an arms supplier. In the past few years, since 1991 and the Gulf War, while America has been scaling back its military, Iran and other Muslim nations have been busily building up theirs.

The core Muslim group of countries—Egypt, Syria, Saudi Arabia, and Iran—now collectively boast of better than five million trained, combat ready soldiers, 3,800 aircraft, and close to 20,000 tanks. The aircraft and tanks represent some of the world's finest hardware from Russia, France, Britain and the

United States. Hard as it is to believe, Egypt was just *given* fleets of US F-15 and F-16 fighter planes by America. This is only conventional hardware. Add to this the Iranian stockpile of nuclear weaponry, purchased from Russia, along with the cache of Russian scientists to design and build a nuclear infrastructure.

The Islamic Message Spreads

At this time, you could argue that not only are the Muslims the most dangerous terrorists in the world, but they may well be on their way to becoming the most dangerous superpower to challenge America and the Russians. America is scaling back, Russia is financially broken, and the Muslims are neither. But that is not all. Islam is spreading its message globally and it is taking hold.

The last decade has seen a dramatic increase in Islam converts. Ten years ago, Catholicism was the largest religion in the world with 622 million followers, followed by Islam with 555 million. Islam has now taken the lead spot from Catholicism with *one billion* followers, or about twenty percent of the world's population.

As one example, only a decade ago, Britain had about 150 mosques; now it has over a thousand. Islam is growing quickly in North America, Australia, France and Germany. There are some 500 centers for Islam in America, and Muslims outnumber Episcopalians and Presbyterians in this country.[26]

What makes Islamic Fundamentalism so disconcerting is its extreme nature. A man who is a true Islamic adherent believes that if he dies while engaged in any effort to promote Islam, not only goes to paradise, but is met by a squadron of virgins at his disposal. While it sounds incredible, this promise has created millions of homicidal maniacs, willing to kill and be killed in the name of their faith.

Interpol

Is this world a safe place? No, of course not. Will it get safer? Probably not in the near future. Right now only one global task force exists that seeks to monitor and attempts to diffuse terrorist activity and that is the British organization, Interpol. Designed to act as an international police force network, Interpol is wholly inadequate, and most heads of state agree that something better is necessary. The trouble is that most countries are only willing to work together to a limited extent, as they are not entirely open to the idea of sharing intelligence. But if there is any chance to deter terrorism of any kind, the up and coming global government will have to address this challenge.

Population & Immigration

As the demographics of the world change, so does the society of the world. Today we have unprecedented population growth, we have a larger group of aging people inhabiting the industrialized world, and we have vast numbers of people moving from impoverished regions of the world to the industrialized nations.

Population

This is a major indicator of change in the Quickening. Until about the beginning of the nineteenth century, it took thousands of years for civilization to produce one billion people. Then, during the subsequent 100 years, by the turn of the twentieth century, two billion more people had sprung into existence. The rate of increase grew exponentially. By 1960, another billion people were added to the population, and only fourteen years after that, *another* billion humans!

With a population currently close to six billion, people are "suddenly" realizing that the earth was never meant to support so many of us. Despite all our global problems—social, environmental, political—we still see fit to bring children into the world at an astounding rate. Based on current trends, social observers estimate the earth will have eight billion people by the year 2020.[27]

Where are most of us? Population growth is unequal throughout the world. Generally, industrialized nations such as America or England are experiencing slow population growth; for just about every person born, someone dies. In fact, the chief factor in the population growth for these nations is immigration, adding about one person every ten minutes.[28] Ironically, in the poorest nations, like India or most of Africa, the population growth is skyrocketing.

India contains about a billion people, and not surprisingly, is one of the most populated nations on earth. India can barely feed the many hungry mouths it has now, much less the many millions on the way. The government can no longer adequately govern this mass of people. And the disparities which exist—sixteen different languages, a variety of religions (Hindu, Sikh, Muslim) that are highly intolerant of each other, and distinct cultural differences—create for India a social, political and economic nightmare.

Some observers theorize that India will break up into a number of independent states on the basis of language, religion and culture. They speculate that each will govern itself and develop its own political and social order. Whatever happens, turmoil will surely persist for years to come.[29]

Africa is not in much better shape than India. In fact, in many ways, Africa is in worse condition. Not only will Africa continue to be one of the world's poorest countries for years to come, but by 2020, based on United Nations estimates, it will try to feed at least two billion people. One reality that could affect or perhaps even prevent this unbelievable population growth is the spread of AIDS. At this point, one in three people in Africa are HIV positive. Life in most of Africa is bleak, and there is little to indicate that this will change in the near future.[30]

China is somewhat of an oddity in the world with respect to her economic situation, population and future prospects. While China has about one billion people within her borders, the country is showing tremendous economic growth, to the point of vying for an economic leadership position in the twenty-first century. Although most of the country is poor, China also has a low fertility rate. The question some social observers ponder is whether or not the birth rate will increase as more of the Chinese population benefit from the growing prosperity of the country. As in the case of other countries, any rise in population will have a significant impact on China.

Aging

Not only should we consider the fact that there are huge quantities of people on this planet, but we should also keep in mind their ages. An aging population has a significant impact on the social atmosphere of a country. Currently, the industrialized, wealthier nations have more people at retirement age or nearing retirement than the poorer nations. Why is this? The birth rate is lower in the wealthier countries; people are having smaller families or are simply having no families at all. That means there are generally more older people.

Poorer nations have the youngest populations in the world because they have a high birth rate. Nearly half the populations of poor countries are people aged twenty-five years or younger. In Kenya, for example, fifty-two percent of the population is under the age of fifteen.[31]

Living Standards

Of course, the rate of aging will vary from country to country, but overall a country which has a population containing large numbers of elderly people will see a change in living standards. As many people become older, there will be fewer people of working age to support the older people and the younger people who exist. Economically, this will slow down the rate at which a country will grow. But that will probably not matter for industrious individuals in a global economic environment, or for those who take advantage of the trend and provide much needed service businesses to accommodate older people.

With fewer working age people in a given industrialized nation, lifestyles will change. The age of retirement will most likely rise. More and more women will work, which of course means less time to raise a family. However, we will see more people working at home (made possible by computers and telecommunications), which may help with some family situations. Continual re-training to enhance existing skills and to acquire new ones will be necessary, and people may be more likely to change careers more frequently; right now people change their career direction about three times in their life.

A renewed emphasis on volunteer work will be encouraged, perhaps by retired people on a part-time basis. As responsible parents see how competitive the world becomes, there will be increased pressure on children to learn skills which will directly influence their ability to earn a good living later. A greater number of college aged kids will be expected to study and work.

What does all this mean? In our already chaotic, work-a-day world, things will just get more hectic. Granted, we will have high tech electronic gadgets and gizmos to cut down on routine or rote work, but demands on everyone are likely to increase. This is also likely to put an added strain on our society. Right now, many families are forced to work simply to survive, and given this burden, the traditional nuclear family unit will continue its decline. It will only become harder and harder to raise children.

Poorer Nations Kids

It could be argued that a younger population could help a country grow. During the Industrial Revolutions of Europe and America, population growth had a positive effect on the economies of those regions as there was a constant demand for workers. After World War II, Japan also benefited economically from having a growing younger population. However, today in poorer nations, a greater portion of the population being younger is more of a disadvantage.

It is harder to build housing and the necessary infrastructure of roads, sewage, adequate water supplies and so on to accommodate more people in poorer nations, especially in the face of such tremendous population growth; the economy simply does not exist to make such advances happen. America, Britain and other nations have poured money into these regions, but nothing has really helped these people on a long-term basis. Even educating these people in the use of contraceptives has not seemed to have an effect. The mouths to feed remain endless and the ability of these people to help themselves is virtually non-existent.

Thus, it seems that the impoverished fate of these poorer nations is all but sealed. If anything, as the younger population becomes aware of the materialism and sophistication of wealthier nations, they are more likely to flee the plight of their homeland.

Legal & Illegal Immigration

More people immigrate from country to country than ever before. Why? Well, each year the world adds about 100 million people to its population, most of these people within the borders of the poorest nations. It is not possible for the wealthier, industrialized nations to absorb all these people, and even if it were, it would only make a small dent in the population explosion of the poor countries. Nonetheless, people continue by any means to escape and begin a new life in another country. In the last fifteen years, the world has seen twice as many refugees, reaching sixteen million, often people fleeing war-torn regions.[32]

America is at the top of everyone's list of places to run. For some reason, Los Angeles appears to be the most popular spot to dive into our cultural salad bowl; with no ethnic majority, this city has one of the most diverse gatherings of people and culture on earth. Some social commentators forecast that if the trend continues, the rest of America will look a lot like Los Angeles in the next twenty-five years.[33]

Europe has also been under siege by immigrants. Hundreds of thousands flee Africa daily for the European continent. They also arrive from India, Turkey, Serbia, even Cambodia. The masses of Asians immigrating have made Australia the fastest growing industrialized country in the world. Japan, traditionally a xenophobic country, is awash with Asian immigrants, especially from Thailand, Malaysia and Bangladesh.

Ambitious Immigrants, Native Backlash

Those who tend to immigrate, whether legally or illegally, are younger, more aggressive, better educated and the most resourceful no matter where they land. And because of the growing need for skilled people in the industrialized countries, immigrants have been put to use. Generally, apart from their sheer numbers, immigrants are contributing members to the society they join. However, social pressures, already at a peak with people of different ethnicity, cultural or lingual backgrounds or religious ideals, have created an interpersonal conflict for these newcomers. The rising tide of Neo-Nazism globally and American militia activity is a backlash in response to the growing numbers of immigrants. Less tolerance and increased violence against immigrants is evident on a worldwide basis.

Open Doors Closing

Right now, many countries mentioned are starting to turn people away. America is the only country whose doors remain open, at least to legal immigration, but illegal immigrants flood across the borders daily. Despite efforts to discourage illegal immigration at the US/Mexico border, the immigrants get through anyway.

In addition, the Japanese mafia, the *yakuza*, and the Chinese make hundreds of millions of dollars providing counterfeit passports, transportation and employment for people who can pay to enter America. For a mere $30,000, an Asian can enter the United States![34] At this point, there will always be people who need or want to get out of their situation in their country. Global immigration shows no signs of abating no matter what measures industrialized nations may take.

Can Government Help Our Ailing Society?

The short answer to that question is that government can realistically do very little. Traditionally, governments have passed laws and created social programs in an attempt to deter certain types of behavior, but were never quite able to prevent social chaos and problems. Take gun control in America. The rate of murders committed with guns is climbing. Liberal politicians seem to think that the solution is to outlaw guns. In reality, guns don't kill people, people kill people. Even if guns were outlawed, there are plenty of other weapons out there; the problem lies not with the weapon, but with murderous people.

What about the escalating drug problem that plagues the world's industrialized nations? Do you outlaw illegal drugs and their use to prevent people from taking them, even though that is likely to make people try even harder to get them? Or do you legalize drugs as in Sweden where they are now finding that open drug use has apparently produced an even higher number of users? Or is it that Sweden's society was going to cultivate more drug users anyway, whether or not drugs were legalized? You can see there are no easy solutions to this one.

The trouble with laws and rules of any kind is that they are mechanical, looking very good on paper, but still needing to be enforced; they do not attend to the underlying problem of those who choose to break the laws. Ultimately, laws do not change the attitudes or behavior of people. Prisons are packed to overflowing. In America, there are more than one and a half million people locked up, and most of these inmates have been imprisoned more than once. Prison clearly does not significantly deter people from committing crimes, nor does it teach them any other way to live their lives.

Flaws in Social Services

It is easy to suggest that perhaps governments should employ the use of laws combined with social services. That perhaps there should be more privatization to handle the burden of criminals. Why not create a program, set up an institution, provide education, intervention, something along these lines? Logically, you might think, "if we had more ways of helping people deal with their personal, mental, psychological and domestic problems, we would have a happier, healthier society." If this is true, why are there more government and privately funded mental health clinics, psychiatric wards, psychologists, social workers and mental health professionals than ever before—and more problems than ever before?

By the time most people reach adulthood, they are not likely to change appreciably. Or they simply find some other vice to replace a previous one. If a person molests children now, they will probably continue to do so for as long as they can get away with it. What is interesting, and sad, to me is how in today's "feel good" society, everyone is so quick to find an excuse for someone else's behavior.

Drunks are the offspring of alcoholics or its aberrant gene, wife beaters are the result of being raised with wife beaters, child molesters were molested as children, and so on. Therefore, it's not their fault. There is a blatant tendency to either deny certain behavior or try to blame someone or something else. No one wants to take responsibility or be held accountable for their behavior.

Another challenge with social services is finding a way to pay for it all; this is especially true for countries where the social problems are so rampant that even the cost to *attempt* to address them is nearly prohibitive. America, Canada, Britain and most of Europe are regions of the world with the greatest challenge in this area. Incidentally, anything paid out for the enforcement of added laws and social services has a direct impact on everyone's standard of living. Remember: the taxpayer and the consumer pay for everything in the end. Of course, there is at the same time the burden of the legitimate issues to pay for, like the growing cost of health care, legal services, insurance and temporary unemployment.

Even Asia is certainly not exempt from the growing trend in crime and divorce. The difference is, unlike much of the rest of the industrialized world, Asia will be able to maintain a higher standard of living and will find it easier to pay for social programs—whether they are successful or not. The Asians are not only making more money, but they are keeping more of it. In distinct contrast, poorer nations of the world really lose on this front. Economically, politically and socially, the poorer nations of the world will not see much relief in the foreseeable future.

A Global Solution?

A global governing body likely to make its appearance on the world scene soon will undoubtedly face the challenge of the world's social afflictions. On the drug front, for example, it is possible that those countries known to produce drug crops such as poppies for opium will be forced to stamp out their drug cartels with the aid of the global police. As for the growing problems of crime and divorce and the overall breakdown of the traditional family unit, no one seems to have any real idea how to effectively deal with such issues. Some have suggested that a new sort of global morality may emerge, perhaps on the basis of some new global religious or spiritual basis.

At any rate, people everywhere should realize that if they do not adopt a different way of living, a different way of treating each other, the very existence of the human species will be in jeopardy. At the very least, everyone must realize that what we are doing now is not working. Something must change and I have a feeling that waiting for a government to effect those changes is not the answer. More likely, the answer lies in the mirror we all look into daily.

5

Religion & Spirituality

Judy Burgess had always known that she could use her mind to do things. Raising two children on her own had become more demanding as she was forced to spend most of her time just trying to make a living. She worried about her children raising themselves. But she had just learned about a mental technique that might help her keep tabs on her children, no matter where she was. It was called remote viewing, a new mind technology her church pastor had told her about.

"God has given us tremendous human potential," he told her. "We just need to learn to tap into it and it can make such a tremendous, positive difference in our lives."

Judy attended several meetings at church to learn about this method. They used relaxation exercises, which to her seemed more like meditation, but anything was worth trying. And it did not cost anything and it *did* help her relax.

A month later, Judy received a call at work from the police. "Ms. Burgess, we have your son here at the station. He was caught stealing CDs at a store." "Oh, no!" Judy exclaimed, fraught with embarrassment and anger.

Judy was not angry with her son as much as she was angry with her situation. She blamed herself for not being there with the children enough. Later that day, after the ordeal of having to retrieve her sixteen year old from the police station, she resolved to use this mind technology. Two days later, she sat quietly in her office and did a little experiment. She decided she would try to "see" where she had left the laundry basket.

With some breathing and a change in heart rate, Judy was able to clear her mind and open herself to a sort of travel sensation. She imagined being in the house, and actually felt as though she were. First she wandered into the living room, scanning the whole room. No laundry basket. But when she went into the hallway, she saw it at the end of the hallway in a corner. Later, she went home and confirmed that she was right. The basket was exactly where she had seen it. "This works!" She said to herself, both in astonishment and feeling a little creepy about it, too.

The next day, Judy tried the same exercise, only this time she looked into what her son was doing. She was amazed at how easy it was to find him, and when he came home later that afternoon, she asked him, "So, Tom, what did you do after school?" "Nothing," he replied, "Just hanging out with Bob." "Have you seen those Chips Ahoy cookies?" He looked as though he were about to lie, then said, "Uh yeah, Bob wanted some." Then she asked, "Did you have a nice time at the basketball court?" Judy laughed softly as he looked at her with a perplexed frown on his face. This stuff definitely worked!

Ω   Ω   Ω

The ground, burning cigarette smoldered in the ashtray for a couple of seconds longer and then went out as Jim Henderson stared at it. He considered that it was entirely likely that this could have been his last cigarette. Until his doctor had told him to stop, he had been smoking since he was eighteen and he was fifty-four now! The Doc had made it pretty clear: any more cigarettes and his chances of kicking off in the next ten years were really good. Jim decided he had worked too hard and too long to just die and leave it behind without enjoying it.

He pushed the auto-hypnosis tape his doctor had loaned him into his cassette player. Supposedly, this would help him stop smoking, but he had heard about this sort of thing for years and always thought it was crap. But, he had to admit, one of the guys at work tried it and it worked and he had tried everything else—nicotine gums, patches, cold turkey, lollipops. Nothing worked! With his headphones on, he lay back in his bed. The technique offered the option of using the tape while sleeping and what could be easier? The only thing you had to "do" was to be open to the suggestions and words on the tape.

The next day, Jim awakened to find himself entangled in the headset of the tape player. He had forgotten he even had the thing on him! Unfortunately,

151

he was running late, and it wasn't until thirty minutes later as he drove down the highway that he noticed he didn't have a cigarette in his mouth. Stranger still, he didn't feel the craving either. "Well, I'll be damned," he muttered, making a lane change. "Maybe that self-hypnosis stuff really does work."

Months later, Jim still had no interest in smoking. He was so impressed by the auto-hypnosis tape, he immediately agreed when a colleague asked him to attend a business seminar on visualization to enhance sales success. After all, it worked for one part of his life, why not another?

Ω   Ω   Ω

In this world where our senses are blitzed by everything, where we can have all the material goods we can carry away, one of the things that we seem to guard the most fiercely is the one thing we cannot see, taste, touch or hear—our spirituality. No matter how the world around us changes, whether it be technologically, economically or politically, we still have this overriding hunger inside of us that we constantly strive to fulfill. What does this intangible yearning mean? *Can* it be answered?

For most humans, life is a daily struggle in which we all fight to resolve challenges on a variety of levels. Perhaps it is not hard to understand our tendency to search for something to confirm for ourselves that it is all worthwhile, that what we do every day *means* something in the end. Whether you call it religion or spirituality, this desire has been inherent since the beginning of man's time on this earth.

Some religions in the world are experiencing a decline in popularity, while others are growing quickly. There has been a distinct move away from "religion," per se, and a surge in the exploration of the spiritual through what is called the New Age movement. This movement has grown so fast and in so many different ways in the last thirty years (with growing interest in the occult, mind technology, and even UFOs and extra-terrestrial life forms) that it makes you wonder where it is all heading. Some have suggested that a world religion or common spiritual union may evolve.

Perhaps people will even attempt to address the growing lack of morality in our world or seek to induce global unity and peace through spiritual consensus. Whatever lies at the end of these paths, an acceleration in spiritual activity is without a doubt an integral factor in the Quickening.

Are You Spiritual?

Granted, there are a number of people in the world who are atheists. They do not believe in God or in the existence of anything spiritual. But the numbers are smaller than you might think. At the very least, most people in the world believe they have a soul or spirit. Demographers agree that upwards of ninety to ninety-five percent of the world population professes a belief in a spiritual part of their lives. In America, some polls have indicated that ninety percent of the population believe in God. Of this fairly large group, many believe in a supreme, omnipresent being, such as the Judeo-Christian God.[1]

Religion, Spirituality, Cults & the Occult

Most people talk about spiritual matters, inter-changing the words "spiritual" and "religious" as if they meant the same thing. This can be somewhat misleading. A Catholic practices their religion of Catholicism and its various traditions and rituals, usually in a church. On the other hand, someone who considers themselves just as spiritual, such as a New Age "channeler," does not practice a religion, but embraces a spiritual view which may or may not in-clude traditions or rituals.

Within the terms of the Quickening, whether or not you practice one of the commonly known relig-ions, or you are simply exploring different avenues of your spiritual side, all of these things engage us in spirituality. In short, we are *all* spiritual, but some of us are *religious*.

Cults

One of the most confusing things is the distinction between what is a religion and what is a cult. For example, Mormonism, also known as The Church of Jesus Christ of the Latter Day Saints, and the Jeho-vah's Witnesses, are considered to be religious from a secular perspective. But from a traditional, orthodox, Christian perspective, these groups are cults. Why? The practitioners of these groups deny the divinity of Jesus Christ and other essentials of Christian doc-trine.

Cults can also be those groups which appear strange or dangerous, with leaders who are abusive, manipulative and illegally control the lives of their followers. The Jim Jones cult is an example of such an abuse of power. All the members of the cult committed suicide under the direction of Jim Jones.

Groups that practice spiritual techniques of an occult nature, in direct opposition to Biblical, Christian principles, are also considered cults. The occult is a study and practice of paranormal and supernatural powers, as well as communication with the spirit world. One practice of the occult is telekinesis, the ability to move objects without physically touching them (Uri Geller is the famous telekinesis practitioner who not only made forks and spoons move, but he could bend them, too!).

Another example of an occult practice is mental telepathy, a means of sending messages to someone else without speaking to or communicating with them in any other way. Practitioners of the occult are also usually involved in meditation of various forms in which they attempt to enter an altered state of consciousness and make contact with the spirit world.

There are religious people who engage in occultic techniques as part of their religious worship, such as Hindus and Buddhists. However, in terms of the Quickening, a cult refers to any group engaged in non-Christian, occultic techniques.

Religions of the World

To place the importance of religion and spirituality within the context of the Quickening (and to avoid being overwhelmed by the vast numbers of religions), we must narrow our focus down to the most popular religions in the world today. Most religious people are adherents to Islamic Fundamentalism (nearly one and a half billion people). The next is Hinduism with one billion followers, Catholicism with 600 million, Buddhism with 540 million and finally Protestant

Christianity with 350 million.² Judaism is of course a major religion and should be included on this list, even though there are nowhere near the number of adherents compared to other religions.

Even within these major popular religions, many sects and smaller groupings exist. Islam can be broken into Sunnis, Shiites and Sufis, among others. Hinduism actually spawned Buddhism, which in turn produced Sikhism and Jainism. Within Protestant Christianity, myriad denominations exist, such as Episcopalians, Lutherans and Methodists. Roman Catholicism has a number of divisions, called "orders," such as Dominicans, Jesuits and Franciscans. Jews are generally split into Orthodox, Conservative and Reform.

Incidentally, in the secular world, it has become common to categorize Christians as both Catholic and Protestant Christians. This is not accurate, particularly in light of their means of salvation and practice, which are fundamentally different. Catholics require clergy intervention for salvation, while Protestant Christians base their salvation on Biblical principles.

It is important to realize that the world is undergoing some dramatic changes spiritually. We can see this by the trend in numbers of people for any given religion.

Islam

Ten years ago, Catholicism was the most practiced religion in the world—a little over 600 million people—and Islam hovered at around 555 million. In the last decade, the House of Islam, or *Dar al Islam*, skyrocketed in growth to the more than one billion it is today. And the growth continues. By the year 2025, at its current rate of growth, Islam is expected to exceed two billion followers, or about one quarter of the earth's projected population at that time![3]

The trend of growth in the Islamic religion is evident worldwide. Islamic Fundamentalism is practiced in seventy of 184 countries of the world. Islam has spread from the sands of the Middle East—Sudan, Kuwait, Saudi Arabia, Jordan—to the African continent—Algeria, Egypt—and further east into Indonesia, Malaysia, Pakistan, Bangladesh and huge parts of India. Islam has also encroached upon traditionally Judeo-Christian areas of the world such as France, England, Australia, Canada and the United States. In England, for instance, there are more Muslims than Methodists. In the United States, there are more Muslims than Episcopalians and Presbyterians.

Why is Islam spreading so widely and so quickly? Experts have a number of ideas, but the general theory is that Islam offers an organized, monotheistic religion with age-old tradition and ritual, combined with a non-materialistic world view. Moreover, it is an alternative to the traditional Judeo-Christian religions, which are apparently no longer as interesting to people around the world anymore.

Catholicism

Catholicism is experiencing a decline in its number of adherents, though not overly dramatic. One sign of this decline is within the Catholic church itself. In recent years, there have been many defections from the church by bishops, priests and nuns. It is also not uncommon these days for any given parish to be without a priest since fewer young men are joining the priesthood. In fact, the numbers of potential re-

157

cruits in North America are so low, a growing number of parishes are forced to hire priests from South America.

Even more serious, European newspapers have reported perverse behavior among priests, nuns and bishops in various cities in America and Italy. These reports indicate a number of cases of satanic pedophilia in which evil rituals involve the sexual defilement of children by various clergy who openly worship Satan.[4]

The Vatican is not immune to these serious challenges either. Apparently, Pope John Paul II has made it known that he is frustrated with his attempts to reform the moral element within the Vatican. Most of the resistance has come from the large network of active homosexual priests and higher level church leaders.

One of the major factors in Catholicism's loss of laity is the church's dogmatic position on divorce, abortion and birth control. At the same time, the church is marked by confusion as it becomes more lenient in its attitude toward homosexuality, women becoming priests, and the marriage of clergy. This leniency is probably an attempt to encourage new adherents and to prevent the loss of existing members. Nonetheless, many people are falling away from Catholicism.

Alienated by its corruption, bored by its traditions and effort to control its members, many people no longer believe that the Catholic church can realistically address their needs in these troubling times. Despite its obvious problems and a slight decline in members, Catholicism is found on every continent of the world, and will most likely remain a significant religion.

Judaism

As with Catholicism, the Jewish faith has experienced a growing disinterest among its followers. Only about twenty percent of Jews regularly attend worship services in the synagogue.[5] Fewer Jews are Orthodox, and a distinct lack of genuine interest has emerged among current generations in regard to the practice of traditions and rituals established thousands of years ago. Being Jewish is not a simple matter of proclaiming a faith in Judaism; it is a way of life, a culture, a commitment.

Many Jews are turning away from their faith altogether, as they are drawn into the New Age movement. Apparently, the monotheism of Judaism does not offer much spiritual freedom. However, what is interesting is that although a Jew may have turned to Hinduism or another religion, many will continue to observe certain Jewish rituals, such as the lighting of candles at Hanukkah or the traditional seder dinner during Passover.

Further, most people who are born Jewish are very supportive of the existence of the Jewish nation-state, Israel. Even more than the Torah or the synagogue, Jews tend to believe that they are all unified, no matter what branch of Judaism they fall into, particularly now that they once again have a homeland they can call their own.

Another significant sign of a diminished interest in the Jewish faith is that more Jews are marrying non-Jews, or gentiles. This has, until recently, been an exception for most of the Jewish people. The older generations are concerned because they believe that marriages between Jews and gentiles could lead to a watering down of the faith and the culture. Despite these internal challenges, Judaism will undoubtedly continue to exist as a significant religion in the world.

Protestant Christianity

In America, a country which has for the last two centuries claimed to be a Christian nation, only about twenty-five percent of the population actually attends a church of some kind regularly. In the 1920s, Christian churches like Presbyterian, Episcopal, Methodist and Lutheran constituted over seventy-six percent of the Protestant Christian population. By the 1980s, these churches constituted less than fifty percent of the Protestant Christian population. The 1990s have only brought more of the same as Christianity witnesses a steady decline in its membership.

Where are all these Christians going if they are turning away from the traditional denominations? The answer is in two directions. Many millions of these people have been drawn to small, unaffiliated, non-denominational churches that emphasize Bible teaching and study. These are churches that have no rituals to speak of, do not conduct church services in traditional church buildings, and the Bible teachers are not adorned in any particular apparel nor given any clerical title. Non-denominational churches have sprung up around the world, especially in North America, England and limited parts of Europe such as Germany, Poland and parts of Russia.

The other direction in which millions of formerly denominational Christians have fled is toward the exploration of the diverse New Age spiritual movement. Evidently, these are people who have felt alienated by their experience with the Protestant

Christian environment. Perhaps they are turned off by the increased political and social agendas of the mainline denominations. Not all Christians see the necessity of participating in abortion clinic protests, nor do they all feel the need for political reform to change a world which even their own Bible says it is clearly not possible to change. Christian groups and organizations such as Pat Robertson's 700 Club and the Christian right are well meaning, if somewhat misdirected.

A confidential survey conducted in the early 1980s revealed that over forty-five percent of ministers and pastors did not believe Jesus Christ was God. Over eighty percent of these same clerics rejected the Bible as the inspired word of God. Perhaps it is no wonder that people have been abandoning the Christian denomination if their own pastors are not convinced of what they preach. In any event, millions of alienated Christians have sought to find an alternative, seeking no doubt one which does not require church attendance and may provide a sense of spiritual satisfaction.[6]

Hinduism & Buddhism

In the past thirty years, these two religions have been marked by explosive growth. Why? First of all, there has been the increase in sheer numbers of people in areas of the world in which these religions have been traditionally practiced, such as India, China, Japan and other Eastern countries. Second and even more significantly, the world has seen an unprecedented increase in Eastern religions among people in countries where these religions are *not* traditionally found.

In America, during the last thirty years, more than 1,000 Buddhist temples, study groups and associations have come into being. The largest concentrations seem to be in Southern California for some reason—over 250,000 people in this region claim to be Buddhists.[7]

There is no reason to believe that the rapid spread of these religions throughout the world will be halted. The mystic elements of Hinduism and Buddhism have been the basis for many of the spiritual practices in the New Age movement. It is Eastern mysticism which seems to keep people interested and tends to draw new adherents to the religions.

The New Age Movement

One-third of the earth's population are members of the basically monotheistic religions of Islam, Catholicism and Protestant Christianity. That's a lot of people. However, the most popular form of spirituality in the world today is a combination of polytheism and pantheism, commonly called the New Age movement. That means *billions* of people around the world practice this form of spirituality. The numbers of people drawn into New Age spirituality are increasing faster than any religion, including Islam.

Polytheism & Pantheism: New Age Building Blocks

Polytheism and pantheism have been woven together to form a foundation for what we today label the New Age movement. Polytheism, the worship of multiple gods or goddesses, is the oldest form of spirituality. These deities usually represent some natural source or power, such as the sun, the moon, a river, the wind or even trees. As an example, Hinduism, one of the oldest known religions, is a polytheistic religion honoring the spirits of nature, especially Mother Earth.

Pantheism is a belief that God is found in all things. Buddhism is pantheistic as it does not uphold the worship of a specific god nor does it acknowledge many gods or goddesses. Instead, it is a religion that venerates all things, and stipulates that all forms of life are sacred and entitled to enjoy life.

New Age Defined

The New Age movement takes Hinduism and Buddhism as its foundation and goes a step further. Basically, the New Age movement takes the idea that a common power or energy flows through all things and combines this with the notion that God exists in all things. This energy-God mixture is the "life-force" which flows through all of us, making us part of God and giving us the potential to become a god.

New Age spirituality also adopts the Eastern religious concept of reincarnation. Reincarnation ensures that you never die, but instead return to earth in some different form depending on how you lived on earth in your past life. How you conduct yourself in this life—your treatment of other people, animals and the environment—can elevate you to a higher level of spiritual attainment. This is where the messages of brotherly love and unity, animal rights and earth awareness enter the picture.

If you practice the various techniques common to New Age spirituality, you can theoretically attain a higher level of self and become a god. By becoming a god, you can escape the interminable cycle of birth and rebirth, and the return in an unknown form.

Unlike the monotheistic religions, the New Age movement allows you to escape death, judgment and hell (New Agers don't believe a hell exists). This may be one of the reasons so many people like the New Age spirituality: you can't go to hell! Another attractive feature of New Age spirituality is its mystical element, including the occultic practices of concentration and meditation techniques.

Enter the Occult

Most people who start off experimenting with New Age spirituality either do not know or do not want to believe that they are getting involved with the occult. The word 'mysticism' is a common euphemism used in place of the word 'occult,' which tends to sound sinister to some people. Whatever they choose to call it, that is what they are doing. This is particularly true once you begin to engage in concentration and meditation techniques. After all, the purpose of meditation is to open yourself to the spirit world by inducing an altered or trance-like state of consciousness.

Indian yogis or swamis are considered to be the best spiritual teachers of these techniques. Tibetan monks, however, are the most revered gurus of New Age tenets. Any one of these spiritual teachers will assure you that meditation is the best means by which you can achieve "godhood." For me, this is interesting, but very scary stuff. For many, many people, this is better than recreational drugs or alcohol, and about as addictive.

Most beginners who try meditation do not have a "significant experience," i.e., a contact with the spirit world, for some time. If you really go deeply into it, however, meditation can lead to a variety of experiences, all touted to be spiritually beneficial. Everyone has heard of some of these phenomena: out-of-body travel, often called astral projection; past life regression (often induced by hypnosis, another occultic technique); channeling; distinct visions about future events; or even direct communication with spirit beings or "spirit guides" (sometimes simply called guides). New Age proponents also contend that the right state of consciousness brought about by meditation can enable you to tap into the life-force and perform such psychic phenomena as mental telepathy, clairvoyance and telekinesis.

Origin of the New Age Movement

You already know that the New Age movement has its basis in Hinduism and Buddhism. So technically, there is nothing new about New Age spirituality; these Eastern mystic beliefs and practices have been around longer than any other known religion. But they were not very well known in Western civilization until the late nineteenth century, when the godmother of the New Age movement, Helena Petrovna Blavatsky founded the Theosophical Society in New York.

After spending a period of time under the tutelage of Indian swamis, Blavatsky promoted and wrote about New Age spirituality. Her most famous book is *The Secret Doctrine*, in which she coins many of the popular New Age phrases and ideologies we are familiar with today. For example, according to Blavatsky, we are all part of the "brotherhood of man," and the world should unite in one belief system, as long as it is not monotheistic, of course. New Agers often proclaim peace, non-violence, love and other positive expressions. An early Theosophical Society statement encourages its members "to oppose . . . every form of dogmatic theology, especially Christian."[8]

Blavatsky's writings became very popular, and many of her works are studied eagerly even to this day by New Age initiates. By 1920, Alice Bailey became a leader of the Theosophical Society and established Lucifer Publishing Company to publish and distribute the literature of both Blavatsky and other writers in the Society. The blatant reference to the devil created a stir and the Theosophical Society changed the name of their publishing company to Lucis Press, still in operation today.

Lucis Press is an important part of the global Lucis Trust organization with headquarters in the United Nations building in New York. In the 1920s and 1930s, the Lucis Trust established branch organizations in various parts of the world. The most influential, as far as promoting the New Age movement, are the Arcane Schools, located in New York, London, Geneva and Buenos Aires, the Triangles and World Goodwill; these organizations provide New Age spiritual instruction and literature, and are even politically active.

America & the New Age Movement

During the 1960s, the Baby Boomer generation invoked a social revolt in America, beginning with the protest of the Vietnam War and their parents' materialism, reaching as far as experimentation with drugs, sex, music and spirituality. Just about everything conventional went by the wayside. America was primed for a full scale introduction and acceptance of the New Age spiritual movement.

On the religious and spiritual front, many millions of these Baby Boomers rejected their parents' traditional Judeo-Christian practices. They were, however, eager to experiment with new religious and spiritual experiences that often mixed drugs (mostly LSD and heroine) with Eastern mysticism.

In 1968, the Buddhist guru, Maharishi Makesh Yogi, came to America to introduce "Transcendental Meditation," or TM, to many of these young people. Yoga, a Hindu-based meditation method, also entered mainstream America in the late 1960s. Both TM and yoga were touted not only as forms of meditation, but as means to relieve stress, reduce blood pressure and heart attacks, and even rescue persons addicted to drugs and alcohol.

In 1966, Anton La Vey, the high priest of modern Satanism and author of the widely distributed *Satanic Bible,* proclaimed that God was dead, and that the 1960s marked the dawn of the Satanic Age. Obviously, this was an extreme example of rebellion against traditional religious and spiritual beliefs. And for most people, this is too overtly evil. But there are those who point out that its source is no less malevolent than the source of New Age spirituality, cloaked in its positive sounding phrases of love, peace, unity and non-violence.

Nonetheless, there was a virtual explosion of interest in the New Age spiritual movement in America during the 1960s and on into the 1970s. Today, this movement has only gained popularity and acceptance, whereas before the decade of the sixties, it was mostly resisted. And just as in many other areas of human activity, America encouraged a trend for people throughout the world, especially the Western countries, to take a greater interest in the Eastern religions and New Age in particular.

These days, literature and instruction on all aspects of New Age spirituality abound. In the last thirty years, Western society has integrated the New Age movement in a variety of ways. There are books, audio tape series, seminars, university courses—even the YWCA and YMCA offer instruction on yoga. Eastern mysticism has been accepted as legitimate in medicine, psychology, education and even the major religions. It has become easy to accept such expressions and practices as "centering," "relaxation therapy," "self-hypnosis," and "creative visualization."

What is really interesting is how New Age spirituality has gained acceptance by the scientific community. Apparently, the Quickening of spiritual matters involves a desire by many people to incorporate the spiritual with science in some way—perhaps to further legitimize their beliefs.

Modern Psychology & Mind Technologies

Psychology has had a significant impact on the development of society in the last fifty years. Many people looking for answers in their lives have turned from religion, resisted anything that appears spiritual, and found psychology. So it may come as a surprise to you when I say that psychology and psychiatry are not as much scientific as they are spiritual. In fact, some have even called the psychology of the mind a secular religion. Of course, most of us want to believe that psychology is scientific, that somehow man has employed a scientific method to grasp the complex world of the human mind, the psyche. Are psychology and psychiatry legitimate branches of medicine?

In medicine, there are legitimate, scientifically based methods used to identify certain diseases of the mind. We have identified diseases which often manifest themselves in peculiar behavior, such as Tourette's Syndrome, Huntington's Disease, or perhaps even brain tumors. These are either genetic or organically based mental diseases and afflictions. In some cases, they can be treated with drugs or by surgery; in many other cases, they cannot be treated at all.

To a large extent, however, most problems in behavior are not genetic or organic. Many people are often depressed, anxious, exhibit compulsive behavior, e.g., alcoholism, drug addiction, overeating, are sexually deviant or prone to fits of violence. The trouble is that these problems are impossible to treat as you would a physical ailment. After all, mental health problems are not something you can measure, weigh, probe or examine under a microscope.

The best you can do with many of today's health problems is a common practice of psychiatrists today: prescribe mind numbing drugs like Valium or Prozac. But these drugs do not treat the underlying problems; they only pull a blanket over the symptoms. They do not prevent someone from being a child molester or beating their spouse.

In an effort to find some way of addressing the common mental health problems in society, psychologists, psychiatrists and other mental health professionals have attempted alternate methods. They have explored non-traditional, non-scientific means of treatment.

Roots of Modern Psychology

Are you surprised to hear that today's mental health professionals are not really engaged in a wholly scientific field? Actually, modern psychology can trace its roots to Eastern mysticism and New Age spirituality. During the nineteenth century, Sigmund Freud experimented with the occultic techniques of hypnosis and the use of cocaine to understand various mental disorders.

William James, often described as the father of American psychology, co-founded the American Society For Psychical Research. James was interested in Eastern mysticism and parapsychology. Carl Rogers, the famous psychotherapist, and Carl Jung, the famous and influential Swiss psychologist, were both interested in the use of occultic methods for emotional problems.

But psychology did not really gain popularity as a way of addressing mental health until after World War II. In 1946, the US Congress made federal funds available for the first time to establish a national mental health care program with the passing of the National Mental Health Care Act. From there, psychology became a legitimate college course, spreading like wildfire throughout the country.

Obviously, this gave psychology and psychiatry legitimacy even though much of what was taught was not based on science. So what are students and practitioners of psychology and psychiatry being taught?

Today, about 100 years after modern psychology began, psychologists are still exploring the depths of the human mind, employing methods derived from Eastern mysticism. Only today, the words used are "visualization," "power of the imagination," and "inner guides" to achieve changes in your life.

Here is something interesting. Most psychologists and psychiatrists deny the existence of God, Satan, angels, demons or spirit beings of any kind. Instead, they attribute any special powers, such as psychic ability, to the mind because of what they like to call "unlimited human potential." By delving into our unconscious mind, they believe that we can tap this potential. As an example, Marquette University psychologists have instructed thousands of people to visualize inner guides to achieve dramatic changes in their lives. Sometimes called "mental imaging," or "transformation," some psychologists believe this is simply a matter of exercising the unlimited power of the imagination.

Mental Imaging Works!

Most practitioners of these methods of mental imaging agree with Norman Vincent Peale's conclusion that "when the imaging concept is applied steadily and systematically, it solves problems, strengthens personalities, improves health and greatly enhances the chances for success in any kind of endeavor."[9]

Methods such as these have been explored and promoted to the mental health world by such organizations as the Foundation For Mind Research, which was licensed by the American government to use LSD to study the depths of the human mind. Co-founder Jean Houston readily revealed that her organization uses ancient Eastern sorcery techniques of visualization to achieve results like those described by Peale.

Support for the use of mind imaging has come from other sources as well. Dr. Beverly Galyean, late psychologist and consultant to the Los Angeles

171

school system, wrote an article in *The Journal of Humanistic Psychology* in which she encouraged the acceptance of these non-scientific methods of treatment. She wrote:

"The ancients of all cultures filled their folkloric epics with tales of visions, dreams, intuitive insights, and internal dialogues with higher beings whom they saw as the sources of ultimate wisdom and knowledge. By accepting as true the narrative of spiritual seekers from all cultures, we now have evidence of various levels of consciousness possible to human beings.... Human potential is inexhaustible and is realized through new modes of exploration (i.e., meditation, guided imagery, dream work, yoga, body movement, sensory awareness, energy transfer or healing, reincarnation therapy, and esoteric studies)...Meditation and guided imagery activities are the core of the curriculum."[10]

Ironically, Dr. Galyean describes meditation and other methods as "new modes of exploration," when in fact they are very old modes.

It appears that psychology has provided a "legitimate" alternative for people who do not want to worship a guru, practice a religion, or be overtly spiritual. Psychology has put this alternative path in terms we can accept by creating the impression that spiritual methods are actually scientific methods of tapping your unconscious mind. They lead you to believe that you are simply employing methods to fully realize your human potential. When you think about this, it is worship after all—of self.

The Cult of Self Esteem

With the help of psychologists, for the last twenty years or so, many of us believe our problems derive from a low self esteem. Supposedly, we do not esteem ourselves highly enough, and this is the alleged basis for so many of our emotional problems.

The fact is, most people esteem themselves very highly! That is why we are so preoccupied with ourselves. We are concerned with everything having to do with ourselves. We worry about our looks: Am I too ugly, too fat? We worry about how successful we are: Am I doing as well or better than the other guy? Do I have more stuff? Do I live in a nicer house? Drive a nicer car? We obsess about how others view us: Do they like me? We lose sleep about whether we are appealing to the opposite sex, how intelligent we are and so on. It all goes back to self without a whole lot of difficulty.

The society we live in during this time of the Quickening caters more and more to self, to narcissism. This is a trend which does not improve things, but only makes them worse. The more we worry about ourselves, the more we drive ourselves crazy at the expense of everyone else around us.

The question that comes up the most frequently is: "What do I get out of it?" Whether it is our relationships, business, in the supermarket, in our quest for entertainment or our spiritual experience, it always comes down to what we can get for ourselves. Two or three generations ago, people were genuinely concerned about their neighbors. Now, they could care less. Most of us don't even know our neighbors! And as things are now, "If I make the effort to get to know my neighbor, what will I get out of it?" Gone is the Christian precept: "Love your neighbor as yourself."

Mind Technologies

In keeping with the trend of "what's in it for me," many of us have been duped into accepting what amounts to just another form of religion: mind technology. Today there is hardly a person alive who has not heard about motivational, self-help gurus Tony Robbins, Zig Ziglar, Robert Schuller, Norman Vincent Peale, Claude Bristol or Napoleon Hill. These people have made fortunes catering to the growing selfishness of people worldwide.

Make no mistake, they are very aware of the cult of self esteem. How else would their books have sold in the hundreds of millions or been translated into many languages for distribution throughout the world? Something like this has never existed in our world before and yet their appeal has only increased over the years. And why not? They offer solutions so anyone can be successful and live a happy, satisfying life.

Obviously, I don't object to people being successful or living happily. It is the means we are willing to accept to achieve our selfish desires that interests me. So what do these self-help gurus teach? Believe it or not, their methods are not really any different than the methods of psychology except that they sell their approach as mind technology. Of course, just as with the claim that psychology is based on science, there is nothing technological at all about these methods; they are spiritual in nature, derived from Eastern mysticism and the occult. Buddhism is a basis for the mind technologies because it promotes the idea that "man's mind is the center of the universe, and the mind has an infinite capacity for change and growth."[11]

Here are some examples of mind technology:

Robert Schuller says: "You don't know what power you have within you! You make the world into anything you choose."[12]   Schuller is not talking about self confidence or the power of applying yourself in the daily tasks of life, but a spiritual power which can be conjured through your mind to achieve success in life.   Napoleon Hill teaches the same gospel. Hill wrote: "You can make your life what you want it to be.... A healthy ego makes you more receptive to the influences which guide you from a region beyond the power of our five senses to know... 'I am the master of my fate....'"[13]

Norman Vincent Peale is also a proponent of accessing spiritual power to create your own reality. Peale asserted: "...Your unconscious mind...[has a] power that turns wishes into realities when the wishes are strong enough."[14]

The reason the mind technology religion is popular is that it works. Business leaders, global corporations, politicians, housewives, students—anyone open and willing to accept these teachings have benefited. The word gets out and the motivational gurus draw millions more in. And our already selfish society becomes even more concentrated on their own selfish needs, only with people seeking to force their will on others through the use of these and other similar methods of the occult.

Scientific Religion

Yes, this is a strange sounding concept, isn't it? Apparently, the world of science has strayed increasingly farther into the realm of the spiritual, especially in the last four decades. This unexpected combination of science and spirituality is gaining acceptance by millions around the world.

Man has always sought to be the captain of his own fate, the master of the universe. Scientists, and those who venerate science, like to consider themselves atheistic, or at the very least agnostic and too sophisticated to accept the existence of a spirit world. They instead choose to believe that man can eventually know all about atomic structure, all about space, will inevitably conquer disease, and can unravel all the secrets of life, perhaps even to prolong it indefinitely.

Man hopes to achieve this through his own investigation, through science and technology. However, scientists are increasingly open to the idea of gaining insights into life's mysteries as the result of contact with higher life forms or some natural force in the universe. In fact, many people seem to have pinned these kinds of hopes on the space program.

This type of thinking has been promoted and encouraged by highly respected men of science, such as Robert Jastrow, the world's leading astrophysicist, and Carl Sagan, the renowned cosmologist. Jastrow has suggested the popular theory that evolution has gone on far longer than the earth has existed. He also thinks it is likely that there are beings which have evolved far beyond the evolved state of humans. Perhaps these beings not only possess vastly greater intellects, but the capacity for omnipotence and omniscience—spiritual capacities—as well.

Both Sagan and Jastrow have declared such confidence in the cosmos that they are able to take the "leap of faith" that such beings can be contacted and may in fact provide humanity with the missing link we have been searching for all along. The hope is that they could teach us to be masters of the universe; in other words, we anticipate that their intelligence and spiritual ability could transform us into gods.[15]

Of course, Eastern mysticism has advocated this belief all along. But instead of outer space, we are encouraged to explore inner space to make contact with highly evolved beings and in so doing become like gods. In this way, we might expedite the evolutionary process of our inner selves by going within ourselves to achieve a higher self, a higher level of consciousness. Many scientists have accepted this because the pseudo-science of psychology has legitimized the exploration of the unconscious mind.

Conscious Evolution

An innate need to achieve a higher self has produced serious attempts by scientists to demonstrate that there is indeed an evolution of the mind. One respected organization in San Francisco, The Institute For Conscious Evolution, is known for its research in this area. Efforts by psychologists and scientists to prove the mind's evolution have involved putting subjects under hypnotic trances to regress to prior lives. Some researchers, such as Jean Houston, describe this as a "remembering" therapy; for instance, she believes people can remember when they were amphibians or apes.

Does anyone really know what the evolution of the unconscious mind is? Moreover, is this science? No certain answers to those questions yet! If anything, though, what these efforts have demonstrated is a New Age belief in reincarnation and hypnosis, and an increasing desire by people to become involved in these occultic practices.

Here is an irony for you: whether they admit it or not, those who accept and promote the idea of contacting what they believe to be a natural force in the universe, as a means of achieving a higher level of consciousness, are actually exercising a religious faith. Their belief is not based on fact and it is not scientific. They are accepting an intangible and inexplicable natural force.

Even Jastrow openly admits that he personally takes a leap of religious faith: "There is a kind of religion in science; a faith that...every event can be explained as the product of some previous event.... This conviction is violated by the discovery that the world had a beginning under conditions in which the known laws of physics are not valid.... The scientist has lost control."[16]

God Versus God-Force

Ideas and notions such as these are easy for scientists to accept because they have invalidated the possibility or need for God by upholding the notion that every event can be explained by some previous event. After all, science does claim to explain all things in terms of natural processes. Therefore, you don't need a God to have created them. God, god-force, or life-force can be thought of as natural forces or energies that we can access through the depths of our mind. This asserts a capacity within each of us to control our own fate if we wish. In essence, we can become gods.

This type of thinking has led to the formation of a variety of religions practiced by millions throughout the world. The most popular among them include Humanism, Unity, Religious Science, Scientism, Positive Confession, Christian Science, and the

Church of Scientology among others. Each of these address the wishes on the part of its members to uphold science, to satisfy personal desires in this life and at the same time to meet an inner spiritual hunger.

UFOs & Extra-terrestrials

There is a growing fascination in this world today with the phenomenon of unidentified flying objects (UFOs) and the possibility of alien life forms, or extra-terrestrials. One way I see this reflected is the popularity of radio and television shows that deal with these subjects, including my own, *Dreamland*, which has doubled in popularity in the last few years alone. Traditionally, this has been an area into which most media do not venture, but there is an obvious demand for a forum to share information and experiences.

I know that the people who share actual experiences with non-human intelligence are not making these things up. The question is not necessarily *whether* these kinds of creatures exist, but the *nature* of such beings.

One of the things that persuaded me was my own personal encounter with what I believe to be a UFO several years ago. My wife and I were driving home late one evening. We were about a mile from our house on a deserted road, and the night air was warm and absolutely still. Nothing could be heard. My wife spotted a craft behind us, hovering over the road, perhaps 150 feet above the earth, and we stopped the car to get a better look.

What we saw was large and triangular, about 150 feet across, with strobing red and white lights. The craft made no noise, and was slowly floating, not flying. It then disappeared over the mountains. As yet, I do not believe I have encountered any alien life forms, but the possibility for it seems very clear.

The UFO Quickening

Have the sightings of UFOs increased in the last fifty years? Definitely. But historically, UFO sightings have been recorded for several thousand years. The Jewish historian, Josephus, near Rome in 66 A.D., recorded that many people saw what they described as "celestial chariots" and "flying shields." In the eighteenth century, the descriptions changed to "phantom ships" and "flying saucers." By the late 19th century, there was a sudden increase in reported UFO sightings, particularly in America. These sightings were collected and published around the turn of the twentieth century in a book by Charles Fort called *The Book of the Damned*. Largely because of this book, Fort is considered to be the father of modern ufology.

The acronym, "UFO," has only been around for about fifty years, coined in 1947 by US Air Force captain, Edward J. Ruppelt. Ruppelt was assigned by the Air Force to oversee its new UFO investigation agency. The Air Force wanted to investigate any possible breach of national security given the increased number of sightings by civilians and military personnel of unusual flying objects.

The most significant sighting, and the one which concerned the Air Force the most, was made in Seattle, Washington on June 24, 1947. A civilian pilot, Kenneth Arnold, reported seeing nine shiny, crescent-shaped craft fly across the sky, traveling at what he estimated to be well over 1,000 miles per hour. This was faster than any known aircraft at that time.

Although most sightings of UFOs in the first few decades of the twentieth century were made by Americans in various parts of the United States, reports throughout the world have skyrocketed in the last five decades. It is estimated that hundreds of millions of people around the world have seen UFOs. But what is a UFO? It is as the name implies: an object which appears to fly and which seems to have no known origin. But is everything we see and are unable to identify a UFO?

According to the Mutual UFO Network (MUFON), about ninety percent of all reports of UFO sightings are identifiable objects, sometimes called IFOs.[17] Generally, these IFOs are weather balloons, a ball of lightning or some other meteorological phenomenon, the landing lights of a distant airplane or even astronomical objects such as a planet or star. So the chances of seeing something that is actually a UFO are pretty slim!

Aliens

If UFOs are real, then who or what is controlling them? All sorts of ideas come up. Everyone has heard stories about aliens or extra-terrestrial life forms or beings from other planets or worlds. With its science fiction movies, Hollywood certainly has not hesitated in concocting various scenarios and possible motives for aliens to visit our planet and interact with humans.

A popular movie in the 1950s was "The Day The Earth Stood Still." At the beginning, a flying saucer parks in the sky within sight of the earth's inhabitants. Earthlings are frightened nearly out of their wits as they speculate about its occupants. Are they humanoids? Are they gods? Are they friend or foe? Then we discover the occupants are attractive and well mannered. But we do not doubt for a minute who is in control. Years later, a whole barrage of movies and television shows include alien life forms.

Humans interacted with aliens as they explored space aboard their own spacecraft, the USS Enterprise, in the 1960s TV series, "Star Trek." Of course, the immensely popular "Star Wars" movie series brought to life a whole variety of alien life forms, some not very attractive, but not always unfriendly. With the 1980s, our stellar alien was E.T., the friendly dwarf-sized alien who accidentally found himself stranded on earth, and was subsequently befriended by a few ordinary American children.

Perhaps one of the more direct movies in terms of addressing an actual meeting with aliens was "Close Encounters of the Third Kind." Leading man Richard Dreyfuss was drawn to the landing site of a space craft containing benevolent alien occupants. This movie dealt with many of the issues of choosing between the safety of remaining on earth and the tantalizing curiosity about other life forms and worlds.

On the other hand, movies such as the 1996 blockbuster "Independence Day" depicted aliens as horrific and transported them in overwhelmingly huge craft, supplying them with intentions of destroying the earth. Of course, who knows what would have happened had we not attacked these aliens, but perhaps these aliens already had some insight into human nature before they arrived at our planet.

With the generous assistance of Hollywood and our own imaginations, I suppose we all have some idea about what aliens look or act like. For most people, the idea of alien visitation seems mortifying and frightening, perhaps thanks to movies such as "Independence Day." Many other people prefer to believe that visiting aliens would be benevolent, and that contact with them would not be a negative experience, but instead might be just what the earth needs in these unsettling times.

The Roswell Case

What could be more intriguing than the crash of a mysterious craft on a remote ranch northwest of Roswell, New Mexico? And this happened only a week after Kenneth Arnold spotted the nine shiny UFO craft flitting across the Seattle sky. Ironic, isn't it? With the Roswell crash in early July 1947 leading the way, there was an increase all throughout the following summer of UFO sightings reported in newspapers. Lending even more credibility was the fact that many of these sightings were made by pilots, military personnel and other trained observers of the sky.

The crash site at Roswell is now famous because it yielded what appeared to be an alien space craft. When rancher Mac Brazel decided to check on his sheep after a night of severe thunderstorms, what he discovered was unusual debris and a shallow gouge in the earth several hundred feet long. Gathering some of the debris, Brazel called the local sheriff, who then notified the commander of the nearby Roswell Army Airfield, Colonel William Blanchard.

An initial press release from Roswell Airfield described the wreckage as a crashed "disk." This press release was transmitted on the wire to over thirty US afternoon newspapers that same day. Almost immediately, the Army retracted that press release and called it simply a weather balloon. At that point, it was too late, even though the government swept in and removed the debris, seeking to dismiss the whole incident. But it was not so easy, particularly in light of the discovery of yet another large piece of the craft which landed away from the site of the gouge.

The story got even more interesting when a base hospital nurse, speaking with Glenn Dennis, a young mortician for a local funeral home, confessed that she had assisted two doctors in performing autopsies on several, non-human bodies. She described how one of the bodies was intact, while the others were badly mangled, and noted the anatomical differences between these humanoid creatures and humans. Shortly after this conversation with Dennis, the nurse, and four other nurses from the hospital, were transferred and their files disappeared.

Since that time, a number of serious, non-government investigations to learn more about Roswell have been undertaken. Despite the fact that the military threatened witnesses with death, many of those who were involved in the recovery of the site have come forward to tell their story. Others, like rancher Mac Brazel, have remained silent, even to their graves.

The Truman administration enacted a policy at that time to withhold any information about this incident and other UFO or alien related matters from the public. The government has certainly been silent about the Roswell case, claiming all related documents have been destroyed.[18]

Alien Autopsy

The most recent controversial development over the Roswell incident has been a film, presumably an autopsy of one of these alien humanoids. Ray Santilli, a British publisher, claims to have purchased a copy of the film from the original cameraman. In August 1995, portions of the black and white film were broadcast on national television throughout the United States, with experts in film making, surgeons and others speculating about the film's authenticity and whether the alien body was real.

The consensus appeared to be that the film and the aliens were genuine. But skeptics still abound, as with anything. The Committee for the Scientific Investigation of Claims of the Paranormal (CSICOP), based in Amherst, New York, asserted that the film was a hoax, pointing to a lack of any prior record of the film. None of the witnesses of the autopsy ever mentioned anything about a motion picture camera present during the autopsy.

Santilli went a step further and provided the Eastman-Kodak company a small piece of the autopsy film to authenticate its age. A company spokesman did confirm that the piece was from the correct time period, but hedged by saying it was not the entire footage and thus was not enough to know for certain whether the autopsy was actually recorded on this film.[19]

Obviously, it is not clear whether these were alien life forms who came crashing to earth. If they were, this means we really are not alone in the universe. This means there is the possibility of extra-terrestrial life and that they are aware we exist. But what do they want? And what *are* they exactly, physical or spirit?

Alien Encounters & Abductions

There are literally thousands of accounts of people who have encountered aliens or claim to have actually been taken away by aliens. I know, many people just choose to laugh it away, without giving any credence to the possibility. But I believe these people have seen and experienced *something.* Just as with the numbers of UFO sightings worldwide, there are simply too many people reporting alien encounters and abductions to be just one big hoax. Granted, people will make things up just for the attention. But those notwithstanding, I believe there are significant numbers of people who are telling the truth. So what have they seen? What have they experienced?

Linda Moulton Howe, an Emmy award-winning television journalist has written several comprehensive books, gathering dozens of alien encounters and abduction stories. Howe provides accounts by credible witnesses, including scientists, military personnel and law enforcement officers. Apparently, most people describe aliens similarly. Their bodies are grey in color, and they do not wear clothing. They appear genderless, and they have hands and feet, sometimes with six fingers or toes. The most notable physical trait described is a set of two enormous eyes, often without pupils or with a vertical slit in the center of the eye, like a cat. Some aliens have been described as very tall, others as short.

For those who are abducted and actually transported to some alien craft or environment, a variety of experiences are reported, everything from being probed to being sexually assaulted. The one common experience shared by these abductees is the impression that these creatures wield incredible powers. Nearly all people who have encountered what they believe to be aliens say they felt this was a strongly spiritual experience. The aliens could appear or disappear at will, they made things move or respond to them with an unseen power, and moreover, it was impossible to resist an alien; it could do whatever it pleased to a person.

Not only is there a growing acceptance of the reality of these experiences, but many more people are beginning to think that these aliens are not necessarily from some other planet or universe. Contrary to the traditionally held belief, now people are starting to wonder if these alien creatures are from another dimension, or if they are spiritual.

Perhaps one of the most well-known accounts of an alien abduction is documented in Whitley Strieber's book, *Communion*. He also described the power that aliens possess, and indicated a sense that these aliens were not just spirit beings, but demons. About his experience, Strieber wrote:

> "Increasingly I felt as if I were entering a struggle for my soul, my essence, or whatever part of me might have reference to the eternal.... There are worse things than death, I suspected. And I was beginning to get the distinct impression that one of them [an alien] had taken an interest in me. So far the word 'demon' had never been spoken among the scientists and doctors who were working with me. And why should it have been? We were beyond such things. We were a group of atheists and agnostics, far too sophisticated to be concerned with such archaic ideas as demons and angels."[20]

Apart from the sense that there is a spiritual struggle, what could these aliens want? There seems to be no clear motive. Perhaps it is as simple as other life forms seeking to study and experiment with humans. Or perhaps it really is a desire to take the souls of people. Perhaps aliens are demons with the commission to identify certain people whose minds and spirits they can control.

It is interesting to note that most people who have had contact with aliens have been involved in the occult. And it is not uncommon for those who engage in such occultic practices as meditation or hypnosis to initiate and make contact with spirit beings. In fact, some occultists have reported contact with spirit beings who have similar traits described by those who have encountered what they believe to be aliens. If they are from the same source, this should not be a surprise. Given that there are many more people now than ever before who are engaged in occultic practices because of the New Age spiritual movement, this may explain the increase in reported alien experiences over the last thirty years.

Crop Circles & Animal Mutilations

What if you refused to believe that aliens were spiritual beings? What if, instead, you believed that they were super-intelligent physical beings from another planet or another solar system? What if you believed that these beings transported themselves with spacecraft far surpassing the technology of man? In some way, you might look for evidence throughout history and perhaps even in the present to validate your beliefs. You might point to mysterious ancient wonders such as Stonehenge on the Salisbury Plain of England, an odd configuration of massive, carved stones which appear to be aligned in some mystical way. Or you might think of the great pyramids of Egypt, built by seemingly superhuman efforts, maybe even an alien race.

Some people believe that there is compelling evidence today of alien activity. In the last twenty years, two unusual worldwide phenomena have been on the rise: animal mutilations and crop circles. Linda Howe has written books and produced several documentaries recording her investigations of these strange anomalies, which she asserts might indeed be the work of aliens. Her premise is that sightings of UFOs have often been reported in the immediate vicinity of mutilated animals or crop circles.

Howe has documented hundreds of abnormal, inexplicable deaths of animals, mostly cattle and horses on the open range. These animals died because of bloodless excisions and the removal of eyes, organs and genitals. Apparently, according to forensic pathologists who examined many of these animals, traditional surgical instruments were not used, but incisions were perhaps the result of an advanced laser technology. Further, it appears no coincidence that this same type of animal mutilation occurs worldwide with the same kinds of animals every time.

Circles or unusual geometric shaped designs are discovered laid in cereal crops around the world, and even in the rice paddies of Japan. The circles or designs are sometimes hundreds of feet long and cover many acres. In nearly all cases, scientists have discovered that the crops were bio-chemically or bio-physically changed. No one knows how these circles appear as they usually form overnight and are not cut; it is not as simple as some guy going into a field with a weed whacker. While there have been hoaxes, these pranksters have been unable to create crop circles with the same precision and undisturbed nature as those circles thought to be of alien origin.

Do these phenomena prove there are aliens in physical form with unusual physical and intellectual abilities? Perhaps there is a strong case that something non-human perpetrates these things. But whether it proves that these aliens are physical or spiritual is still not clear. It is also unclear as to whether they are spiritual with the ability to manifest things in physical form. And why would super-intelligent beings do these things in the first place, on an increasing basis in the last twenty years?

Monuments on Mars?

Several distinguished scientists, Robert Jastrow and Carl Sagan included, have supported the idea that evolution has gone on longer than the earth has existed. They have supported the theory that there may be super-intelligent beings out there, and that physical evidence of this may be found on one of our known planets.

Richard Hoagland, author of *Monuments of Mars*, has studied and gathered what he calls scientific data on several provocative photos of the surface of Mars taken by NASA's Viking probe in 1976. These photos show certain formations which appear to be unusual compared to the rest of the geologic features on the Martian surface. Hoagland contends that these formations are artificial, not unlike the pyramids of Egypt or the Sphinx. In fact, he goes so far as to say that these structures may have been constructed by some alien race thousands or even millions of years ago. He also notes the possibility is the same for Europa, a moon of Jupiter, as seen in Voyager mission photos.

Are there artificial structures on Mars or Europa? Well, NASA doesn't seem too interested in finding out if there are, as they have allocated no money toward a project of this kind or indicated they will pursue this possibility. Hoagland and others seem to believe that this is part of an American government conspiracy to prevent the world from knowing the truth. If we ever do find out the truth, does this prove that alien beings are only physical with super-intelligence? Again, it is difficult to be conclusive, as the answer to one question only leads to another question.

Even though the government has historically been silent about the possibility of extra-terrestrial life, some efforts have been made toward direct, purposeful contact with aliens. NASA temporarily funded the NASA Search For Extra-Terrestrial Intelligence (SETI), which attempted to intercept radio signals from anywhere in the universe, perhaps from some alien civilization. After a year of not receiving anything, NASA discontinued the program.

What Does It All Mean?

Sitting back and reflecting, you can see that there is obviously something going on in our world not readily visible to most of us. However, UFO sightings and encounters have definitely increased, although the news media still generally avoids the subject. And yet, there are more TV shows than ever before featuring reports and stories about such things: "X-Files," "Unsolved Mysteries," "Strange Universe," and "Dark Skies" among others. Despite the fact that millions of people are interested in these subjects and have had some UFO or alien related experience, media sources have remained resistant to legitimizing it.

Will aliens make themselves conspicuous? And if they do, what will happen, mass panic or calm acceptance? It is anyone's guess where all this is leading.

The Paranormal & Supernatural

History has shown that people are not only spiritually or religiously inclined, but have always had a fascination with the supernatural. The supernatural refers to things which occur beyond the visible, natural elements, especially in relation to a spirit realm. This realm is generally the paranormal, that is, it cannot be explained scientifically. Paranormal experiences are weird and unexplainable, and many of us are intrigued by them.

The level of interest in things of the paranormal has led some people to seek to develop their own abilities and perform supernatural feats. The Berkeley Psychic Institute in Berkeley, California is one example of a "school" that provides training to anyone who wishes to develop psychic abilities. Through meditation techniques, they teach you how to engage in clairvoyance, mental telepathy, out-of-body experiences and more. They claim that the techniques at which you become proficient can help you succeed in life and even give you more energy to achieve your goals.[21] Sound familiar? It should. Psychic training is another brand of New Age spirituality, just like mind technology, and even uses essentially the same methods.

Those who promote and teach psychic ability attempt to explain this in scientific terms, even calling themselves parapsychologists and preferring to think of themselves as scientists. Many of them hold advanced degrees in real sciences, such as physics, chemistry and mathematics. In endeavoring to demonstrate their seriousness and scholarly attitude, they often seek to disassociate themselves from what they deem to be controversial or frivolous topics— UFOs, astrology, searching for Bigfoot, witchcraft, paganism. The irony is that they choose to ignore what is really the same source for psychic abilities. In short, it is all spiritually based and occultic.

Ghosts & Hauntings

Ghosts and apparitions exist and houses can be haunted. Of that there is no doubt. In fact, this is another area in which the interest level is rising. One example of this actually changes the way we plan our vacations! In America, your vacation can include staying at various hotels and houses *known* to be haunted. In Estes Park, Colorado, you can stay at the Baldpate Inn, where there are resident ghosts, lit cigarettes tend to mysteriously extinguish, and mixed drinks fly across the room.

Or take a two hour tour through various haunted properties in the famous French Quarter in New Orleans, Louisiana, courtesy of Hauntings Today Investigations & Ghost Expeditions. Their team of parapsychologists will make sure this is a getaway you'll remember! Apparently, the spirit realm has now become a form of entertainment.

What *are* ghosts? Some people suggest that ghosts are demons who only pretend to give people the impression of being good. Most ghosts seem harmless. Still, to observe a ghost is at the very least disconcerting if not downright scary. Many people insist that most of the ghosts are good, but good or bad, how healthy is this curiosity in hauntings? And why do ghosts appear to people anyway?

Clairvoyance & Remote Viewing

Ever wonder what another person is *really* thinking? Some people *know!* They have an ability called clairvoyance, or mental telepathy. Through meditation techniques, there are people who have developed this ability to such a high level that even the Russian and US governments have become interested. In their attempt to justify research funds, perhaps, and to add credibility to their work, these people call this scientific remote viewing.

It may surprise you to find out that, particularly during the 1970s and 1980s, the CIA funded the Stanford Research Institute (SRI) for research and instruction in the area of remote viewing. The remote viewers have "seen" a variety of things, many in relation to national security interests, and have been tested for and produced a high accuracy rate. Of course this works. It works because these people are actually transporting themselves spiritually to some remote location to investigate what is called their "target." Some New Agers call this an out-of-body experience or astral projection, but remote viewers prefer to call this occultic practice technology.

Ingo Swann and Harold Puthoff were both developed psychics before they helped form the SRI programs. Their connection with L. Ron Hubbard's Church of Scientology is well known, and in fact, many early SRI participants—ranging even to military personnel and US congressmen—were Scientologists and practitioners of the occult.

Millions of dollars were granted to SRI and eventually the military stepped in more fully to manage the projects. Major Ed Dames and General Stubblebine were two such managers. Stubblebine directed SRI and later broadened the activities at SRI to include tarot card reading and the New Age occultic practice of channeling.[22]

One of the more well-known remote viewers, an SRI participant in the 1980s, is Courtney Brown, the founder of the Farsight Institute. In his book, *Cosmic Voyage: A Scientific Discovery of Extra-terrestrials Visiting Earth*, Brown reveals that he made contact with what he believed to be aliens during the course of his remote viewing experiences. There are those who suggest that what Brown and others like him have actually done is contact spirit beings while in a meditative trance. This is not an uncommon occurrence for someone who has been developing their meditation skills for years. But is this really science and technology?

Prophecy & Precognition

The closer we have gotten to the year 2000, the more people claiming to be prophets have appeared. Of course, there have always been prophets throughout history. People with these abilities usually have dreams or visions, and varying degrees of accuracy, anywhere between eighty and 100 percent. Two thousand years ago, Biblical prophets were the most common, and hundreds of years ago it was Nostradamus. In the last century, names like Edgar Cayce and Gordon Michael Scallion have replaced prophets of old.

The turn of the century seems to be a popular time to bring out the doomsaying prophets. It was that way around 1900 and it is that way as we approach 2000. Prophets of today predict that the end of the century will bring all kinds of doom in the form of natural disasters, weather changes, warfare, disease, etc. At this time, perhaps more than at any other time in history, I wonder if these prophets are right.

Where do these psychics get their abilities? Psychic experts assert that precognition abilities can be learned. For centuries, the Celtic people in Scotland and England passed on their knowledge of these abilities, a practice continued to this day. Dr. Roderic Vickers of Star Concepts, Ltd., a psychic abilities organization, believes that everyone is born with this ability, but that "just like a muscle, you may not have developed it to its full potential yet."

And how do you develop your precognition or psychic abilities? Vickers makes it sound pretty easy:

> "It works for you. You do not have to do anything but relax and become aware. If you are aware...you go with the energy, go with the flow.... You may see images; you may hear messages; you may provide the hand through which a person on another [spiritual] plane will write. You may sense a happening far from where you are. You may just hear about it, in advance or as it is happening, as some will say, 'My little voices told me.'"[23]

Going with the flow does not sound very scientific to me, but I do know that these abilities are real and people can predict things with a fair amount of accuracy. This is yet another occultic practice that has gained a great deal of popularity in recent years. The psychic telephone hot lines, credible or not, have exploded, especially in the United States.

In these uncertain times, people want to know what the future holds. Perhaps they hope to be assured that everything will be all right. So far, I have never heard of someone going to a psychic who tells them something negative like "tomorrow your husband will run away, you will lose your job, and you will be hit by a bus." At least, they probably didn't go to that psychic more than once!

Near Death Experiences

Probably one of the most disturbing things to a human being is the uncertainty we face toward death. We want to believe that there is something beyond death, perhaps to allay our fears of the unknown. Many people have reportedly been near death, left their bodies and returned to life, and we have been fascinated by the details of what happens to them. Experiences like these are often called "near death experiences," a phrase coined in 1975 by Doctor Raymond Moody, Jr. in his book, *Life After Life*. Dr. Moody gathered dozens of near death experiences and interviewed at length those people who had these experiences.

According to Dr. Moody, near death experiences are usually characterized by several common elements. First, there is the feeling that your soul or spirit has left your body, and you are hovering over yourself. This is followed by the feeling that you are progressing through a dark tunnel or space. Emotions become intense, from bliss to sheer terror. You then approach a golden or white light at the end of the tunnel that draws you to it, evoking a feeling of love or goodness.

Some people hear a voice telling them, "It is not yet your time." You may then meet a deceased loved one or some spirit being, often described as "beings of light," as you review major and trivial events of your life. Somehow this must give you insight about life, and maybe you are even given a deeper understanding of the whole life process. You then reach a boundary—a cliff, a fence, a body of water or some other barrier—which you cannot cross, especially if you are to return to life. At this point, people have described being given the decision of whether to return to life, or are simply brought back. Your spirit folds itself back into your body.

Is this truly a near death experience? Is this someone who has died and headed toward heaven or some afterlife environment? Does this truly provide an insight into the beyond? Most people who have had these experiences want to think so. A Gallup poll in 1982 estimated that at least eight million adults in the United States alone have had this experience. Some experts believe that by now the number in the US is closer to thirteen million, which you can add to the many millions worldwide with the same experience.

This does not necessarily prove what happens after you die. What this *does* prove is that millions of people have had a common spiritual experience. Dr. Moody has indicated that these experiences are possible even without being sick or near death; in fact, those who practice meditation or other methods of inducing altered states of consciousness are also able to have near death episodes. An increase in these experiences may be the result of more people in the world engaging in the practice of meditation or other occultic techniques. The more popular the New Age spiritual movement, the more strange spiritual experiences people have.

One World Religion?

The desire for peace, a union of humanity and a concern for the environment can very likely induce a desire in the world for not only a global governing body, but also a worldwide religious or spiritual consensus. Proponents of the New Age movement, particularly the leaders of the Theosophical Society, have long been advocates of both a one world government and a one world spiritual union. They have actively participated in the World Constitution and Parliament Association (WCPA), one of many global government advocacy groups. The Theosophical Society is also in support of the proposed United Nations spiritual charter to achieve world peace and unity. Pope John Paul II has in recent years repeatedly called for world ecumenism, hoping to bring the religions of the world together despite their differences in doctrine and belief.[24]

Clearly, there has been an increase in the spiritual "broad-mindedness" among the people of the world. Nearly every religion, cult, mind technology or spiritual movement is perceived by people everywhere as true and acceptable according to one's own conscience. Even some mystic Muslims and certain denominations of Protestant Christianity have become more open in recent years.

Furthermore, one of the strongest areas of emphasis in the majority of today's popular religions or modes of spirituality seems to be that narcissism is acceptable and good. Developing one's human potential and developing a higher awareness of self is ideal. We are all "one" spiritually, as we can all tap into the same spiritual or global mind.

The Bible prophets make some very interesting predictions about spiritual developments with respect to a one world government as the world heads toward its end. The Book of Revelation not only predicts that there will be a one world government dominated by a global ruler, but it suggests that this may come about because of certain spiritual and religious developments in "the last days," or as I call it, the time of the Quickening.

Apparently, even though this global leader will certainly possess wit, charisma and will exercise control over the majority of the world's military, this may not be enough to gain the support of all the people on earth. Instead, it will require a massive spiritual influence to accept this man not just as a ruler, but as a spiritual leader. In fact, he will be possessed by Satan himself to demonstrate supernatural powers. And since not even that will convince everyone,

> "God will send upon them [all people of the earth] a deluding influence so that they might believe the lie...," giving "authority over every tribe, people, language and nation...to him [this ruler, also known as the 'beast' or the 'Antichrist']. The Bible says it very simply: "And all who dwell on earth will worship him...."[25]

Is this what is happening in the world today? Are we becoming part of a spiritual and religious ecumenical movement to prepare us to unite as one spiritual body? Are we heading toward a time when God will allow us to be deluded into thinking that a man will not only be our spiritual leader or guru, but will also rule the whole earth? This and all our other forms of religion and spirituality give us a lot to ponder.

6

Environment

Eric Stone had been employed by Exxon for twenty years and now they were letting him go. That's the thanks he got! Admittedly, he had been somewhat of a hothead in the past, allowing co-workers to provoke him. But this was the last time he would get away with it; he was out of a job. He felt this weird bubble of rage inside of him, and he vowed to show them that they could not just dispense with him so easily.

Several months went by and Eric met Helen, a woman who had been involved in a number of Greenpeace demonstrations. He attended their meetings and enjoyed being a member of such an accepting and environmentally concerned group. Eventually, Eric picked up and read some literature by a German philosopher and environmentalist, who advocated turning back history to a simpler, healthier lifestyle. That *really* impressed him. Besides, cars and computers were evil and the world would be a better place without them.

After weeks of meetings, Eric and Helen were invited to join a few of the members in their homes. Before long, they revealed to Eric and Helen their plans to blow up an oil refinery. Eric became very interested and excited, intimating his own knowledge of the Exxon refinery, located about twenty miles outside of town. In a short while, a plan was made and all the necessary equipment had been assembled. One member, Joe, was a Vietnam veteran with explosives experience.

On the night of the mission, Eric and Helen dressed in black clothing and ski masks, joining Joe and another couple, all dressed similarly. "Are you ready to teach these environmental traitors a lesson?" Joe asked the group. "Yes!" came the resounding reply.

After snipping their way through a chain link fence, the group scurried to various strategic areas of the oil refinery, carrying plastic explosives and a detonator that Joe had designed. Minutes later, the explosives were mounted and the detonators set. The group ran clear of the refinery fence, heading for their cars.

Fifteen minutes later, the first explosions were heard for miles around, all the way back to the bar the group had gathered at afterward. Toasting their success, Eric sighed with satisfaction, feeling completely vindicated.

$$\Omega \quad \Omega \quad \Omega$$

Cheryl felt the muscles in her calves as she stretched. Tying her hair back, she walked out of her apartment to the street where the sun was already burning through the morning mist. It was going to be another hot one! The only way she could run was to get up at seven am or the heat and traffic was just too much.

Going at a steady pace, she jogged her way to the Pacific Coast Highway, where at some point she would reach the asphalt bicycle path running from Huntington Beach to Newport. As she ran, she felt herself get warm and her muscles loosen; it was a nice day to run, but the air was thick and yellow, even though the ocean was so close.

The first mile was relatively easy. She wanted to make it a six mile day, so she paced herself. After the second mile, though, she began to feel an unusual tightness in her chest. Then a side ache started. At first she thought she might be running too fast, or not breathing enough. Maybe she was a little dehydrated. Cheryl slowed down and tried to adjust, but the tightness was growing worse and beginning to hurt. Experienced and stubborn, she willed it to pass and kept running.

A quarter of a mile later, Cheryl started to get dizzy, feeling the dark edges of faintness. She had to stop. Leaning over, her hands gripping her knees, she struggled for breath, wheezing and coughing, unable to get enough air. About 100 feet ahead of her was an oxygen dispenser. She walked to it, groping for a quarter in her fanny pack. Dropping the coin in, she placed the plastic mask over her nose and mouth, inhaling deeply.

Cheryl felt better after a few minutes, but not without being alienated by the experience. Here she was, twenty-three, in excellent shape and a distance runner. It finally struck her that southern California smog was worse now than she had ever seen it.

Growing up in Huntington Beach, she knew it was getting bad, but not like this. For the first time in her life, she began to have serious thoughts about leaving the state.

Ω   Ω   Ω

No matter how you turn it, the number one problem when it comes to the environment around us—the air, the water, the soil—is *people*. From day one, we have busily manipulated the environment to our own benefit—polluting when necessary, dumping all manner of manmade substances wherever we see fit, destroying forests, damming rivers, extinguishing animal species—without a thought for the consequences. We have been taking up more and more space to accommodate our growing populations and from this fact spring most of our environmental problems.

The reality of our environmental problems is that they are getting worse, not better. And why is that such a surprise? There are now nearly six *billion* people on this earth. That means more people producing consumer waste, creating smog by driving what amount to more cars, having babies, plowing sections of land under for their office buildings or homes. Let's wake up! This kind of behavior doesn't translate into an earth that will last forever and anyone who believes that it does is seriously deluded. The Quickening is a time of reckoning for our environment and despite the clamor of optimists, the future is undeniably grim.

Why Are There More People?

We have managed to control certain aspects of our environment. This in turn has led us to have longer life spans by being able to use the environmental resources to our advantage. For thousands of years, until as recently as the nineteenth century, people were lucky if they lived to be forty years old. Life expectancy increased because we recognized the need to clean up our living environment, especially in the growing urban centers of the world. We greatly improved methods of sanitation, hygiene, garbage disposal and water treatment. We learned to produce food more efficiently, and we developed inexpensive vaccines and medicines to control most disease and illness.

As a result, people live longer. And even though people technically have smaller families, the population of the world is witnessing an unprecedented, almost nightmarish growth. This has naturally fostered environmental challenges since the earth was never meant to hold this many creatures! Some have even speculated that in the face of these collective challenges, we can read the end of our own species.

The Environmentalist Agenda

Everyone wants to live in a clean environment—*everyone*. We all want clean air, relatively pure water, lots of healthy vegetation, animals to admire and appreciate and so on. But somehow, the environmentalist groups, such as the Sierra Club and Greenpeace, want us to believe that they *care* more than the rest of us.

The truth is, most environmentalists have one primary agenda: to make money. They have on their mind the matter of how to find the funds from government, industry and private citizens to keep their operations going. Many environmental groups can be more ideologically and religiously motivated, but they all attempt to achieve their goals by creating alarmist propaganda that plays on our emotions. They want us to donate money because we feel guilty for exploiting the environment or because we are scared by the condition of the environment or even because their commercials bring a tear to our eyes.

Granted, some of these environmental groups busily produce nice products. I have always enjoyed the beautiful greeting cards, calendars and books that the Sierra Club produces, but I also remember that it all goes to their bottom line. Many of these groups go about the arduous task of political reform to save certain species, valued forests and other acreage. The trouble is, these liberal groups pretend to be something they are not and are not any more concerned about the environment than the rest of us. Furthermore, some of their fringe members use questionable tactics to make their point.

Eco-Terrorism

In recent years, many environmental extremists have engaged in various forms of 'eco-vandalism.' Maybe you remember the Greenpeace boats cutting through the nets of commercial fishermen off the coast of Alaska, blowing up utility equipment, or environmental activists handcuffing themselves to age-old redwood trees in northern California, or the many nuclear reactor site demonstrations throughout the world. Thankfully, most of these have been peaceable, but many have also resulted in violence and arrests.

But the 'theo-ecologically' motivated groups do pose a potential danger. Just like religious extremists, these groups, governed not so much by an environmental agenda as a religious-cult agenda, are just as capable of terrorism and hurting people to achieve their aim, to "save the planet." The Golden Age environmentalists, influenced by German theorist, Rudolf Bahro are one example of a theo-ecological group. These people are pantheistic (i.e., God is in all things) and believe that from the beginning man communed with nature in a so-called "Golden Age."

During this Golden Age, life seemed to proceed quite nicely, until the technology "Devil" defiled the world. According to these Golden Age proponents, we must now pursue a "Paradise" of perfect, sustainable harmony between nature and man, or we will face "Armageddon."[1] The idea of destroying our technological advances to go back to the Golden Age is perfectly acceptable to these people. If possible, they would rather that humanity return to the Middle Ages when God ruled the medieval mind and humanity and nature were supposedly in balance. Terrorism, rationalized in their minds for the achievement of this path back to this ideal age, might very well be one way to demonstrate such bizarre theo-ecological convictions.

Bear in mind that eco-vandalism and eco-terrorism exist hand in hand. And terrorism is a highly effective way to gain global attention for even a small group of zealots. Inevitably, another Chernobyl or another Exxon Valdez incident will occur and perhaps instigate such extreme behavior with disastrous human consequences likely.

American Consumerism

Whatever angles environmental groups decide to approach the destruction of the earth from, it still comes down to a basic fact: our society is a pack of consumers. Nowhere is this more evident than in America. At the turn of the twentieth century, America was the architect of industry, and we invented consumerism with the mass production of low cost goods.

With the progression of the century, there was no end to the variety and number of goods available, from radios and refrigerators to automobiles and tires to outfit them—all things which didn't exist before the twentieth century. When these products became easily affordable, everyone had to have them, first America, then the rest of the world.

Americans have developed the fast paced world of consumerism to an art. We are literally the epitome of the "throw away society." We don't think about purchasing a TV or a car and keeping it for a lifetime; we use it for a while and then just throw it "away," eager to go out and buy another, better, bigger, newer version, which we will also include later in our cycle of throwing away.

This applies to all kinds of products, not just household appliances. Think about it. Nearly everything we eat or drink comes wrapped or canned or bottled in some throw-away, non-perishable container. Most of us don't or can't keep clothing forever either. One hundred years ago, people had a few items they would wear, maybe a pair or two of shoes, which they kept for years. Today, we replace clothing annually, monthly, daily. Where does it go? We throw it away!

As the world economy becomes more fluid, so do the products we manufacture. Moreover, rather than mass production of one item and the storage of excess inventory, we use computers and sophisticated tracking technology to maintain smaller inventories of each item. This sounds good, but the flip side is that we are producing a greater variety of products! More stuff!

And the consumption of products is not just limited to Americans and people of other Western countries, but has now extended itself all over the world. Communism is going away, and the demand by hundreds of millions more people for disposable goods has replaced it. For example, during the 1980s, one-third of the Chinese population purchased a color television. That's hundreds of millions of TVs that twenty years ago did not exist!

More people, more products, and with our global economy, more people with money to spend. Disposable products have already proliferated far beyond anything before in history and there's no sign of it stopping. There's no end in sight for the amount of stuff we will buy, use for a while and then throw away, somehow expecting there will always be a place for it to go. In Europe and Japan, the average family discards about a ton of garbage a year. Americans, not to be outdone of course, produce no less than two tons of garbage per family a year.[2]

Not Enough Room!

By the year 2025, more people will live in cities than occupied the whole earth ten years ago! But the challenge of finding enough space to accommodate the growing world population is a very real problem in burgeoning metropolitan areas of the world *today*, not just one we can put in our back pockets and worry about in twenty years.

According to the World Resources Institute, only one-third of the world's population was urban thirty-five years ago. Now, more than 150,000 people are being added to urban populations in developing countries every day. The greater metropolitan area of Tokyo has twenty-seven million people, Sao Paulo, Brazil has nearly sixteen and a half million, and Bombay, India has fifteen million. These are only a few of the world's mega-cities today with populations exceeding eight million; thirty-three more mega-cities will explode into existence in the next twenty years. More than 500 cities will reach one million or more people in the next few years as well.[3] This is not normal, all these people, and it will have consequences.

Experts say that with these growing numbers of people inhabiting cities, there will be a tremendous increase in the urban poor. In fact, it is believed that these people will live in worse conditions in the cities than the rural poor. Vast slums will exist in all those cities containing one million or more people. A good example of this trend is Latin America. Between 1970 and 1990, the numbers of urban poor in Latin America increased from forty-four million to 115 million.

And this problem will exist no matter how rich a country may be; of course, we will see more urban poor in the poorer countries like India and Africa. In the next five years, you can expect to see the size of major cities in developing countries to double what they were in 1980. The result will be a strain not only on the means of housing so many additional people, but also on the ability of the infrastructure to provide adequate sewage, sufficient water supplies, utilities and other basic needs.

Smog

One of the most direct side effects of this increased number of people in cities will be auto and industrial emissions. For most Western, industrialized cities with stringent emission standards, smog has actually diminished somewhat in recent years. However, auto-intense cities such as Tokyo, Los Angeles, Mexico City and Bombay will all continue to suffer from heavy smog. And as the number of motor vehicles increase to accommodate the growing population..., well, you can see where it is going. Smog will take its place as a significant problem in the years ahead.

Just how many more cars will be on the road anyway? In about the next ten years, another *billion* motor vehicles will be on the road! In the United States, the number of miles driven in motor vehicles climbed forty percent in the last decade, largely offsetting an increase in vehicle efficiency. For fast growing cities like Bangkok, there will be no relief either; every day more than 400 more vehicles are added to the traffic jams.

Smog is something we are going to have to get used to, apparently, but the long term effects are becoming evident already. Historically, smog has always existed, even at a limited level. People created smog with fires for thousands of years. Two centuries ago, railroads began belching more smog into the environment. But humanity has not seen anything like the vehicular smog of the last fifty years. We can thank smog for eye irritation, crop damage, severe reductions in visibility and the rapid deterioration of rubber products. Moreover, there is now plenty of evidence of specific health problems induced by constant exposure to smog.

Ask any American where they think the worst smog problem in the country is and one of the top five answers will be Los Angeles. The Los Angeles County Medical Association of Physicians cited that ninety-five percent of them recognized in their patients the existence of a "smog complex," involving eye irritation, inflammation of the respiratory tract, chest pains, coughing, shortness of breath, nausea and persistent headaches.

Just under ninety percent of these same doctors observed that patients with respiratory diseases were more susceptible to the effects of smog, and eighty-one percent believed that smog contributed to cancer of the lungs and the respiratory system. Not a real big incentive to live in Los Angeles! But there is nowhere to run from this problem.

People have also died from too much smog exposure in a brief time period. In 1930, a five day period of intense smog in Belgium's Meuse Valley killed sixty-three people. In 1948, a three day period of smog in Donora, Pennsylvania killed twenty people and caused illness in 7,000. And three heavy episodes of smog in London during 1948, 1952 and 1956 killed nearly 5,000 people. This establishes an uncomfortable but very real precedent for what happens when smog levels get out of control. Emission standards have been created in most Western countries, but are almost non-existent elsewhere. The world has not seen the end of such environmental tragedies.[4]

Garbage, Garbage Everywhere

So much of what we produce is non-perishable, so it's no surprise that we have a serious challenge when it comes to getting rid of our refuse. Things as common as aluminum cans take 4,000 years to break down, and plastic is not biodegradable at all! If you combine all the municipal, industrial, agricultural and mining waste from the United States, it adds up to about 180 million tons a year! By the year 2000, it is projected to be over 216 million tons.

Our old solution of burying it in the ground so we don't think about what we don't see won't work anymore either. More than half the landfills in the United States are already at or on the verge of capacity. Rural inhabitants are even now resisting efforts on the part of mega-cities worldwide to encroach on their land to dump more garbage. Some cities haul their garbage hundreds of miles before finding a place to dump it.[5]

Many of you probably remember a few years ago when New Jersey had a huge barge with garbage on it floating along the Atlantic coast and eventually down to the Gulf coast trying to unload its cargo. No port would even let them near! It would be humorous if it were not so pathetic. Elsewhere in the world, things are not much better. The Germans have over 50,000 landfill sites, and now they believe that the chemicals in these landfills are seeping into their groundwater. The rest of the world is experiencing the same dilemma.[6]

Alternatives to landfills have been suggested: recycling, composting, and incineration are among these ideas. And cities have employed these methods to some extent, but people are simply producing more garbage than cities can handle. Besides, there is only so much you can practically recycle, compost or incinerate, both on a financially feasible level and on the level of human nature. In fact, only about twenty percent of our garbage can be taken care of by these alternative means anyway.

Right now, the two greatest challenges are managing all the stuff we throw away and protecting our groundwater in the process. Groundwater is the primary concern since seventy percent of it is our main source of usable water. Methane gas is another problem engendered by landfills. This chemical has the potential of exploding and destroying nearby structures; in addition, the presence of methane gas can also lead to fires and intensified air pollution.[7]

Obviously, the garbage situation is not a promising one. It is an eternal catch-22: humans produce, humans consume, humans throw away, humans produce....

Chemicals & Other Gunk

In the last fifty years, man has made the world his chemistry lab, manufacturing over 70,000 different chemicals. Only a small number of these chemicals have been tested for their effects on people and the environment; in other words, we have no idea how bad some of this stuff is for us! And what may be illegal to use in one country is legal in another, like the highly toxic pesticide DDT, which is illegal in the US, but legal in Mexico. So although the US does not grow crops sprayed with DDT, we do import a variety of produce from Mexico which is doused in this poison.

No one is safe from the chemicals we are exposed to on a daily basis. And with more and more people coming on the scene, the use of chemicals is bound to increase as the need for food sprayed with such toxins increases.[8]

Pesticides

Mass-scale commercial farming has been successful in large part because of pesticides and artificial fertilizers. Without pesticides, it might be impossible to produce crops unaffected by pests. But farmers are not the only ones using pesticides; many home gardens, public parks, golf courses and other common areas are soaked in these bug-eradicating solutions and powders.

Here's the problem: pesticides travel through the air, get into the ground and the water, and even into living organisms. This makes it pretty likely that humans in the area will either inhale, drink or ingest pesticides in some form. Along with DDT, people around the world are also exposed to other common dangerous pesticides and pesticide by-products such as DDD and methyl bromide. DDD breaks down in the soil to become DDE, and either one of these poisons can be found in root and leafy vegetables, fatty meats, fish and poultry. They also have a knack for building up in the fatty tissues of animals and people with often fatal consequences later.

With prolonged exposure to these poisons in food, people become very ill. The most likely afflictions include damage to the nervous system, which can invoke excitability, tremors and seizures. Methyl bromide, used legally in the United States (we consume about 28,000 tons annually), especially on strawberries, grapes, tomatoes, peppers, and nut crops, can induce additional health hazards.

High doses of methyl bromide can lead to nervous and respiratory system failure, as well as severe problems in the lungs, eyes and skin. Initial indications may include weakness, despondency, headache, nausea, visual impairment, vomiting, numbness, muscle spasms and lack of balance. Extreme cases have resulted in death.[9]

These are only a few of the sometimes lethal pesticides we choose to spread into the environment. But again, our growing demand for food for our growing number of mouths means we must continue to use the methods we know, unless we find something better.

Cleaning Agents

If you have ever watched afternoon television, soap operas and the like, you know that the commercials are mostly directed toward housewives, whom the advertising agencies still believe put a great deal of emphasis on cleaning their homes. Thousands of the untested chemicals manufactured all over the world are used in our household cleaning products, everything from floor, window and oven cleaners to soaps and detergents. The chemicals in these products end up in our water sources, the soil and evaporate into the atmosphere.

Ironic, isn't it? Hygiene and sanitation are two of the reasons we have been able to prolong life in the past century. Now we are discovering that all this cleanliness may result in the deaths of some of us. Yet another cruel twist in our Quickening world.

Lead

The water we use every day is moved through a complicated infrastructure above, below and around us. Much of this is done using lead piping. Unfortunately, in many cities, this lead piping is aging and pretty far down on the list of things to be repaired. This creates a major problem for anyone who drinks water, takes a shower, or cooks: lead poisoning.

Lead poisoning is dangerous at any level of exposure; however, it is our children who are most vulnerable in this area. Their younger bodies absorb and retain lead more easily and in larger quantities than those of adults. Even at very low levels, children can experience reduced IQs, impaired learning and language skills, loss of hearing and reduced attention abilities. High levels of lead exposure damage the brain and the central nervous system, the very foundations of humans. For adults, blood pressure can increase and some impaired function is possible. How do we make this a priority among the many other problems in the world around us?[10]

Fresh Water: A Rare Commodity

Theoretically, we could feed the world for the most part, if we chose to. But this will become a growing challenge in just a few years because of the exploding population and the demands on fresh water for irrigation. Fresh water is the most immediate concern today, above and beyond food. For one thing, fresh water is usually the first thing contaminated by our heaping garbage sites and the chemicals that leach into the ground and into our underground aquifers.

Although seventy percent of the world is covered by water, most of it is not fresh water. Of the fresh water that actually exists, seventy-five percent of it is held in the polar ice caps and glaciers—not exactly the most convenient source. You take for granted that fresh water is readily available, but it becomes scarcer every day, and that fact is starting to catch up with us.

For many people, the solution is to simply not drink the water in their city; they buy it bottled, shipped in from somewhere else. But they still bathe, cook and water their plants and lawns with tap water. Water filtration systems have also become a popular way to ensure that your water is at least passable. City officials will argue that the water is safe to drink, that it just tastes a little funny, or smells a little unusual (like rotten eggs, for instance). Some are clever and suggest that water smells and tastes weird because of the unique mineral deposits. Actually, they are right. However, these are unhealthful heavy metals and a variety of other organic and inorganic toxins from landfill seepage.

For now, tap water may be acceptable to use for some things, but eventually it may no longer be considered fresh water. Or the water supply may become non-existent.

Drip, Drip, Gone

Imagine turning on your faucet and hearing only a groaning pipe, feeling only a cold rush of air through the spigot. Water shortages are not a new phenomenon. People who live in areas like Nevada and southern California are forced to use their water sparingly; for example, you cannot water your lawn or wash your car on certain days lest you get caught and fined. Australians have the same challenge; they have to pipe in their limited water supply over hundreds of miles of desert.

Egypt is the poorest country in fresh water. Elsewhere in the world, countries such as China, India and Pakistan use most of the available fresh water for irrigation to raise crops and feed the billions of people in these regions. India uses ninety-seven percent of its fresh water for irrigation; they drink, cook and bathe in the remaining three percent, which is more often than not contaminated and alive with diseases like cholera and typhoid.

Dams & Irrigation

The world is in the middle of a ongoing paradox of saving and spending when it comes to its water supply. Over the last forty years, we have built an inordinate number of dams; of the approximately 100 dams built in that time, seventy-five percent were built since 1955. And it's still not enough!

The situation in China is so desperate that soon they will be forced to dam parts of the Yangtze River to divert water to the semi-arid northern provinces. When it takes place, this will be one of the largest, most expensive damming projects in the world. Further, it may bring much needed water to these areas, but will not come without a price; a few of the negative environmental and human repercussions are flooding, the displacement of established villages with millions of inhabitants, and the destruction of rare vegetation and many other forms of wildlife.[11]

Other dams will be built around the world as well, in response to the demand from growing cities. Already under construction or in the planning phase are the Gabcikovo Dam on the Danube River in Slovakia, dams at the Blue and White Niles, dams at the upper reaches of the Tigris and Euphrates Rivers near Turkey, and the Euphrates by Syria, and a division of water from the Sea of Galilee into Israel's National Water Carrier. As more and more people come into existence, we are being forced to literally carve up beautiful, natural regions of the earth all in the name of our survival.[12]

To further our dilemma, we are faced with the fact that for thousands of years, the people in most regions of the world have practiced inefficient irrigation methods. Farmers have been notorious worldwide for over-irrigating and wasting up to one-third of the water they use. With the distinct possibility of water shortages increasing in the next few decades, governments in nearly every country must avoid wasteful water practices.

One way that already exists is to increase the cost of water, usually in favor of the farmer. As an example, a farmer in Arizona might pay one cent for a cubic yard of water, while the city of Phoenix will pay twenty-five cents. Since most people understand things better when you put them in terms of money, maybe this will transform water into a bargaining business.[13]

Toxic Seepage

Speaking of Arizona, the groundwater there is all but undrinkable! Why? High levels of toxic organic compounds are seeping in from Mexico. Even parts of the world that have traditionally had plenty of fresh water, like Europe, have begun to be concerned as they see the heavy metal content in their water rise steadily. Finland, Sweden and Denmark have all noted a marked increase in their water's heavy metal content, attributing it to landfill seepage. Some of this seepage is coming from as far away as the sewage systems of St. Petersburg, Russia. And not only is the fresh water contaminated, but the oceans of the world are polluted as well, destroying huge beds of kelp and plankton, and eliminating many species of fish, birds and other wildlife.

By the year 2000, at least twenty-five cities in the world will have populations in excess of eleven million people. Of these cities, five of them are in industrialized parts of the world, and will either have severely rationed fresh water sources or have no available water at all. The other twenty non-industrialized cities will in fact have *no* practical, clean source of fresh water.[14]

Enough Natural Resources?

While water is becoming scarce, we are having no problem using our other natural resources either. For years, environmentalists have howled about relentless strip mining, deforestation by greedy lumber companies and the rapacious nature of oil companies when it comes to the earth's petroleum. Our problem is not our capacity to produce things and the energy needed for the manufacture and distribution of these products, but how to get rid of these things once they are made.

Energy Sources

Most of what we use for energy is still plentiful; natural gas, for instance, should last at least another 200 years, and coal is easily good for about sixty more years. Even petroleum is not lacking yet, despite what millions of people thought who sat angrily in line during Jimmy Carter's pseudo-energy crisis of the 1970s. The fact is, for now, anyway, there is plenty of liquid petroleum to supply up to eighty percent of the world's energy needs.[15]

New oil reserves have been discovered in the last few years, and our existing reserves turned out to be bigger than initially estimated. The greatest sources of coal and petroleum are in America, China, Russia and the Ukraine. Moreover, scientists have been developing cost efficient methods of extracting oil from coal. The only real negative is that reserves will begin to feel the pinch in about twenty years as we add billions more vehicles and people. We can happily use petroleum, but it does have atmospheric consequences.

Electricity is plentiful as well, given our hydro-generators and nuclear reactors. Of course, nuclear power has not been the great source of electricity that some hoped it would be thirty years ago. Some countries, like France, derive most of their electricity from nuclear power, and the United States derives more energy from nuclear power than from gas or hydroelectric and all other renewable power combined; it has not been a significantly viable electricity source in other countries, though.

The main reasons for this are cost, safety and means of disposal. Nuclear reactors are not cheap to operate! They are also not completely safe; as with anything run by humans, mistakes are always possible and are made—remember Three Mile Island and Chernobyl. And as far as nuclear waste disposal, that is one political issue that seems to have no solution, especially since no one wants it in their backyard.

Solar and wind energy work mostly for localized use, a minute source in the big picture of the world's electricity. Half of the world population uses wood to generate energy, wood which people gather themselves. Strange as it may seem, this source of energy has been free for most poor people in the world. Now even wood is growing scarce as the protection of forests has been plunged directly in with the other environmental issues.

Trees, Minerals & Other Resources

A peculiar balance exists when it comes to the use of resources. In general, any resource, whether it is rain forests or forests of any kind, minerals, or deep sea fisheries, when exploited by private enterprise are usually not in danger of exhaustion. On the other hand, those resources exploited by governments, owned in common, or not owned by anyone *are* vulnerable to over-exploitation. What this boils down to is that as long as a private company has control over its own resources, the company will usually make the effort of preserving its interest. To a lumber company, it makes no sense to harvest all the trees and have nothing left to harvest; instead a lumber company is more likely to replant trees in such a way that the future will yield an ongoing crop for them.

Rain forests are in the public domain of South America. This has led to nothing but trouble as people burn and butcher these lands for temporary use, moving on once the land's nutrients are depleted. Since these forests are crucial in extracting carbon dioxide from the earth's atmosphere so humans are able to live, you can imagine what damage this has wrought. And the rain forests are not replaceable.

This also rings true for public lands, like national and public parks, and any areas that have been set aside by the government for public use. What is it about these lands that people feel so free to deface them? People apparently have no remorse about throwing their trash—cans, fast food wrappers, cigarettes, rubber tires—all over it. Perhaps this is an indication of human nature, that we don't know how to appreciate something beautiful until it is completely in ruins and just a memory in someone's photographs.

In some ways, when it comes to land set aside in the public "trust," as they say, people are merciless, running like bulldozers over anything and everything in their way and leaving destruction behind them without a second thought. Perhaps again, we have no incentive to preserve these lands because our *money* is not at stake, because it doesn't *cost* anything to pillage these places of quiet beauty.

Rising Temperatures

All of us have awakened in the morning and looked outside, admiring the colors of the land and the sky. Unfortunately, more often than not these days we are looking at a thick layer of brown-black haze. The air we breathe is not getting any better, and even the climate of the earth is undergoing dramatic changes because of what are called "greenhouse gases." Greenhouse gases are motor vehicle smog and industrial emissions that combine to create a gas blanket surrounding the earth, warming it much like a greenhouse.

Smog consists of carbon dioxide, carbon monoxide, ozone and other nitrogen oxide based gases. Industrial emissions are mostly the result of industrial incinerators and various waste processes that continue to dump deadly toxins like beryllium, benzene, cadmium and mercury into the sky. Of all the greenhouse gases, however, carbon dioxide is the greatest culprit when it comes to warming the earth because it is the best at holding the sun's solar heat in the upper atmosphere of the earth.[16]

Some recently industrialized countries have been in a better position to start with a clean slate, to avoid a certain amount of this greenhouse gas pollution. They can monitor industrial pollution with tight controls, fining businesses for over-pollution when necessary. For established industrialized countries, it is harder to stop industry and undo the damage. This is why cities like Los Angeles and Mexico City will always contribute to the greenhouse gas problem. Ultimately, however, all cities in the world will create motor vehicle smog, contributing to the larger problem of global warming.

The Intergovernmental Panel on Climate Change recently concluded that greenhouse gases have induced global warming and indicate a distinct "human influence on global climate." This has been controversial because there are those who resist the idea that we are experiencing disturbing weather patterns as the result of global warming.

People who do believe in the idea of global warming also think that the polar ice caps and glaciers are melting and will eventually submerge coastal cities worldwide. Cities like New Orleans, Venice or Bangladesh could be under water forever. It is true that an unusual number of icebergs have been breaking away from Antarctica in recent years.

The earth *has* undergone dramatic changes in temperature over the course of its history. And it is known that even a minute fluctuation in the overall temperature of the earth can send ripples of change throughout the world climate. But the pace at which temperature changes have been occurring lately is notable. Today, most experts agree that a marked increase in the earth's temperature has been seen in the last half of the century. While the increase has only been a few degrees, it still has a dramatic effect on the overall world climate.

As long as the earth has existed, the greatest source of temperature change has come from volcanic eruptions. Volcanoes spew vast amounts of ash and debris into the air, creating a cloud that collects in the upper atmosphere and traps the earth's heat. We have seen a remarkable number of volcanic eruptions in the last fifty years, along with the destruction of the rain forests (which normally convert twenty-five percent of all polluting carbons into bio-mass), and a buildup of greenhouse gases generated by cars and industry. Combined, these have raised the earth's temperature. In fact, it is entirely possible that these types of alterations in the balance of the earth have been responsible for the many storms, hurricanes, tornadoes and other unusual weather patterns in recent times.

Global warming is most likely out of our control. If there are more volcanoes erupting, who can stop them? And we are certainly not about to stop producing greenhouse gases—that would be *far* too inconvenient for most people. Industry will continue to create these gases because money nearly always assumes a greater importance over the environment. Of course, remember, we have an additional billion motor vehicles that will collect on the world's highways, too, in the next twenty years. So this part of the Quickening will not be stopped.

The Ozone Controversy

The ozone layer is a very thin (only one-eighth of an inch thick) shield that protects the world from excessive UV rays from the sun. Without the ozone layer, the world would be virtually uninhabitable. And should the ozone layer be destroyed for any reason, it is gone forever.

What will happen as the ozone layer continues to deteriorate? The world will see a dramatic rise in cases of skin cancer, cataract problems and blindness, suppression of the immune system and a direct threat to our food supply. For every one percent of the ozone depleted, about 100,000 to 150,000 people suffer from cataract-induced blindness globally.[17]

Australia is in a particularly bad situation with the ozone; it is estimated that as many as two-thirds of Australians will develop some form of skin cancer in the next decade. To date, about three percent of the ozone has been destroyed, and some believe that at its current rate of destruction, we could see up to eight percent destroyed in just a few years.[18]

Should We Worry?

We have some pretty sophisticated equipment that we have used to measure the ozone layer, whether it's from the ground, the sky or in space. Scientists from the United Nations Environment Programme (UNEP) are among those who have conducted these types of studies and concluded that "record low global ozone levels were measured over the past two years." UNEP Executive Director, Elizabeth Dowdeswell indicated that this was not a good sign, especially since an overwhelming amount of the deterioration has been attributed to greenhouse gases; theoretically, humans have some control over this.

When it comes to naming specific agents responsible for the destruction of the ozone layer, there are names we have all heard on the news: chlorofluorocarbons (CFCs), hydrochlorofluorocarbons (HCFCs), hydrofluorocarbons (HFCs), methyl bromide (the pesticide discussed earlier), industrial chlorine and various halons. CFCs, HCFCs and HFCs have been the refrigerants used in air conditioners and refrigerators all over the world.

In the late 1970s, the first ozone "holes" were detected over various parts of the earth, particularly over the Antarctic. Did this stop the world from producing ozone-depleting gases? Did we feel any amount of alarm or responsibility for this? Apparently not, because we kept driving our cars and our industry kept running the way it always did, and by 1992, the holes had gotten bigger.

Concern finally bloomed into a meeting of the major industrialized countries of the world in Copenhagen with the goal being the reduction of these gases. The document that resulted from this meeting was called the Montreal Protocol, and placed emphasis on reducing industrial chlorine and bromine. Many countries complied, but continued their use of CFCs. America banned the use of CFCs, but we still use methyl bromide (a class of bromine) for agriculture. The other factor that this meeting could not address was the existence of millions of products containing CFCs before the Montreal Protocol, and eventually these gases will have to escape into the atmosphere as well.

By the turn of the century, UNEP predicted that the levels of atmospheric chlorine and bromine will begin to diminish. However, this is outweighed by the increase of the CFCs which is inevitable.[19]

Again, however important the influence of greenhouse gases on the ozone, volcanic debris also play their own major role. The 1991 eruption of Mount Pinatubo in the Philippines has had the most dramatic and negative effect on the ozone in recent years. Some experts believe that this underscores how vulnerable the ozone layer is and how all the more important it is to eliminate chemicals known to destroy the ozone.

What Can I Do?

According to UNEP, there are several ways that humanity can at least put an end to man's destruction of the ozone layer. We can eliminate all methyl bromide, we can eliminate all HCFCs, and we can prevent CFCs and halon chemicals from being released by existing equipment and products. Furthermore, *all* these measures must be done *now*. This is pretty idealistic, and not very practical, but that is the best the world can come up with for now.[20]

Environmentalist Complaints

The environmental groups *love* the ozone. Why? It is one of their favorite ways of scaring the rest of us into giving them money. Now, there have been those who have sought to correct these groups, to convince them that the ozone layer is not really an issue. They claim that things are not really that bad, that the deterioration is not as severe as everyone makes it out to be, and that this whole CFC thing is nothing but propaganda.

Well, obviously, just as with the global warming problem, there is nothing we can do to prevent the eruptions of volcanoes and their proven destruction of the ozone. But we do have control over the production of greenhouse gases. Quite frankly, though, can we honestly believe that *everyone* will correct their behavior *immediately* to prevent further damage to the very thing that protects all our lives? Given human nature, I don't think so. Or perhaps it is really not that bad anyway and there is nothing to get stressed over. In the meantime, while we are all thinking about it, I'm wearing my sunglasses and sun block outside.

Avoiding Fallout

Nuclear proliferation, something most people prefer just to deny the existence of, is the one scourge of the earth for which man can credit himself for his own colossal brilliance and stupidity. No other animal on earth is smart enough and stupid enough simultaneously to create something that could completely destroy his own species within a matter of hours. Not only that, it produces the type of pollution that once it gets started, it just keeps killing and killing. You can't see it, but it's there, everywhere. And yes, we did it.

There are literally tens of thousands of nuclear warheads littering the world, either in silos, aircraft, battleships or nuclear submarines. Every major city in the world is targeted, especially in the Western countries, by someone, and usually more than one bomb has a city's name on it. If just one goes off, we instantly have a type of pollution we can't deal with. How can you overlook the serious threat of nuclear installations that exist to produce the plutonium for nuclear warheads and the more than 400 nuclear reactor power stations throughout the world?

No one knows how to properly dispose of nuclear waste. Some countries are so perplexed by what they have wrought, there are instances of ships throwing drums of the stuff into the ocean! You don't just walk away from this kind of creation and pretend it doesn't exist; eventually, this *will* come back to haunt us.

Chernobyl

Why did the Chernobyl accident occur? One very distressing answer is operator incompetence combined with a technical flaw in the system. In April 1986, two explosions destroyed the core of Unit 4 and the roof of the reactor building, sending a shower of hot and highly radioactive debris into the air. The destroyed core was exposed to the atmosphere. More than two dozen people within close proximity to the site died within a week. Hundreds more who were involved in controlling the subsequent fire were hospitalized days later with whole-body doses of Acute Radiation Syndrome.

That wasn't even the worst of it. About fifty tons of radioactive fission products and debris rose more than half a mile into the air and were blown by a prevailing northwest wind. The radioactive fallout was broadcast thousands of miles, into areas of Scandinavia, Poland, Germany and other parts of Europe. Crops were contaminated along with many other food stuffs, much of which was unwittingly distributed to other parts of the world, including America. Thousands of people in the years to come will develop leukemia and a variety of cancers all because of a disaster that took seconds.[21]

See how easily that happened? What is really unnerving is the thought that it can happen again, anytime, anywhere. Another accident like that could be even worse, could claim more lives, could have more far-reaching effects. Someone could make a mistake, or perhaps an act of either well-intentioned or lunatic terrorism—even an earthquake could

233

cause such a disaster. Dozens of reactor sites worldwide are either sitting on or in close proximity to known fault lines.

We can't undo this. Yes, nuclear reactor power stations have ceased construction in most parts of the world. But some of the world's most dangerous countries—Libya, Iran, Korea—are busy constructing nuclear installations to build their own nuclear warhead arsenal. In weapon form or not, the stuff is out there, with no place to bury it or throw it away, no way to make it disappear. And next time, there might not be a second chance.

Global Environmental Control

The growing concern over the environment could spur the formation of a global governing body. The United Nations has called for such unity over the years and so has the World Bank. Several meetings of the countries of the world have also addressed concerns over the environment, and world leaders everywhere have discussed the concepts of global efforts and agreements. At the world environmental summit in Rio de Janeiro in 1992, all sorts of impressive sounding commitments were made. Even former President George Bush boasted of being "the environmental president." Other than talking, nothing significant has happened in regard to a global environmental effort.

Otherwise, laws have been passed by many Western countries outlawing a variety of chemicals, to bolster emissions standards, and to clean up rivers and beaches. These measures do work to a certain extent. The air in Tokyo and London has improved slightly. In northwest Europe, the governments have cleaned up badly polluted rivers and put sanctions on industry. The mistakes of the past are not corrected so easily and these efforts are good, but not enough.

Pollution persists, albeit unevenly, throughout the world. The worst spots will continue to be the poorer and less developed countries, but the world definitely shares some global problems. The climate is changing, the ozone is diminishing, fresh water is becoming scarce and what does exist is being poisoned, radioactivity moves across borders, international fishing waters are over-exploited—the list goes on and on.

Then there is the question of when and where the next Exxon Valdez oil spill will happen, or the next Chernobyl, or some other disaster. This doesn't even include natural disasters, like Mount Pinatubo or Mount Saint Helens erupting again, or the effect of the next big earthquake.

Environmental Laws & Taxes

The world may yet come together to tackle these global environmental concerns. Theoretically, measures such as pollution taxes could be imposed to pay for the technology and effort to clean things up, and sanctions could be levied on countries and megacorporations that continue to pollute. Obviously, there will always be someone or some company that will pollute, just like there will always be someone who speeds in their car. But we have seen that the law can be enforced and even huge fines are meted and paid. Exxon paid billions to clean up and pay fines after the oil spill. And laws have been broadened to prevent or discourage pollution.

Taxes on a variety of polluting products are also gaining popularity around the world. Sweden taxes pesticides, Norway taxes non-recyclable containers and Italy taxes plastic bags. A system of tax credits to companies who use recycled products is now being implemented in some European countries.

In the end, self-interest will take precedence, even at the expense of everyone else. Powerful, highly financed oil companies and auto manufacturers have no incentive to participate. Why would they want to discourage driving and the use of petroleum? This easily applies to chemical companies and other merchants of environmental destruction. These industries have the money and the means to make something bad not look so bad. If they do violate the law and are caught, it may simply be easier and less costly in the long run to pay and go on. Moreover, let's not forget that politicians are greatly influenced by the money of industry lobbyists.

Governmental means of addressing environmental problems will be adopted globally, perhaps under the auspices of a global environmental council. In a way, it could ensure enforcement of the laws if all countries recognized the need to participate actively. After all, the survival of our species is at stake. It is clear that ignoring the environment and just hoping it is just not that bad or that it will just go away is not the answer.

7

Disease & Famine

Cynthia was the epitome of a happy bride. She dearly loved her husband, Bertrand, and after four years of dating, their honeymoon in the Bahamas was like a dream; they were together constantly, and always had a wonderful time. Cynthia and Bertrand spent hours talking about their future together, planning the type of house they would have, where they would live and how many children they wanted. At twenty-seven, Cynthia had been married before and gone through a string of dead-end relationships before that. Both she and Bertrand were amazed to have found each other, that special someone they could share a wonderful life with.

Two months after the honeymoon, Cynthia was mystified by the fact that she could not get pregnant. Bertrand cheerfully went and had himself checked out by his own doctor. The results came back completely normal; he was absolutely capable of having children. With a nasty twinge of worry in the back of her mind, Cynthia finally decided to see her doctor. Until then, she hadn't believed there might be something wrong with her. After all, her sister had three children and her brother had one, so it didn't seem to be anything that could be genetic.

After going through a number of tests, her doctor called Cynthia with the unfortunate news that she could not have children. Apparently, when Cynthia was much younger, she had become infected with chlamydia, a sexually transmitted disease that had been there so long it had rendered her infertile. Crying as she hung up the phone, Cynthia could not understand how this had happened. In her whole life, she hadn't slept with more than a half dozen men.

Ω Ω Ω

It was a beautiful summer day, but the humidity in Philadelphia was already stifling. Still, John had the day off and was determined to plant his begonias in the front yard. Even wearing a short sleeve shirt and khaki shorts, he was sweating profusely as he pushed his wheelbarrow to the garden.

Throughout the day, John turned over soil and dug holes for his favorite kind of plants. In one area of his yard, it was shady and he particularly enjoyed working there. As he labored, every so often gnats fluttered around his head, and he would swat them away in a good-natured fashion. Eventually, he noticed a mosquito hovering, and he swatted at that, too, but it immediately came back. He swatted it again, this time trying to snatch it with his hand. It evaded him, but came right back, aggressively, as

238

though angered by his audacity in attempting to kill it. Then it seemed to disappear in a gust of wind.

Sighing, John resumed working, pulling his water hose to the garden and spraying his plants happily. As he was about to go inside, he felt an irritating itching sensation on his neck. Like a reflex, he slapped his neck. When he brought his hand back, the palm was smeared with bright red blood, probably his own, and the quivering carcass of a crushed mosquito. This was like no mosquito John had ever seen before, distinct, tiger-stripe markings on its body. He washed his hands clean and went inside.

Several days later, John awoke feeling very tired and feverish. Thinking he had a cold or the flu, he stayed home from work, but the next day he was no better. That evening, as he watched the news, the woman broadcaster announced that an apparently drug-resistant form of malaria had struck the Philadelphia area. A dozen people had been hospitalized and one elderly man was in critical condition. There was no known treatment of the disease, and as the announcer described the symptoms, John felt a wave of terror pass through his body.

Ω   Ω   Ω

One of the most insidious things to realize about disease is that the things that cause it are sometimes impossible to see and even harder to stop from running rampant. Whether you are talking about viruses, bacteria or parasites, humans, innocently going about their daily business at the grocery store, the gas station or the shopping mall, spread disease. How many times have you watched someone leave a bathroom without washing their hands, on their way to eat a meal? Have you ever been next to someone when they have sneezed? Ever felt fine one day, and the next you can't keep anything you eat in your system? Truthfully, what do you really know about disease, anyway?

Most people seem to take their health for granted, particularly in the Baby Boomer generation. Why? The Baby Boomers were the first generation in human history to benefit from modern day vaccines and medicines that combated disease. In fact, until about the turn of the twentieth century, people still died from common infections, like a deep cut or an abrasion, neither of which are considered life-threatening injuries today.

The Baby Boomers, those living in the Western world especially, grew up in a sanitized, immunized environment. For children to die at an early age was unusual. And even more remote was the idea of dying from some exotic disease no one had heard of before, like malaria or tuberculosis.

Ignorance Is Not Bliss

In America, the general public has predominantly been oblivious in the last fifty years to pandemic (global) diseases, let alone an epidemic (local). What was there to worry about? We had every confidence that the gurus of medicine had the answer to big problems in a vial or a syringe. As for the symptoms of the common cold, that doesn't kill you, and advice is plentiful from mothers everywhere on how to cure this malady. Pleasant as this notion of control over disease may be, it is a delusion in our world today.

Scientists are puzzled by the many new viruses, such as Hanta and Ebola, and mutations of viruses and bacteria emerging, some we thought we had conquered twenty or thirty years ago. Medical science is stunned by the re-emergence of so-called "old" diseases we thought were merely a part of history. In the last ten to fifteen years, pandemic diseases are resurfacing even in the Western world. Cholera, diphtheria, malaria, tuberculosis and yes, even the bubonic plague, are coming back, carving inroads into our smug confidence in survival. Only now, it's not so easy to beat them back. Many of the "miracle" drugs that worked in the past are failing us now.

With the growing world population encroaching on undeveloped areas that harbor these unleashed monsters, the increased world travel and the sexual promiscuity fostered in the 1960s, anyone can and will be susceptible. Our fate as a species is much more precarious now than ever before.

Disease Versus Man

Microbes, a shorter word for microscopic organisms, such as viruses, bacteria and parasites existed long before man. And it is entirely possible that they may yet outlast us. What, exactly, *are* microbes? Ironically, microbes are an integral part of the ecosystem; they are as vital to life as water, oxygen and the sun. Many microbes are capable of killing other creatures and in fact seem to serve no other purpose but destruction. However, many more microbes are critical for the survival of many species, even our own; without certain types of microbes, we would die.

For example, there are microbes that exist in our intestines specifically for the purpose of breaking down the food we eat. Nearly seventy percent of human excrement is alive with bacteria! Most of the microbes we inhale or ingest, or which enter our bodies by some other means, do not harm us; we are usually not even aware they exist. But when they do make their presence known, that gets our attention real fast!

Sooner or later, everyone gets a cold or suffers from the flu. Despite all our advances in medical science and all our efforts for a sanitized living environment, we still get these illnesses. Have you ever wondered why? It is not, as some people think, because you went outside with a wet head or because you didn't wear a coat in freezing weather. Microbes have entered our body, invisible intruders we have no way of stopping.

Medical science has not found the cure for the common cold; we can only take medicine to deal with the symptoms. Sure, pharmacies and grocery stores stock antihistamines and aspirin prolifically, but these are not cures; these drugs only help us survive the recovery processes. It is our body's immune system that is hard at work fighting the unwelcome presence of these organisms. Common microbial intrusions are easily combated, otherwise humanity would have been wiped out a long time ago.

The Black Death

In the past, humanity has come very close to extinction, much closer than many people like to admit. Other microbes, far more lethal than the common cold, have scourged the earth. Historian William McNeil of the University of Chicago indicated that

242

over the last thousand years, each time humanity has made a dramatic step forward in exploration or trade, in the settlement of new regions of the earth, and in surges of population, their vulnerability to diseases has increased. Perhaps the worst of the pandemic plagues were the infamous bubonic plagues, commonly referred to by the people of the Middle Ages as "the Black Death."

Few diseases in history have inspired as much terror as the Bubonic plague. Caused by a bacterium (singular of bacteria) called *Yersinia pestis*, the host, the one who carries the disease, is usually a rodent, such as a rat or squirrel. These animals are not usually affected by this bacterium, but their fleas are and that is how humans are infected.

Victims of bubonic plague experience enormous swelling of the glands under the arms or in the groin area. The bacteria enters the bloodstream, poisoning the blood, inducing bleeding and clotting disorders, followed by meningitis and pneumonia. Once pneumonia has developed, it is not unusual in a victim's struggle for enough air to cough and thus create an airborne version of the bubonic plague.

Although bubonic plague has historically devastated humanity for the past one and a half thousand years, the first outbreak was traced back to the year 541 AD, during the reign of Justinian, the Roman emperor. In the two centuries that followed, plague epidemics killed an estimated forty million people. And this was just the beginning. By 1346, the plague struck Europe with such a vengeance it produced one of the worst threats to the human species in history.

When twelve Italian galley ships entered the Sicilian port of Messina in 1346, they carried sailors who had come from Asia Minor, where they were infected with the plague in any number of cities. Soon, the streets of cities in India, Armenia, Syria and Mesopotamia were littered with plague stricken corpses. The plague knew no geo-political boundaries, assaulting China and leaving millions dead there as well. From Sicily, the plague slammed through Europe, extending to Ireland and eventually Iceland.

People then didn't travel as quickly or in as vast numbers as today, but there was enough movement among the population to create an enormous worldwide death toll—an estimated one-third to half of the world population at the time was obliterated by the bubonic plague. It affected every aspect of life and even contributed to the downfall of several empires, including the Roman, Byzantine and Mongolian.[1]

The bubonic plague is an example of the worst pandemic mankind has yet experienced, but historically, many epidemics and pandemics have affected the world. Millions have died from tuberculosis, malaria, cholera, smallpox and others. In the last 100 years, a fervent amount of research and effort has been spent trying to cure such diseases. Vaccines and medicines have been developed, but the battle is not over.

Viruses, Bacteria & Parasites

In recent years, emerging viruses have received a lot of attention from the media and other concerned sources. The human immune deficiency virus (HIV), which causes acquired immune deficiency syndrome (AIDS) is one example of this. But despite their virulence and sometimes horrific effects, viruses are not the greatest concern to medical science. Scientists point to bacteria and parasitic microbes as the greatest threat to humanity today. What exactly is a virus, a bacteria or a parasite? What are their differences? And why are they so hard to control?

Virus Defined

Different experts in the field of virology will give various definitions of the virus. In simple terms, the consensus is that a virus is not a living organism. It contains genetic material, either a strand of RNA or DNA, is sheathed in a coating or shell of protein and knows only one thing: to reproduce itself. A virus may seem vicious, but it cannot see, feel or think. It has no sense of morality. In order for a virus to reproduce itself, it needs a host with living cells into which it can weave its genetic structure; this host can be a plant, animal or human.

The process is not an overly complicated one. Once inside the host, the virus attaches itself to a cell, entering it chemically, and basically takes over that cell. The problem arises when the virus spreads within the host, causing the host to react, to become sick in most cases. Viruses are not the disease, they are the agent that induces the disease. The greatest challenge is that a virus does not respond to drug treatment, and it is this fact that experts contend will make viruses hazardous to humanity.

Bacteria Defined

Usually many times larger than viruses, bacteria can be seen under a compound microscope. While viruses were not seen until the highly powerful electron microscope came into use in the 1920s, Anton van Leeuwenhoek viewed bacteria in 1674 with a hand held magnifying glass. A bacterium is a living organism with a cell membrane and the ability to replicate itself given the right environment.

For some bacteria, the best environment for survival and reproduction is in human waste, but bacteria can also subsist elsewhere in a host, human or animal; many even exist in the earth's soil, between rocks, or thousands of feet below the earth's surface, feeding on whatever they can find. As with viruses, bacteria induce disease or infection, and are often the "germs" that infect a cut or abrasion.

Parasites Defined

Parasites are usually larger than bacteria and can be seen easily under a compound microscope or by the naked eye. As the name of this microbe implies, a parasite is an organism that lives on or within another organism, plant or animal, without contributing anything to the subsistence of its host. Now, you could say that bacteria and viruses fall into this category as well, but scientific tradition has ruled this out. Protozoa and ringworms are examples of parasites. Malaria is considered to be one of the world's most common and complicated parasitic diseases; it exists because of four species of parasites, the two most lethal of which are *Plasmodium vivax* and *P. Falciparum.*

To understand the malarial parasites, parasitologists must possess a broad knowledge, extending far beyond that of simple tropical medicine. The scientists studying parasites must know its life cycle, the insect that typically carries it, the environment of that insect, and the various warm-blooded animals the parasite typically infects, as well as diverse things like rainfall patterns, human migrations and changes in monkey population.

Taking Control

Make no mistake—we are not in control. These microbes rule in a variety of ways. For one thing, the sheer numbers make it impossible to find and control all of them. Add to that fact their tendency to mutate, producing a new strain of themselves, perhaps immune to drugs produced for the initial microbe strain. Population also plays a role in our difficulty in winning over microbes; many are surfacing for the first time as they come out from previously undisturbed habitats or regions of the world where they were not previously found—nightmarish in densely populated areas.

Many of these microbes have spawned some of today's emerging diseases. For example, two new hepatitis virus strains have resulted in the most lethal cases of liver cell cancer ever. A new version of the bubonic plague bacteria has sprung up, and the malarial parasite *P. Falciparum* has developed a strain resistant to chloroquine, the drug we have used in the past to eradicate the disease.

Humanity's Fight Against Disease

The first person to link bacteria with disease was Louis Pasteur, a French pioneer in bacteriology, in 1864. From that point forward, so much was learned about these organisms that 100 years later, most students of medicine and biology considered the study of bacteria a dead field. In 1928, Alexander Fleming, a British scientist, discovered *penicillin*, and for the first time, humanity had a means of killing bacteria. But penicillin did not become available for general medical use until 1943, when it emerged as an anti-bacterial agent and earned the name "miracle drug."[2]

Biological and medical research had a surge of Quickening in the 1940s and 1960s, when cures were found for many of the microbial diseases. The same year that penicillin became available to the public, two drugs for the treatment of tuberculosis were also discovered: *streptomycin* and *para-aminosalicylic acid*. The discovery of a barrage of anti-bacterial drugs followed quickly on the heels of the tuberculosis drugs, and could be used to treat every known bacterial infection. Even certain viral drugs, called *interferons*, were affecting viral infections, which up to that point had appeared untreatable.

With a whole crop of effective vaccines and medicines under our arms, developed and distributed around the world, global campaigns were waged against some of the deadliest diseases known to man. In 1967, the most feared plague virus, smallpox, was assaulted, as 250 million people during that year were vaccinated by the World Health Organization (WHO) in an effort to prevent the disease. Tuberculosis was also one of the great challenges of the twentieth century, but it, too, was beaten back with our advanced medical knowledge. Other diseases like bubonic plague and malaria were thought to be safely on their dusty shelf in history, while we assured ourselves that typhoid, polio, leprosy and diphtheria were on the way out as well.

False Confidence

With all these successes, it is no wonder that by the 1960s, the world was brimming with the confidence that deadly microbes could be conquered. In fact, in December 1967, US Surgeon General William H. Stewart formally stated that infectious diseases were now defeated. President Richard Nixon reflected this mood of confidence as well when, in 1971, he pledged $100 million for cancer research now that infectious diseases were cured. The miracle of modern medicine ensured that he had nothing to worry about as far as disease was concerned.[3]

Despite this glazed eye complacence of the world, the Quickening of events had a direct effect on our susceptibility to disease. No one expected that the population of the world would explode the way it has! Consider that between 1930 and 1960, the world's population jumped to two billion. By the early 1970s, another billion people were added, and twenty years later, three billion more! This is totally unprecedented. And of course, with the added population, the cities then grew to become mega-cities, encroaching on rain forests and other regions never before disturbed.[4]

It is no accident that the very regions that have exploded in population growth—Africa, India, Latin America—are the very regions where the pockets of deadly diseases have originated in the past and today. The rapid increase in travel means there are more people than ever moving across the earth. If anyone goes to a country and becomes infected by a new virus, they can spread it to another part of the world within a few hours—it just takes one plane ride. The 1960s also saw the sexual revolution, another big invitation to spread the variety of venereal diseases like never before, and it has done just that.

Eroding Optimism

Sooner or later, people have to wake up and face reality. The optimism over the advances in medicine began to erode during the 1970s. In 1967, we saw one of the first signs that medicine would not go un-challenged forever. There was a sudden outbreak in Germany of what was known as Marburg, a virus with origins in African monkeys that were used for research; the virus caused hemorrhaging and even-tually death in most cases. Although a handful of people died from this, it was as though the world sought to ignore these cases and little attention was given to it. Many people thought it was merely a fluke.

In August 1974, the world was shaken by an epi-demic of a severe bacterial disease called meningo-coccal meningitis, highly contagious and airborne. The outbreak occurred in the burgeoning, twenty million person city of Sao Paulo, Brazil. Before it was over, thousands had died. At the time, there was even serious concern that someone might get on a plane and spread this unwanted specter to other parts of the earth.

The following year, 1975, nine years after the first outbreak, the Marburg virus returned, banishing delusive hopes that it had disappeared into the jun-gle; a young Australian man visiting South Africa died from the vicious virus. The medical community was greatly disturbed by Marburg's re-emergence.[5] The mysterious American Legionnaire's disease in-voked a global stir in 1976 when it made 182 people sick and left twenty-nine dead. That same year, peo-ple were stunned as one of the most lethal new hem-orrhagic viruses emerged from the jungles of Zaire, Africa: Ebola virus. Not long after, the US government alerted the public to the possibility of a large influenza epidemic.

The 1980s were not much friendlier in terms of new diseases, bringing another virus from the realms of Africa: HIV, the precursor to AIDS. It was this virus, affecting gay men from California to New York, that really got the attention of the American public, the media and medical experts the world over. Americans, who typically feel that things never happen to them but to someone else in some other country, preferably far away, began to worry. After all, what might show up on their shores next? And what if there's something out there worse than AIDS? By 1993, one and a half million Americans had contracted HIV and the American government had spent twelve billion dollars for AIDS research, education and the treatment of those afflicted with AIDS.

Facing the Truth, Raising Awareness

Medicine, it was proven by all these new diseases, had not conquered all, and many informed, concerned scientists realized this by the late 1970s. The emergence of these new and ominously threatening diseases reflected not isolated instances, but a global trend. Something had to be done. In 1982, Dr. Richard Krause, head of the US National Institutes of Health made it clear that those diseases of the "past," once thought to be defeated, could very well return in new, drug-resistant strains. In addressing the US Congress on the matter, Krause asserted that "plagues are as certain as death and taxes."[6]

Even in the face of fear and uncertainty, and the nature of humanity being what it is, change was slow to come about, or even to be proposed. It was not until 1994 that a plan to increase awareness and respond to outbreaks of disease was developed. The US Centers for Disease Control and Prevention, commonly called the CDC, in Atlanta, devised this plan. Eventually, this plan would be broadened to address emerging diseases around the world, as disease is obviously not just a regional concern, but very much a world issue.

The question that remains is whether the noble efforts of the CDC have made any kind of a difference in the forward progress of diseases today. Many of its critics argue that its effects upon controlling diseases have been minimal. In the meantime, many new diseases—as many as thirty in the past twenty years, according to the World Health Organization—continue to emerge, and many new microbes and variations on the old have invaded humanity's supposed realm of safety.

Emerging Viruses

Mankind's challenge in defeating viruses comes with a virus's inherent ability to mutate very quickly, as well as it's tendency to elude treatment by modern day drugs. This makes viruses increasingly dangerous. Another one of the most fearsome properties of some of today's viruses is that they can be spread through the air, making them "airborne." What does this mean? An airborne virus can travel through the air on dust or sneeze particles, landing on someone's hand, which then goes into their eye or their mouth. Or you can inhale a virus. It happens all too easily.

Obviously, there are viruses in existence today too numerous to discuss, but among the most lethal and rapidly emerging ones are dengue, influenza, hanta, filoviruses, hepatitis, and HIV. The hantaviruses and filoviruses are only two examples of viruses that can invoke hemorrhagic fevers; a variety of these deadly killers exist: yellow fever, lassa, rotavirus, machupo and oropouche.

Dengue

Dengue virus, pronounced "den-gay," is one of the fastest movers among the viruses today, emerging from the tropics. Earliest outbreaks occurred during the 1950s and 1960s in Manila, Philippines, and later in Bangkok, leaving hundreds of people dead. The worst epidemic to date occurred in May 1981, when Havana, Cuba saw thousands of its people fall victim to dengue. The dengue disease, known as dengue hemorrhagic fever, is invoked by any one of four dengue virus strains. Related to the yellow fever, dengue is carried by the female mosquito, *Aedes aegypti*. Symptoms range from pinpoint-sized red spots, where bleeding surfaces through the skin, to severe hemorrhaging, shock and high fevers.

In 1985, a cargo ship from Japan carried more than just its load of tires; stowed away was an even more aggressive carrier of dengue and yellow fever, the tiger mosquito. This mosquito eventually found its way to seventeen US cities during the 1980s. Imbued with a determined will to survive, the tiger mosquito feeds on nearly any warm-blooded animal, man or rat; the more timid *aegypti* mosquito only feeds on humans. At this time, there is no cure for dengue, and the best that can be done is to eliminate areas in which the mosquito is known to breed. This is not the most encouraging solution, and scientists anticipate that outbreaks could occur at any time in North and South America.

Influenza

The most highly contagious, airborne pandemic disease ever known is influenza. Over the centuries, it has killed millions of people in nearly every region of the world. The worst pandemic occurred as recently as 1919, and America was high on the hit list: 500,000 Americans died and over ten percent of the American work force was bedridden. That same pandemic took the lives of twenty-one million people worldwide at a time when there were fewer than two billion people on earth. The only reason that the disease didn't claim more victims and spread more quickly was the lack of efficient transportation—trains and ocean liners were the best way to get around then—and the fact that fewer people traveled.[7]

Influenza is a champion of self-preservation and disguise. Symptoms of emerging influenza strains resemble common flu symptoms, but with deadlier consequences. Usually carried by wild water fowl, influenza exemplifies today's emerging viruses with its ability to mutate into new strains. Vaccines exist, but in the face of changes in the influenza virus, they are losing their effectiveness. With its over-populated cities, it may be no surprise that China is one of the most common regions from which the new influenza strains have emerged.

Today the world waits expectantly for the next major influenza pandemic. Based on historical precedents, the medical community is aware that the world is actually overdue for an influenza outbreak of major proportions. Once it starts, it is theoretically possible to develop a vaccine and immunize millions of people. However, according to experts, it could take up to six months for pharmaceutical companies to produce and distribute enough of the vaccine for the world's vast populations. What this most likely means is that people in the Western world will not suffer as much as people in Third World and other underdeveloped countries. But all it takes is one person hopping on a plane to get the whole influenza virus rolling through the whole world. *Billions* of people would die, and very quickly.

Hantavirus

The world's first encounter with the hantavirus was during the Korean War. Nearly 3,000 American soldiers became ill because of the virus, 121 of them eventually dying. Victims of hantaviruses commonly experienced weakness and fatigue, vomiting, diarrhea, headaches, fever and eventually kidney failure. Years later, it was learned that the hantavirus could also induce a variety of ailments including muscle pains, hypertension and kidney dysfunction. The first identified hantavirus was called the Korean Hantaan, and it was carried by field mice. Infection with the virus occurred when a person inhaled or was in the presence of the dust of rodent excrement.

Twenty years later, during the 1970s, eleven additional strains of the hantaviruses were discovered in Europe and various parts of Asia, also attributed to rodents as the carriers. A few of the more disturbing outbreaks in America were in 1986 when a Mexican worker died of a hemorrhagic strain of hantavirus, and then in 1993 when a Navajo Indian and his fiancee also died of a hemorrhagic strain.[8]

Interestingly, as Korea and the United States became trading partners over the years, more cases of hantaviruses were reported; apparently, Korean cargo ships arrived at American shores carrying rats

255

with the hantavirus. Now it is known that rats and a variety of wild rodents that inhabit North America have also become carriers of the hantavirus.

American microbiologist James DeLuc and others concluded in the early 1990s that the different types of hantaviruses have been responsible for the increased rates of hypertension and kidney disease among Americans living in the poor inner cities, especially African-Americans. This is a problem that isn't easily remedied as the living conditions are squalid in many of these areas, thus encouraging a higher rat infestation.[9] The CDC has also acknowledged the problem of growing cities as a contributor to the recurrence of the hantavirus; in the face of population growth, it is entirely likely that America and other countries will at some point face an epidemic of hantavirus in the near future.

Filoviruses

Anyone who has read *The Hot Zone* by Richard Preston or seen the movie *Outbreak* has felt the deep-seated fear of a filovirus. Our imaginations have been unwillingly captured by the idea of a virus that acts so quickly, is highly contagious and can destroy a person through massive hemorrhaging. Among the filoviruses, there are four that stand out most prominently today: Ebola Zaire, Sudan, Tai and Reston.

In general, filoviruses affect monkeys, apes and humans, with the exception of Ebola Reston, which does not cause human illness in its present strain. Zaire has a ninety percent fatality rate and Sudan has sixty percent; Tai has not occurred frequently and there is not sufficient data to know its lethality.

Usually string-shaped with a hook or loop at one end, filoviruses are highly pathogenic and capable of epidemic transmission. Symptoms start with fever and muscle aches, and proceed to respiratory problems, severe bleeding, kidney failure and shock. Ebola is a particularly nasty filovirus in that it leads to what is called 'bleeding out,' a condition in which a person bleeds from injection sites, the gastrointestinal tract, skin and internal organs—there is no reversal at this point, and there is no cure for Ebola.

The first outbreak of Ebola was in 1976, and the major outbreaks have luckily been few and far between—so far. In May 1995, an outbreak of Ebola struck Kikwit, a city in Zaire with a population of 600,000, about 250 miles from Kinshasa, the capital of Zaire. The number of cases grew and grew as Ebola spread its tentacles to neighboring towns, finally infecting close to 300 people and killing approximately eighty percent of them.[10]

You can be pretty sure that at some point we can expect a major epidemic of Ebola. Why? Conditions for an epidemic exist in places that struggle to finance their healthcare systems and do things like re-using needles. Conditions exist in places where humans don't have proper sanitation, decreased immune response because of a disease like AIDS, where social customs encourage interaction with the dead. Remember, we don't even know for certain what carries the Ebola virus! The only reassuring thing about the Ebola viruses is that their virulence and ability to spread is limited because victims die so quickly.

Human Immunodeficiency Virus (HIV)

If you know nothing else about HIV, you know that it is the virus that causes AIDS. Two known strains of HIV exist: HIV-1 and HIV-2. Generally, HIV-1 is the strain found most commonly in North America,

Europe, central Africa, Asia and Australia, while HIV-2 seems to be limited to Africa. AIDS is one of the most frightening and controversial diseases in this century. Once diagnosed with AIDS, your chances of survival are very slim, and there is no cure. A viral suppressant drug called AZT is one of the most common methods of treatment for the symptoms, but carries with it some serious side effects.

Another of the controversial issues within the AIDS problem is the high cost of newly developed drugs. Many of the people who have AIDS are at poverty level or below, or are in poor, underdeveloped countries that have no way of providing their citizens with such medicine.

While it may take several years for AIDs symptoms to appear, once they do appear, they strike hard. The AIDS victim becomes progressively weak, listless and gaunt with the loss of appetite; this is why AIDS victims so often die from a common cold, because their immune systems simply do not have the strength to fight anything off.

HIV and AIDS originate in Africa. Today, the whole world feels the effects of AIDS, which can truly be called a pandemic disease. At least 190 countries have reported cases of AIDS to the World Health Organization, and it is likely that the reported numbers are higher in reality due to under-reporting. The United Nations reported in November 1996 that AIDS is gaining momentum in Europe and Asia, and described the spread of AIDS in India as explosive.

Just what are the numbers? In 1996, estimates placed the number of people with AIDS at twenty-two million, and the number of people newly infected with HIV at over three million. Since AIDS has the lethal ability to go undetected for many years, pregnant women have passed the disease on to their children; today more than one and a half million children have contracted HIV this way. Most of these children die before they are five years old. By the year 2000, it is estimated that over forty million people globally will have AIDS just from HIV-1 alone, and in the meantime, many more will have already died.[11]

Although AIDS may have started out as strictly a sexually transmitted disease, it has since proven to be transmitted in other ways, mainly through the blood. Tennis player Arthur Ashe died several years ago as the result of contracting HIV from a tainted blood transfusion during heart surgery. HIV can be transmitted through the use of unsterile syringes, and not just among drug addicts, but in negligent medical facilities, particularly in poorer countries.

Overall, most people still contract AIDS sexually. In the US, the controversy over AIDS is that many of its victims have been promiscuous young homosexual men, but in Africa, the disease has split itself fairly evenly between men and women; homosexuality is not as common in Africa. In many cases, African men have picked up HIV from prostitution and general promiscuity.

You would think that with the tangible fact of millions of people infected with HIV and AIDS, people would learn a lesson in awareness and caution. This has not been the case. Recent studies indicate there is a new surge in unprotected sexual activity among a new generation of homosexual and bisexual men in America and Britain. What seemed to happen is that when AIDS became an issue in the early 1980s, there was a brief period of decline, but after the initial concern wore off, everyone went back to their routine behavior. Even though their behavior is dangerous and people are dying around them from not being more careful, it seems that people just don't believe that it will happen to them.[12]

Emerging Bacteria & Parasites

Most of the bacterial and parasitic diseases in the world today are not strangers to humanity; they are old, familiar names, emerging quickly into the world in new, more virulent and drug-resistant strains. A few are more lethal than others, with the ability to strike anywhere, at any moment.

Tuberculosis

During the course of the last 200 years, the bacteria that causes tuberculosis has led to the death of one billion people worldwide. Now there is a drug-resistant strain of the bacteria which is airborne and highly contagious. Moreover, the disease can affect any organ of the body, although it usually settles in the lungs and destroys them. The World Health Organization has been at war with the disease since the 1960s, and a significant decline had been noted; it is now returning as a pandemic disease. Globally, there are close to two billion people infected with tuberculosis, fifty million of which are infected with a drug-resistant strain.

Tuberculosis has increased in recent years, making hundreds of thousands of people sick every year, in part because infected people from poorer countries have immigrated to industrialized countries, especially from Africa into Europe. The Africans have 171 million people who are infected with tuberculosis; many people with AIDS also have contracted tuberculosis and this only spreads the disease even faster. No cure exists and none are on the horizon either.[13]

Cholera

The world is not yet rid of its old, pre-hygienic nemesis, cholera, the waterborne bacteria that has been around for centuries. In 1991, a new chlorine and drug-resistant strain of cholera called El Tor Cholera entered Latin America when the ballast tanks of Chinese cargo ships were discharged off the coast of Peru. The cholera got into the seafood, which people later ate and became ill from. India and certain parts of Africa are still badgered by cholera when waste from humans and animals pollutes the fresh water supply, which is already limited. This is a serious and growing problem in poorer countries, especially since as many as three billion people in the world battle an ongoing fresh water shortage and live with inadequate toilet facilities.

Malaria

The malarial parasite is a protozoan called "plasmodium." Victims of malaria are doomed once they have the disease; they either fight the high fever, acute anemia and delirium, and come out on the other side of it to live with its chronic fatigue and weakness for the rest of their lives, or they succumb to the strength of malaria and die.

Plasmodium has of late developed into a drug-resistant strain; in addition, the mosquito that carries plasmodium and infects humans has also become resistant to the pesticides that used to kill it. Consequently, there are more people dying of malaria today than thirty years ago; in 1996, as many as three million people throughout the world died from malaria.

Although countries where the populations are increasing exponentially are at the highest risk for malaria—Africa, South America, Asia—industrialized countries like America are not as safe from malaria as you might think. It is simple for an American, returning from a trip overseas, to bring back a little more than what is packed in his suitcase! In 1994, migrant workers in Southern California experienced an outbreak of malaria, and another outbreak recently occurred in New Jersey, blamed on local mosquitoes.

Virologists and biologists believe that the global warming trend will very likely cause a migration of mosquitoes known to carry malarial parasites to different areas of the world; this kind of movement by these little pests could cause a serious threat to the world in the years ahead.

Venereal Diseases

Diseases that you can't necessarily see tend to get swept from people's minds more easily than sensational diseases, like Ebola, with its dramatic method of destruction. Even though diseases brought on by human behavior, particularly those transmitted sexually, are not in the news every day, they exist daily at epidemic levels throughout the world.

The 1960s seemed to be a turning point in America, and quickly the world, as far as sexual promiscuity was concerned. The advent of the birth control pill and an increased laxness in people's attitude toward sex naturally contributed to an increase in sexually transmitted diseases, or STDs. Marriages occurring later in life and people having sex at an earlier age were also factors in this increase. Because humans are governed by their emotions and by the "it won't happen to me" attitude, it is no surprise that sexually transmitted diseases have run rampant.

Syphilis & Gonorrhea

Syphilis got a great deal of attention 100 years ago from the media of the day. By World War II, syphilis seemed to lose its ominous nature with the discovery that penicillin was a cure for the disease in the early stages. Syphilis is sinister because it starts with a rash that could be from anything, while its bacteria build up at the base of your brain, destroying the spinal cord and your neurological system, eventually driving you crazy.

Gonorrhea was also a problem that was essentially eliminated by penicillin, again providing that the person was treated in time. With gonorrhea, victims saw a greenish-yellow discharge from the genitals, fever and painful urination; long term, gonorrhea could cause sterilization and pelvic inflammatory disease (PID), which is chronic and can destroy the uterus if left untreated. Before antibiotics, thousands of people in America died from both these diseases, but funding by the government for education and the distribution of drugs seemed to get things under control.

The American medical community had concluded by 1970 that these diseases were easily cured and were essentially defeated. This ended virtually all efforts at educating people about the dangers of syphilis and gonorrhea, and people grew complacent, as if the diseases no longer existed. By the early 1980s, gonorrhea and syphilis had returned at epidemic levels, ranking as the top two infectious diseases in the US with two and a half million new cases each year. Women have especially suffered from gonorrhea, which can lead to pelvic inflammatory disease. To make matters worse, new strains of antibiotic-resistant gonorrhea and syphilis have appeared.

Chlamydia

Cases of chlamydia, another bacterial STD, have risen dramatically since the 1970s; there are an estimated three million cases of chlamydia each year. A bacteria that grows in the pelvic area and urethra, the disease is worrisome, particularly because of how easy it is to spread it throughout your body. If you touch the infected area and rub your eye, your eye will become infected. Even a fly could land on a person's eye and transmit the disease by landing on someone else. Infected mothers can transmit it to their children, and a treated person can easily be re-infected.

Again, women suffer the most from chlamydia in that they are likely to develop pelvic inflammatory disease. In addition, it is not easy to discern whether you have chlamydia and the infection can last for years if untreated, causing sterility in many cases. Elsewhere in the world, chlamydia is even worse; Britain, Europe and Africa have seen chlamydia sharply increase since the 1980s, but it is in the Fiji Islands where chlamydia truly reigns—an astounding forty-five percent of pregnant women tested positive for chlamydia.

Herpes & Genital Warts

Herpes and genital warts are viral STDs. Hard as it may be to believe, herpes simplex one (HSV-1), which produces cold sores on the mouth, appears to have infected nearly everyone in North America and Europe. A survey taken in 1980 revealed that at least ninety percent of the North American population has been infected with HSV-1 at some point in their lives.

The more dangerous of the two known strains of herpes is herpes simple two (HSV-2). Usually transferred sexually, the virus hides for years, showing no symptoms, or it surfaces periodically to produce painful blisters near the genitals or anus. If you should happen to spread these herpes to your eyes, you could impair your vision or induce blindness. There is nothing nice or friendly about this virus. Mothers who give birth to their children with an active herpes outbreak risk death or brain damage to their child.

Although there are drugs to suppress herpes, it is not curable. Since the 1970s, cases of herpes have increased worldwide. Between 1966 and 1981, the number of Americans treated for HSV-2 increased by nine times. By 1986, it is estimated that at least sixty percent of men in key US cities were infected with HSV-2. Other countries have seen an average twelve percent increase in HSV-2 cases each year, and about 500,000 people are infected worldwide.[14]

Genital warts are similar to herpes in that they are highly contagious and have steadily increased to epidemic proportions globally. At least twenty-five percent of Americans are infected with the genital wart virus, but do not show symptoms (though they may eventually). Genital warts can develop in the mouth, genitals and anus, and are bumpy tissue that look like miniature heads of cauliflower. Babies who are infected by their mothers at birth can have genital warts grow in their throats. Drugs treat genital warts, but like all viruses currently known to man, there is no cure. Each year, millions of people become infected, and there seems to be no decline in sight.

Hepatitis

Growing numbers of people around the world are also being infected by the hepatitis virus. Hepatitis is an inflammation of the liver, occurring in three or more forms. Hepatitis A is transmitted by food or water contaminated with excrement; it can also be contracted by the use of improperly sterilized hypodermic needles. Outbreaks of Hepatitis A often occur in army camps and in institutions where small children are crowded together, like schools or orphanages.

Previously named serum hepatitis, Hepatitis B is a form we only recognized around the time of World War II. Epidemic in parts of Asia and Africa, Hepatitis B is transmitted by injections transporting a virus-bearing serum, commonly during blood transfusions and by contaminated syringes. The virus is also present in other body fluids and thus can be transmitted sexually. With 300,000 new cases each year in the US alone, and 300 million people infected worldwide, Hepatitis B is more common and more contagious than even AIDS.

Hepatitis C is not as commonly spread by sexual means because the concentration of virus is not as high as that of Hepatitis B. Nevertheless, there are three and a half million cases of this virus in the

United States; many people are in fact unaware they have it, and for some reason, it seems to target poor people the most frequently. One major factor about Hepatitis C is that it can be chronic in up to fifty percent of the patients infected.

Interestingly enough, in 1977, an Italian physician, Mario Rizzetto, identified a virus—first called the delta hepatitis virus, now known as Hepatitis D—that requires the presence of Hepatitis B in order to transmit itself. This delta virus has occurred worldwide and is responsible for major epidemics. Finally, there has been a form of hepatitis found commonly in the Indian Ocean, Africa and underdeveloped countries called Hepatitis E, which is similar to Hepatitis A.

Symptoms of all forms of hepatitis are fever, weakness, loss of appetite, digestive upset and muscle pains. Jaundice appears, intensifying after a few weeks, and a person can convalesce for as long as six months. Internally, hepatitis causes swelling and tenderness, and is capable of permanent damage to the liver. The worst part of hepatitis is that it can be chronic, and is known to encourage an increased rate of miscarriage and difficult labor in women. The drug Interferon has been used with some limited success, but hepatitis is something that is here to stay.[15]

The Future of STDs

Despite the epidemic levels of many STDs, there appears to be no decline in the sexually promiscuous behavior of both men and women in the world today. And many younger adults are not even thinking about abstinence or using any form of protection like a condom. Perhaps they believe, as people do, that their youth somehow protects them, or gives them a shield of invincibility. And yet, with their friends and the people around them already suffering from such diseases, it really makes you wonder why they continue this kind of lackadaisical behavior.

Biological Warfare

Although there are only a few reported instances in which biological agents were used during war in this century, biological terrorism is a very real concern in our world today. According to an October 31, 1995 report by the US Senate Permanent Subcommittee, the Aum Shirin Kyo cult leader, Shoko Asahara, responsible for the release of sarin in 1995 in the Tokyo subway, led a small group to Zaire during an Ebola outbreak. Ostensibly, this cult was there to help Ebola victims, but the Subcommittee report reveals that they were actually there to collect samples of the deadly virus to culture and use in a future biological attack. Pretty scary when you consider how uncontrollable a mutative virus like Ebola can be!

During the summer of 1995, white supremacist Larry Harris used phony stationery and his credit card to order the bubonic plague bacterium from a biomedical supply company in Rockville, Maryland— the American Type Culture Collection. The order was processed without question, and Harris was caught by the FBI only because of his own impatience, hounding the company only four days after his initial order was placed.[16]

Biological agents are considered to be one of the least costly and most effective means of destroying an enemy. Simply cultivate a highly contagious and lethal strain of virus or bacteria and launch a warhead into a select city to release the agent. Some have called biological warheads "the poor man's nuclear bomb."

Despite signed agreements, such as the 1972 Biological Weapons Convention, to ban the development and use of biological agents in war, the world has more in development and existence than ever before. As of 1995, you can count seventeen countries that develop biological weapons, and of course, the most dangerous, unstable rogue nation-states are among them: Iran, Iraq, Syria, Korea and Libya. The US no longer develops biological weapons, choosing instead to concentrate on nuclear weapons for the last fifty years.

Not only are biological agents inexpensive, they are also easy to make. Kathleen Bailey, former assistant director of the US Arms Control and Disarmament Agency, is persuaded that "a major biological arsenal could be built with $10,000 worth of equipment in a room fifteen feet by fifteen feet."[17] The most likely agents developed may include anthrax bacteria (you just need to inhale an amount the size of a period), botulism bacteria, bubonic plague and the Ebola virus. The prospects for controlling such a threat are not promising.

Gulf War Syndrome
Now here is a controversial issue with no real conclusion at this point. What *is* it? No one really knows. After testing 10,000 plus Gulf War veterans, the US Institute of Medicine has concluded that there is no mysterious disease behind the Gulf War syndrome. According to the US Pentagon, symptoms

vary widely from respiratory, digestive and skin diseases, to fatigue and memory loss.

Some have speculated that Gulf War syndrome may be the result of chemical exposure from the discharge of chemical bombs, or pollutants from the burning oil fields in the desert, and have even suggested that symptoms are a reaction to insecticides used during the war. The Pentagon seems to assume that these veterans are suffering from stress not uncommon to those who have fought in a war, similar to a post-war traumatic stress syndrome that has afflicted service men and women in the past.[18]

Famine

Theoretically, the world is capable of producing enough food for all its people, but the fact is that nearly one billion people are starving today. Unfortunately, this number will only get higher as more people are added to the world's population. Africa and India face the greatest challenge in feeding their hungry; in the next decade, the demand for food will increase by seventy percent in Africa, and this will invariably mean more starving people.

Most of the food shortage problems we face today are from an inefficient means of distribution, political unrest, economic instability and most of all, too many people. As for teaching the people in these parts of the world to raise their own food, this has either not worked at all or worked with such a limited amount of success as to barely make a difference in their overall situation.[19]

Food production will lower in just a few years. Why? Of the world's population, one billion depend upon fish as a main staple in their diet. Today, however, the world is over-fishing and polluting the world's marine stock to such an extent that already twenty-five percent of the fish stock has been depleted. Salination of irrigated farm land is yet another factor in reducing the world's ability to produce food; this is an especially serious problem in China, India, Pakistan and Egypt, countries that account for one-third of the world's irrigated farm land. In the next few years, more and more of this land promises to become useless as over-watering and poor drainage force mineral salts to the surface of the soil. Once salinated, the soil cannot be reclaimed and plants will not grow.[20]

Environmental hazards will also have an increased effect on the world's capacity to produce enough food for its exploding populations. As the ozone depletes, this will affect the ability of plants to grow. Continued absorption by the soil of heavy metals and other pollutants combined with wasteful irrigation practices will continue to reduce the world's fresh water supply. Drought will subsequently plague much of the world's farm lands and plants will not have a chance of growing.

As you can see, we're going nowhere fast with this issue, struggling in the face of damage that is already done, and still forced to acknowledge that we cannot stop these practices; unless more people stop coming into the world, we will always have more people to feed!

The Fattening of America

Here's an irony for you: while the rest of the world is starving, America is besieged by an epidemic of obesity. An estimated sixty-one million Americans between the ages of twenty and seventy-four are at

271

least twenty percent or more over their desirable weight; this figure has increased to include thirty-three percent of all Americans. Why? That's simple, Americans eat too much junk food, i.e., candy, cookies, cake, too much food high in fat content, i.e., hamburgers, corn dogs, pizza, and too much food in general.

While we are busily shelling out our money at the fast food window, we are simultaneously spending it in obscene quantities on weight reduction products and services—some thirty-three billion dollars annually—because of what we're buying at the fast food places. Despite the fact that obesity increases our risk for heart disease, cancer, diabetes and high blood pressure—Americans spend one and a half *billion* dollars annually on obesity-related high blood pressure problems—we refuse to mend our ways.

It is not just our adults that are obese, either. Americans seem to be raising some of the most obese children in the world; a recent survey showed that the number of obese children, ages six to seventeen, in America has more than doubled in the last decade, from five percent in the 1960s to over eleven percent during the 1990s.[21] Comparatively, there are presently about 193 million children in the world below five years of age are actually underweight, and that number is expected to rise to 200 million in the next twenty years.[22] More than half of the fourteen million hunger-related deaths among the world's children are because of malnutrition and moderate undernourishment.[23]

The biggest problem in America seems to be that we are so overwhelmed by choices. We have had it too good for too long, and have literally become fat and lazy. While children in Africa starve and wonder where their next meal will come from and when they will be too weak to eat, our hardest decision is whether to go to McDonald's or Burger King. Is there something we can do about this?

Global Food Effort

The greatest challenges in our near future are the dwindling fresh water supply and shortages of farm land. And provided we can resolve those issues, we also need to address new technological methods for farmers globally in order to achieve more productive crops. Things seem to be at a virtual standstill right now, as we all look at someone else to fix the problem. The World Bank has called for cooperation on the part of all countries to participate, and perhaps come to an agreement of pooling funds and resources to develop the necessary technology and implement it all over the world.

In 1974, Rome held a world food conference in which it was declared, "...every man, woman and child has the inalienable right to be free from hunger and malnutrition." This is a good idea, but not entirely realistic, particularly when no global plan exists to achieve such a goal. All that we really have right now in the fight against famine is hope.[24]

Global Solutions For Disease

Outbreaks of disease occur all the time in this world, and this is one of the biggest challenges in monitoring and controlling disease. There are only a few global health organizations to shoulder the responsibility for the entire world's health, including the United Nations, the World Health Organization,

273

the Centers for Disease Control and the Pasteur Institute. Even though these organizations are involved, they are all past existing limits as far as
money and manpower.

One of the biggest indications of a Quickening
world is the rate at which these diseases keep occurring and the severity with which they strike. We live
in a world that just waits for the inevitable pandemic
to happen. Or perhaps it will be several pandemics
at once. The anticipated influenza outbreak could
occur, while a new strain of Ebola boards a plane
bound for New York's JFK Airport. Perhaps an unusually hot summer will bring out the aggressive tiger mosquito, overwhelming the world with malaria
and plague outbreaks, spinning out of control and
taking millions of people's lives with them.

It has been suggested that an entirely new global
disease organization be established to oversee all
these existing organizations. Each country could
contribute a disease tax, not unlike the global effort
to address the world's environmental concerns, and
from that global fund, special medical forces would
be trained and equipped to deal with world medical
crises. But then, someone still has to find vaccines
for newly emerging diseases, diseases which could
very likely continue to elude cures. With our increasing populations, the problem of disease looms
even larger, a fearsome reminder that we are not in
control.

8

Earth Changes

Astronomy had always been Dolores Dening's favorite preoccupation. Lately she had been fascinated by comets and asteroids, and spent more and more of her time gazing through her high-powered telescope into the heavens. There was a controversy going around these days about a new comet which seemed to have come from nowhere; someone in Australia had spotted it first and named it "Tazmania." Apparently, it was quite large, perhaps ten miles across, and moving quickly. Speculation was thrown back and forth as to whether the comet was heading toward the earth.

In the months that followed, Dolores watched every night, until finally, after six months of observation, the comet could be seen during the day. Everyone around the world was watching. Dolores observed Tazmania carefully, taking measurements and trying to estimate distance, speed and direction. So far, she believed the earth was its target. Most people wanted to believe it would not hit the earth, or that it would disintegrate when it reached the atmosphere, but it only seemed to gain speed as it drew closer.

Weeks later, the world's scientists expressed concern that the comet was now a real threat to the earth's inhabitants. Plans were made to blow the comet out of the sky with nuclear warheads, but many people argued against that because of the effect it would have on the environment. Religious people around the world united to pray, and world leaders assembled and discussed nothing else but the comet.

As the truth became clear, a strange neurosis affected people throughout the world. Dolores was not surprised by this, and somehow she knew instinctively that the comet was going to strike the earth, perhaps the east coast of the United States. If it hit, the impact would be the equivalent of detonating a large nuclear device. Tens of millions of people would be killed.

The US president tried his best to calm people, urging them not to panic. To have confidence that something could be done. That everything would be all right. Dolores watched through her telescope. She knew that nothing could be done. She knew that in a short while, the world would never be the same.

$$\Omega \quad \Omega \quad \Omega$$

Jerry McRae had just moved to Memphis from Los Angeles to start his new sales job near the cotton exchange downtown. Memphis was a beautiful, clean city, and he liked the idea of being so close to the Mississippi River. He was also very happy with his new home, an old brick warehouse renovated into fairly elegant condominiums. From his living room and kitchen on the sixth floor, he could watch the river traffic and beyond, the east bank of Arkansas.

From his new home, it was a quick bike ride to his tenth floor office at the Turley building. As he stopped for coffee at the nearby Peabody Hotel, he overheard people talking about a small tremor that hit the city a few days ago. To Jerry, it was nothing, since he had grown up in Los Angeles. What did surprise him was that Memphis was prone to earthquakes at all.

One day, fatigued and ready to go home, he suddenly felt his bike jerk to the left and he actually lost control. Was he so tired he could not ride a bike? Stopping to steady himself, he realized that the ground beneath him was rocking. At the same time, he heard a rumbling sound. Windows exploded in a shower of glass and he watched bricks fall from the sides of buildings.

Everyone was standing in the street, their faces stricken with fear and excitement. Sirens cried from various parts of the city, and Jerry wondered at the people who had run out into the street, not knowing any better. He shook his head. First Los Angeles, now Memphis. Wasn't there any place where the earth didn't move?

Ω   Ω   Ω

We are basically living on a thin crust on top of a mostly molten globe, so is it any wonder that we are so drastically affected by the changes in the earth? With the various cracks and crevices in our globe, we are besieged by cataclysmic volcanic eruptions and violent earthquakes, more now than ever before. When the earth releases energy, it changes the face of the earth, and it changes the climate of the earth as well. For instance, volcanic ash thrown into the earth's atmosphere has a direct effect upon how much sunlight the earth receives and affects weather patterns, sometimes dramatically.

What we need to realize is that there are forces around us we have no way of controlling. We cannot stop the force of a hurricane that destroys a coastal town, we cannot stop a whirling tornado that whips a building from its foundations like it was made of match sticks. The solid ground underneath our feet and the sky above our heads have surprises in store for us, in greater quantities now than ever before.

The Earth Quickens

These days, we are affected by volcanoes and, to a lesser degree, by the pollutants we add to the air. But unlike in the past, we are now experiencing an unprecedented number of disturbances on our earth. We are seeing more volcanoes erupt, a record number of earthquakes throughout the world, stronger hurricanes and more of them, more tidal waves and tropical storms. We have seen longer, colder winters and hotter summers, increased floods and harsher droughts, and increased wildfires. Why us? Why now?

Some people believe that there has been more material put into the atmosphere during this century than since the beginning of recorded history. They believe that this has played a major role in the greenhouse effect, as well as inducing some very unusual weather patterns. Both man and nature have been responsible for these anomalies of earth behavior.

Then, as if that were not enough, threats from outside our atmosphere come in the form of enormous comets, such as the recently sighted Hale-Bopp comet. Of course, while most are quick to reassure the world that the possibility that a comet would hit the earth is slim, scientists have not completely ruled out this scenario. Why not? After all, plenty of evidence exists that large rocks and other debris have hit the earth in the past. Surely we cannot be so arrogant as to think that just because the earth is home to humanity no comet or asteroid would dare to hit us!

Clearly, our world is undergoing some physical changes. Even if everything else was fine, (i.e., a stable world economy, the way we govern ourselves, the way we treat each other), which it isn't, this is a destructive reality we cannot ignore or deny. Everyone, everywhere is affected. For instance, when an earthquake happens, you cannot say it did not happen. Something is going on within and around our planet and we better keep our eyes open for what's next.

Volcanoes

At any given time, there are several active volcanoes erupting in different parts of the world. Or there are volcanoes waiting to erupt. In the past, it was common to refer to a particular volcano as "inactive" or "extinct," but I don't think we have that luxury anymore.

In California, everyone seems to be waiting for "the big earthquake," but they don't seem to realize that they are just as likely to be wiped out by a volcano; in fact, one could lead to another. Just southeast of San Francisco, near the California-Nevada border, Mammoth Mountain is located, the center of which is a popular ski resort. But Mammoth is also the center of a large flow of molten lava, or "magma," steadily creeping to the surface at a very fast pace of two inches per year.

Should Mammoth Mountain erupt some day, it is entirely possible that it would be a significantly larger eruption than Krakatoa. Some 700,000 years ago, Krakatoa was formed when 140 cubic miles of lava and ash exploded into the air, burying half the continent. The most recent explosion of Krakatoa was in 1883, and accounted for the deaths of some 36,000 people. The last time that supposedly quiet Mammoth Mountain erupted was 200 years ago. Many believe it is quite likely to erupt again given the amount of magnum and the speed at which it is moving; when this happens, three feet of volcanic ash and lava will blanket the area for seventy-five miles. The wind will carry hot ash all the way to San Francisco and Los Angeles like a heavy snowfall, and glass windows will shatter all over northern California from the force of the blast.[1]

That's not all. A blast from Mammoth Mountain would be so loud that those within 100 miles could have their hearing permanently impaired. To make matters worse, the sun would be blocked out enough to cause temperatures to drop globally to record lows *for an entire year!* Even after we recovered from that kind of a disturbance, things would not completely return to the way they were previously. Besides the effects of the lava and ash, such an eruption could invoke major earthquakes, tidal waves, floods and fires. Evidently, Californians have a lot bigger problem to look forward to than they realize.

Recent Eruptions

The earth has evolved in such a way over time that there are distinct regions which tend to exhibit most of the volcanic and earthquake activity. These regions are collectively known as the "Ring of Fire," and include all the islands in the Pacific Ocean (e.g., Hawaii, the Philippines), and the coasts of continents which end at the Pacific Ocean (e.g., Latin America, the Western United States, including Alaska, British Columbia, the eastern coast of Russia, China and all of Japan). If you look at a world map, you will notice that these regions of the world have the highest and most rugged mountain ranges; of course, this is where you will also find the most volcanoes, active or inactive.

However, having said this, an interesting development has taken place in the last several decades of this century, even in the last few years, that challenges this geologic benchmark. The world is experiencing increased volcanic and earthquake activity in areas which have generally been considered inactive. For example, as recently as the summer of 1996, the ancient Soufriere Hills volcano on the Caribbean island of Montserrat suddenly came to life after sitting quietly for more than a thousand years. It began with an initial puff of ash, and was followed by several days of steam explosions and ash bursts into the air; this went on for a month, intensifying tremors and activity as each day passed.

Finally, on August 21, a strong burst of steam and ash exploded from the top of the volcano, sending volcanic material nearly two miles into the air and darkening the capital city of Plymouth for thirty minutes. In anticipation of far worse circumstances, the city began evacuating its people. Their concern was legitimate: a little over ninety years ago, the Pelee volcano on the island of Martinique (in the same island chain) erupted, killing 20,000 people in the nearby town of St. Pierre.[2]

Mount St. Helens

If there is a good example of the power lying under the volcanic Cascade mountain range, it would be Mount St. Helens, which exploded in 1980. The Cascade range, which runs south and north along the western US from Northern California to the southern part of British Columbia, Canada, is just a few hundred miles north of Mammoth Mountain; this doesn't sound like a coincidence, does it? The St. Helens eruption, which people are still talking about to this day, destroyed much of the wildlife and vegetation in the area for miles around; only a few people were killed in this eruption since most of the densely populated cities like Portland, Oregon were out of range. Nevertheless, Portland residents were in fact shoveling ash much like you would shovel snow!

On average, history indicates that the volcanoes in the thousand-mile range of the Cascades are only supposed to erupt once or twice a century; however, in keeping with the Quickening, this trend has increased. In the last two centuries, Cascade range volcanoes have erupted seven times. There is no telling, really, when another volcano could erupt; the difference this time, of course, is that there are more people than ever living in areas close to these volcanoes. Moreover, many of these volcanoes are heavily sheathed in snow and ice; this is important to note because, should these volcanoes heat up, even long before an eruption, melted snow and ice mixed with sediment could create tremendous flooding and destruction.[3]

Mount Pinatubo & Other Volcanoes

So-called "extinct" volcanoes are really making a comeback recently. In June 1991, one of the recent, most violent volcanic eruptions occurred in the Philippines when Mount Pinatubo blew its top off. The eruption was so forceful that it shot volcanic debris and sulfur dioxide gas up to fifteen miles into the atmosphere; it is believed that this debris was enough to literally reduce the sun's radiation and have a significant effect on the world's climate.

More recent, unexpected eruptions occurred in 1996, including the Loki volcano near Reykjavik, Iceland, which spewed a geyser of ash, steam and gas nearly two miles into the atmosphere, and covered sixty miles of glacier with ash. What makes this an unusual eruption is the force that it took for this volcano to blast its way through 800 yards of ice. Since there were no populated areas in the vicinity of the volcano, no deaths occurred from this eruption; however, flooding was a great concern among those downstream from rivers fed by the glacier.

Late in 1996, just twenty miles south of Guatemala City, the Pacaya volcano erupted, as described by Reuters news service, with "rare strength."[4] No deaths were reported, even though rivers of lava and a thick column of ash spewed from the volcano. Within a few days of the Pacaya eruption, the Santiago volcano, just twelve miles southeast of Managua, Nicaragua, started rumbling for a day and then gushed gas, ash and lava; again, no one was close enough to be killed or injured. Experts said that the Santiago volcano erupted lava last in 1986 and expect that it will erupt again soon, perhaps with greater destruction this time.

Elsewhere in the world, a number of volcanoes are brewing. The most famous include the Mount Spurr and Redoubt volcanoes in Alaska, and the Kilauea and Mauna Loa volcanoes in Hawaii. What is dangerous and foolish is that the people living near these volcanoes have become complacent, as if these geologic behemoths could never be a hazard. These days, with the increased volcanic activity in various parts of the world, and the increased populations in the vicinity of these volcanoes, there is more of a danger than ever before.

Volcanoes & Airplanes

In the last decade, volcanic debris has become a growing concern to the aviation industry. The amount of debris that volcanoes blow into the air has a direct effect upon the performance and safety of aircraft. These days, it is such a concern that pilots are given instruction to re-route when they head toward skies known to contain an unusually high volume of volcanic ash. This may sound silly, but I assure you it is not.

Since the early 1980s, seven jumbo jets carrying hundreds of passengers lost power flying through clouds of volcanic ash. Now, in these cases, pilots were able to re-start the engines and land safely, so I suppose this would only make the news if one of these aircraft crashed; nonetheless, the damage to these aircraft was in the tens of millions of dollars. The world aviators have since been trying to track volcanic debris in the atmosphere because they fear that someday, a plane engine might not re-start, and the world will know how serious this new hazard is.[5]

Earthquakes

Most regions of the earth that are in the Ring of Fire are likely to experience earthquakes, but like volcanoes, geologic history is being re-written as the world is experiencing earthquakes in new places. What is an earthquake? Beneath our feet are vast regions of rock which exist as plates; these are called "tectonic" plates, and they are locked together with weak points between them, much like a chain link bracelet or necklace might be. Pressure, previously unreleased energy, is exerted on these plates as the magnum beneath them moves, and the energy is either released slowly, imperceptibly, or suddenly, in the form of earth movement, or an earthquake.

Faults, such as the famous San Andreas in California, are the weak points along two plates at which energy is likely to be released occasionally. The longer it takes for the release of this pent-up energy, the more energy builds up and when the resistance of the plates against each other gives in, an earthquake happens. The more energy that is released, the stronger the earthquake.

Measurements are taken of the intensity of an earthquake with a sensitive device called a Richter scale. This instrument measures from one to nine, nine being the worst and most destructive earthquake scientists think possible. Generally, in terms of structural damage and loss of life, any earthquake beyond a six on the Richter scale is fairly serious. And if the initial quake is not enough to shake people up, there are usually dozens of what are called "aftershocks," which are essentially the plates settling back onto each other; these vary in strength.

The Earthquake Quickening

You can find faults all over the earth. Of course, the Ring of Fire is where most of the faults are, but there are plenty of them in other regions, like Europe, the Middle East, the Balkans or the Mississippi Valley and the eastern part of the US. In the past, earthquakes in these regions have been considered fairly rare, but during the twentieth century, earthquakes are occurring in these regions more than ever, and at very high intensities.

Before the Richter scale came along in 1935, people could only report earthquakes which they felt, usually of a magnitude three or higher. The intensity of earthquakes could only be estimated by subjective observation, based on damage, injuries and death to people. Experts believe that the estimated higher magnitudes of earthquakes are probably accurate, because it is easier to estimate a more intense earthquake than a mild earthquake. Since 1935, the existence of seismic equipment and the number of people have both increased; it can be argued that the apparent increase in earthquakes stems from the increase in earthquake reportings.

However, there are those who indicate that for those earthquakes people feel, our historical record is probably a fair reflection of earthquake activity in populated regions. Therefore, when this data is compared to activity in the same regions during the last century, you can contend that there really have been more earthquakes in recent times.

For the strongest earthquakes, the record shows an average of one great earthquake per year with a reading of 8.0 or higher on the Richter scale. In 1992, however, there were two great earthquakes. At the minor earthquake level of three or less, there has been a substantial increase. In just the past decade, the number of minor earthquakes has tripled (about 5,000 in 1994), and there has been about a twenty percent increase in strong earthquakes at the strong earthquake level of 6.0 to 6.9.[6]

Whether you choose to accept or reject the trend of increased earthquakes, it is clear that the world has definitely been experiencing greater destruction to life and property than ever before in history because of earthquakes. This fact no one can deny.

Recent Earthquakes

The most recent earthquakes give us an idea about how destructive high intensity earthquakes can be, especially in areas of the world that are densely populated. Perhaps the most recent, highly publicized earthquakes were the Northridge earthquakes in northern Los Angeles, California. In January 1994, a series of earthquakes reached a six point seven on the Richter scale and had aftershocks ranging from four to five. Northridge was considered to be the worst earthquake in US history since the San Francisco quakes of 1906, which were about an eight point three magnitude.

Fifty-seven people died in the Northridge quakes and over 1,500 were seriously injured. More than 12,500 buildings and other structures were damaged, and nearly 50,000 people were left either homeless or with little or no water. Eleven major roads into downtown Los Angeles were closed, and several massive freeway overpasses collapsed. The only thing that saved the city of Los Angeles from more in terms of human costs was the fact that it occurred very early in the morning of a holiday and not during the day.[7]

Only five years earlier, in 1989, the Loma Prieta earthquake struck about sixty miles south of San Francisco. The Loma Prieta quake was a scary seven point one on the Richter scale, claimed the lives of sixty-two people and injured over 3,700. Both the Northridge and the Loma Prieta quakes were the result of energy released from one fault, the San Andreas. And Californians are told by seismologists and other earth scientists that neither of these quakes were the "big one." No, this is still somewhere in the near future, perhaps the next decade, and it is expected to exceed eight on the Richter scale.

One of our greatest challenges as far as earthquakes are concerned is their unpredictability. You do not know where they will happen (the point of origin, called the "epicenter"), when they will happen or how intense they will be. All you can really do is expect that they will happen, nearly anywhere there is a fault. Californians are more or less ready for earthquakes, and the structures in which they live and work are usually designed for earthquakes that reach the six or seven range on the Richter scale. But what about other parts of the US and the world that are not so prepared, mentally or structurally?

Earthquakes in Diverse Places

Biblical prophets predicted that in the last days of the world, we would see an increased number of earthquakes in unusual places. Nostradamus also foretold of earthquakes and other natural disasters at a time in the future when he believed the world would undergo a very dramatic transformation. Gordon Michael Scallion, who some have called a modern-day Nostradamus, has made similar predictions, putting emphasis on the chance that the world's coastlines would change. Scallion predicts that cities like New Orleans and Miami will simply be submerged in the ocean and no longer exist.

In many respects, we could be experiencing a precursor today of what is to come in the future. The central part of the US is woefully unprepared mentally and structurally for earthquakes, although faults run through the Mississippi Valley that were active nearly two centuries ago. Cities like St. Louis and Memphis are prime targets for earthquake disasters, and in recent years, small tremors have been felt by the populations in this part of the country. Seismologists warn that the worst is yet to come.

We have seen earthquakes occur in unexpected places throughout the world, creating chaos and destruction. One recent earthquake in October 1996 was in Cyprus, with an epicenter in the Mediterranean and a Richter scale reading of six point four. Many people in this area had never before experienced an earthquake and it was fortunate that there were no deaths or injuries.[8]

The fact is, the larger the populations of those regions hit by earthquakes, and the less prepared they are for them, the greater the likelihood of death and destruction. Other highly populated places on earth in which earthquakes are unusual, but have happened recently include Armenia, New Zealand, China, Italy, Egypt, India and Australia. No place is safe from the power of the earth.

Take Tokyo, Japan, for instance, that has too many people crammed into their city among buildings that are not safe from earthquakes. Even the soil upon which buildings are built there is soft and would "liquefy" during an unusually intense earthquake. Liquefaction is a seismologist's term to describe soil which literally shakes to the consistency of sand during an earthquake. As a result of this, you can imagine that it would only take a few seconds for buildings to actually shift off their foundations and collapse!

Anyone who has gone through an earthquake knows one thing for certain: you are very, very helpless. You have the sense of tremendous power under your feet over which you have absolutely no control. Most of us want to pretend we are the master of our environment, but we are completely vulnerable to an earthquake. The only thing we can do is to be mentally prepared for what will no doubt be a frightening experience at any level on the Richter scale.

Hurricanes & Tropical Storms

Since records have been kept of storms, no period of history has ever seen a greater number of hurricanes and tropical storms than in recent years. Each year for the past decade, the US has experienced at least one or two dangerous hurricanes, and many throughout the year that cause severe tropical storms even if they do not reach land. During 1995 and 1996, there were twenty hurricanes, the highest number recorded in two consecutive years. Pay attention, this is a definite trend.[9]

Why is this happening? In the past, out in the western Pacific Ocean, a regular, cyclical weather condition takes place called "El Niño." El Niño, which means "Christ child," is a warming of the waters in this part of the ocean, starting around Christmas and lasting perhaps twelve to eighteen months. Conversely, the normal cooling period is called "La Niña," or "the girl."

As a rule, whatever happens in the oceans also happens in the earth's atmosphere, as hot, humid air from the surface of the ocean rises to produce tropical storms. This hot, humid air rises tens of thousands of feet and becomes caught up in high altitude jet stream winds. These jet streams travel across North America and even affect the jet streams over Africa. North American jet streams normally produce a series of tropical storms and rainfall, a fairly common weather pattern. However, since the 1980s, and especially during the 1990s, this pattern has changed dramatically, perplexing scientists the world over.

What exactly have the results of this shift in the weather pattern been? For five years in a row, from 1990 to 1995, the world was affected by a persistent El Niño, the longest on record. This is believed to be responsible for everything from the monsoons to the tremendous hurricanes in the South Pacific, including those that hit Hawaii during 1995, and even severe droughts in Australia and Indonesia.

This El Niño brought torrential rains to North America, becoming indirectly responsible for the devastating flooding of the central Mississippi Valley in 1993, considered the worst in American history. This flood killed forty-eight people and created about twenty billion dollars in damage. This is only one example of the chaos that this long-lasting El Niño has created.[10]

US Storm of the Century

Record snowfalls throughout the United States can also be attributed to El Niño. In 1993, the record snowfall levels and severe weather was touted as the "storm of the century," as we had seen nothing like it before. But what we didn't know was that the "Blizzard of 1996" would top that so-called storm of the century. For example, the greatest snowfall during one storm fell on Philadelphia—a record thirty-one inches of snow, surpassing the 1993 record by twelve inches.

In another 1996 storm, LaGuardia International Airport in New York recorded twenty-four inches of snow, exceeding the normal level of twenty-three inches for the whole season! Pocahantas County, Virginia was buried under forty-eight inches of snow in one storm! That's four feet of snow in just a couple of days.[11]

The prodigious amount of snow eventually melted, creating the worst flooding from melting snow in the history of the Mid-Atlantic and Northeast states, and resulting in the deaths of 187 people and three billion dollars in property damage. The worst flooding in the history of the Northwest part of the US came during the 1996-97 winter season, killing thirty-six people and causing billions of dollars in damage in portions of Northern California, Nevada, Oregon, Idaho and Washington. Torrential rains flooded parts of Texas, Oklahoma, southeast Louisiana and southern Mississippi, causing six billion dollars in damages and claiming the lives of thirty-two people in the process. All of this severe weather and destruction is believed to be a result of the unusual El Niño cycle.[12]

Hurricane Andrew

Most hurricanes that hit the US are generated from the Atlantic Ocean off the coast of Africa, gaining strength as they head for the Caribbean. Eventually, they hit the small islands or move on to wreak havoc along a US coastline. Tropical storms graduate to hurricane status once they reach a certain magnitude of churning water, wind speed and ferocity. The most ferocious hurricanes can reach speeds in excess of 165 miles per hour, churning tons and tons of water and debris. Hurricanes are categorized in this way, according to their strength. A category one hurricane is dangerous, but not as dangerous as the most powerful hurricane, a category four.

The unusually warm waters of the North Atlantic are believed to be responsible for the unprecedented wave of high category hurricanes in recent years. One of the most devastating of these recent hurricanes was Hurricane Andrew in 1992, a category four hurricane. Sweeping into Dade County, Florida and narrowly missing Miami, Andrew left unbelievable destruction in its wake, finally petering out on the coast of Louisiana.

Immediately after the hurricane, more than 500,000 people were left without power, phones, water and adequate sewage facilities. As many as 250,000 people were left homeless, thirty-eight people were killed and the total cost of cleaning up Andrew's damage was twenty-seven billion dollars.[13]

Global Storms & Floods

The United States has not been the only country in the world to be graced by increased storm activity. In 1995, Europe experienced unprecedented torrential rains and flooding of a number of major continental European rivers. The Netherlands had the worst of it; parts of South Africa also had torrential rains, but in this case, the rains were welcome as these areas are usually quite arid. Nonetheless, this is another example of how the weather patterns of the world are changing.

Since 1993, torrential rains and flooding have occurred periodically in Bangladesh, northern India, Japan, Korea and Nepal. None of this extreme weather activity has been attributed to El Niño or the unusually warm Atlantic waters, but instead to volcanic debris and other atmospheric pollutants. In the past few years, earthquakes and volcanic rumblings are also believed to be the sources of two huge, destructive "tsunamis" (a series of very large waves) that hit the coast of Java in June 1994, and the coast of the Philippines in November 1994.[14] Storms, floods and tsunamis are hitting areas of the world where they not only have not experienced such things on a regular basis, but where they have plenty of problems already without the weather!

Droughts & Wildfires

Globally, temperatures have risen in the last few years. In fact, 1995 was the world's warmest year since records first were kept in 1856. According to the NASA Goddard Institute for Space Studies in New York, the average temperature was 59.7 degrees Fahrenheit. While this may not seem that astounding, consider that the short period between 1990 and 1995 beat out the decade of the 1980s, which was previously the warmest decade to date. This is slightly mysterious to scientists.

Director James Hansen of the Goddard Institute commented that "the 1995 figure was all the more remarkable...because it was established at a time when two natural warming influences were neutralized: the solar energy cycle was at a low ebb; and the warming effect of El Niño...was offset by a turn to cooler-than-normal conditions in the tropical Pacific later in the year."[15]

What does this change in temperature mean for us? In the United States, we have seen an increase in severe droughts and heat waves. The severe drought of fall 1995 to summer 1996 in the agricultural region of the Southern Plains resulted in four billion dollars in crop damage. The Southeastern states were devastated by a drought in summer 1993, producing one billion dollars in damage. But by far the worst drought in the last decade was in 1988, when an estimated 10,000 people died from heat stress, and about forty billion dollars of damages was incurred.

It is disturbing to see extreme weather records on the rise, especially when there is neither any clear reason that anyone can agree upon, nor anything that anyone can do. In winter, temperatures have been colder than ever and the summer has brought unbearably high heat. In already parched areas of the earth, heat followed by drought only made the situation worse for the people living there. For some people, drought hit them unexpectedly.

Areas of unusual drought include large portions of Brazil, southern Paraguay and northeastern Argentina, where precipitation was down seventy-five percent from the normal levels during 1996. During 1995, central England, a country known for its refreshing rains, had a heat wave during July and August with the highest temperatures recorded since 1659. Scotland and Wales were also bent under record-breaking heat and drought, unprecedented since 1766. Russia and central Asia suffered their hottest year ever in 1995. From fall 1994 to summer 1995, Tunisia, Algeria, southern France and Spain had record drought conditions. It seems that no place is safe from the whims of heat and drought.[16]

Raging Blazes

Obviously, a drought severely cripples the agricultural potential of the affected area. Added to this, abnormal temperatures, increased dryness and gusty winds can result in an increased vulnerability to fires. Not surprisingly then, areas of the world stricken by drought have also been besieged by a record number of fires. In fact, there has been a distinct rise in brush fires in recent years, especially in Australia, Argentina and Southern California. During 1996, unusually dry conditions spurred some of the most devastating wildfires in decades in the US; more than a dozen major fires destroyed hundreds of thousands of acres in Arizona, Colorado, Montana, Nevada, Utah, Wyoming and Idaho.

It seems that Southern California cannot get a break when it comes to weather and natural disasters. Fires have burned consistently in this area in the past, always leaving thousands of acres blackened. The fires of 1993 were even worse because they burned so close to residents of the Los Angeles basin. In ten days during October 1993, over 300 square miles and 1,000 structures were destroyed by fires. Experts predict that the higher temperatures, increased dryness and strong Santa Ana winds will only re-ignite dangerous fires, probably every summer from now on.[17]

Tornadoes

Tornadoes have also followed the pattern of the Quickening, increasing in intensity and frequency, and occurring in states that don't usually see such weather anomalies; for instance, tornadoes hit California, Delaware, Louisiana, Maryland, Colorado, New York and Ohio. As for those states in the so-called "Tornado Alley," including Texas, Kansas, Missouri and Oklahoma, increased tornado activity has broken all previous records. The devastation and chaos created in these areas was more than anyone could have been prepared for.

What is a tornado? All of us have heard tornadoes called "twisters," and the reason is that they look like funnels and consist of cyclonic winds of very high speeds, rotating around a low pressure center. Tornadoes in the south spin clockwise, while those in the northern states spin counter-clockwise. The funnel at its broadest point can be between 100 feet to a mile and a half wide.

Most smaller tornadoes last only a few minutes, reaching wind speeds of about 100 miles per hour, and traveling less than a mile before dissipating. However, that doesn't necessarily mean their damage is any more welcome than a larger tornado that can last hours, reaching speeds of 260 miles per hour, and travel over 200 miles.

Many of us who saw the movie *Twister* heard in the course of the tornado chasers conversation the terms F4 and F5. Tornadoes are given a rating based on their strength and potential destructiveness, just like earthquakes and hurricanes. The classification ranges from F0, a "light" 72 mile per hour tornado, to the F5, packing winds of 260 miles per hour or better—what was called in *Twister*, "the hand of God."

Truthfully, though, tornadoes do not need to reach such heights to wreak havoc. In the last thirty years, the average number of tornadoes has been about 800 per year; that changed by 1992, when the number went up to 1,300 per year. Apparently, an increased number of thunderstorms over North America, brought on by El Niño, can claim partial responsibility for the higher numbers and intensity in tornadoes lately. Just one more indication that the earth changes are happening all around us.[18]

Why the Dramatic Weather Changes?

Why is the world having to endure such extreme changes in the weather? Volcanoes and air pollution and their contribution to the greenhouse effect is one explanation, and holes in the ozone is another. Experts have suggested that an unusual amount of activity on the sun, such as solar flares and pulsars, may have something to do with it as well. And although we do not know why El Niño has been acting differently, or why there are unusually warm waters in various parts of the ocean, something is unquestionably going on, something we have to call the Quickening.

Astronomical Hazards

All manner of moving bodies exist in our universe. Our planet earth is constantly spinning and moving, as are other planets in the solar system. The sun and moon are planets that are important to the earth because of their effect on the atmosphere and all life forms that call the earth their home. These two moving bodies are not the only things to affect the earth, however; in the past, and undoubtedly in the near future, comets, asteroids and meteors have and will continue to play a significant role in our changing world.

Slight differences do exist between comets, asteroids and meteors. Comets are typically huge balls, several miles across, consisting of various types of ice and rock debris. Asteroids can be just a few miles or dozens of miles across, and are usually made up of different types of rock and metallic elements. Meteors are normally much smaller than both comets and asteroids, sometimes only a few feet wide, and consist mostly of rock or metallic elements.

Many astronomers believe that some time in the past, comets have collided with our earth, contributing water to the earth's oceans, and leaving distinct marks upon the planet called "craters." Funny thing is, craters are all around us, but we don't think of them in that way; most of us probably don't even think of how the earth became the way it is!

There are some serious craters in our world. In Bavaria, the Ries crater, fifteen miles in diameter, is believed to be the result of a comet or meteor. In Yucatan, Mexico, a giant, ancient crater called the Chicxulub crater is 112 *miles* in diameter, and believed to have been formed by the impact of a large asteroid millions of years ago. Can you imagine the effect that landing would have had on modern-day Mexico? In northern Arizona, a nickel-iron meteor produced a crater about 4,000 feet in diameter and 600 feet deep.

What about objects that actually hit the earth recently? On October 9, 1992, a twenty-seven pound, stony meteor streaked across the sky from Kentucky and punched a hole through the end of a parked car in Peekskill, New York. A little farther back in time, February 12, 1947, chunks of a thirty-three foot wide meteor struck the earth in the Sikhote-Alin Mountains of eastern Siberia. It originally weighed about 150 tons, but broke up in the earth's atmosphere, producing over 100 little craters as small as a yard in diameter, to one as large as eighty-seven feet wide.[19]

These are just a few examples of rocks, metallic boulders and ice that have fallen to the earth. Our solar system is constantly invaded by all sorts of debris. Over 7,000 asteroids have been identified, and several hundred more are discovered each year. It must be the idea that something large could come out of space, crash through the earth's atmosphere and land in a populated area that excites people. The potential for destruction captures our imagination.

Consider that it would only take a relatively small asteroid, say, six miles wide, to hit the earth and affect the entire ecosystem. In the immediate vicinity of the impact, tremendous shock waves of heat and fire would be generated, combined with earthquakes, hurricane winds and trillions of tons of debris thrown everywhere. A darkness would shroud the earth and the temperatures would drop globally for months. All this from a "small" chunk of rock!

Lately, there has been a great deal of excitement over the now famous Hale-Bopp comet, which came into view in July 1995. Speculation ran wild over whether this might be the one to hit the earth. In the meantime, of course, it was determined that Hale-Bopp was not going to cross earth's orbit or make a threat. As far as we know, there are no immediate threats to the earth at this time, but scientists and astronomers do not rule out the possibility. In fact, many agree that something from space could suddenly enter our solar system and set itself on a collision course with the earth. We will see; maybe we will be lucky.

Global Preparedness

Finding a way to prepare for the Quickening earth changes appears to be one of the greatest challenges in our world today. What else could be so unpredictable, yet so easily ignored? To some extent, we can prepare for earthquakes, provided they are not too high on the Richter scale. We can build specially reinforced buildings and educate people about what to do in the event of an earthquake, such as diving for cover under a solid piece of furniture, or standing in the threshold of a doorway. For areas vulnerable to hurricanes, we can build houses which are likely to withstand most such storms, and devise evacuation routes. For areas prone to flooding, you can move or build your house on stilts like they do in the swamplands of Louisiana. For tornadoes, the best advice seems to be not to live in a trailer park!

In other words, for most natural disasters, we can take some common sense, practical measures to ensure our safety. Unfortunately, as with so many

301

things in our world, people are stubborn and wishful, and sometimes not very realistic. Rather than move from an area known for flooding, or near a volcano, they would rather pretend the threat doesn't exist. Then they lament when everything they own is destroyed or a loved one dies.

On the other hand, some of us are willing to take our chances, come what may. We realize that our circumstances, economically or otherwise, make it impossible to move, or to take certain precautions. In any event, we cannot run away from the planet we are standing on, a world which is quickly becoming an increasingly dangerous place to live.

A Final Word

What does the future hold for us, the inhabitants of this blue marble called earth? You can see by now that the world has been undergoing a Quickening of all aspects in the last 100 years, and particularly the last thirty. Some parts of the Quickening are positive, many others are not. For example, on the positive side, we can see advantages of a world with a somewhat diminished threat of Communism. In this respect, the disunity of the former Soviet Union is a good thing. To a greater extent, more than at any time in human history, the people of the world have attained a little more freedom.

Generally, we can consider the advances in technology to be a positive part of the Quickening. We are able to communicate more efficiently, more freely. We can share our knowledge almost instantly, and relate with others no matter what part of the world they live in, even if we don't speak their language. Economically, our world has benefited from the growing political freedom and technology. Globally, more people than ever before are likely to benefit from these developments. For these positive trends in the Quickening, we should be grateful.

The Law of Nature

Unfortunately, as much as we would like to think otherwise, the many challenges of our world today can actually nullify the positive aspects. The greatest and most immediate concerns involve the growing likelihood of sudden, unpredictable natural disasters as well as pandemics of incurable diseases. No one can predict a highly volatile volcanic eruption or an extremely violent earthquake, not any more than anyone can predict the time and place of an outbreak of a new Ebola virus or even a new strain of HIV.

Apart from the obvious destruction from a volcanic eruption or a major earthquake, there are less blatant, but equally present problems. Any such natural disaster in key cities of the world, such as Tokyo or Los Angeles, will have repercussions on the financial stability of the whole world; after all, these cities are critical centers of global finance. What would happen to computer systems and files if a major disaster were to strike? Are the tall buildings built in the last twenty or thirty years able to withstand a major quake? What if a strain of virus or bacteria strikes a major city and there simply isn't a cure to handle it?

Threats from nature will persist, and may even become more serious in the years ahead if current trends are any indication. As for the environment, our natural habitat, upon which we depend for our survival, is being severely abused merely to propagate the existence of more and more people, which it is not capable of supporting anyway. What of the fact that fresh water becomes more scarce daily? You cannot ignore this problem.

The most important resource in terms of providing energy to run our world is petroleum. For now, we have plenty, but in a few decades, perhaps less, we will have a problem with this as well. We take for granted how easy it is to fill our car up at the local gas station, but what if there was nothing left to fill the car up with? The very notion that water and petroleum could last indefinitely is ludicrous, but most people do not give it a second thought. Do we honestly think that our children's children will have all that we now have? Not likely, and I'm not just talking about water and gas either.

Growing Pains

Food will eventually become a scarce commodity, a distinct possibility in the next twenty years even. Sounds hard to believe now, especially when you go to the grocery stores and the shelves are lined to capacity, but it is not inconceivable. There are just too many people, and we will simply begin to run out of food to feed them all. Most people do not realize that even in America, the supermarkets we depend upon for our food are literally only *days* from empty shelves. It would take less than a month for most cities to be completely without food.

Any natural disaster, which could hit any region of the world at any time, would render a city helpless, isolated even, if the roads were impassable, for instance. Even America, accustomed as its people are to having everything all the time, could quickly become a public war zone should it be a question of acquiring food.

Personal & Social Responsibility

The world may enjoy more freedom than in the past, but at what price? For with more freedom comes the need for greater responsibility from people. The trouble is that increased political and social freedom has had a degenerative effect on the moral fiber of humanity. Increased liberal legislation and public attitude in the last thirty years has undermined Judeo-Christian values and moral obligation. Traditions have been challenged and lost, replaced by aberrant behavior and conduct, e.g., drug abuse, sexual promiscuity, and abusiveness toward others. Laws reflect the acceptance of turning away from tradition; divorce is easier, abortions are easier, homosexual activity is practically sanctioned and the mention of God or prayer has been outlawed in public schools. Secular humanism is the trend of the Quickening, but this has had the backlash of creating a narcissistic population bent on having its own way.

Somehow we have forgotten how to care about others outside of our own immediate circle, or at least how to be decent to them. People we associate with on a daily basis, in business, at the store, even on the street, must be able to give us something of value, or they are of no use to us. Even in our personal relations, there is a underlying transience and cynicism. Marriage is no longer something you need to commit to forever in this throw-away society since you can always find someone new, someone better.

We have children we do not know how or have the time to raise, so we send them to daycare or some other substitute. It amazes me when people say the choice not to have children is selfish or self-centered.

What is selfish is to have children without thinking before having them, without looking more than a few days ahead. If more people thought about their actions and perhaps made a choice not to have children, or to get their lives straightened out beforehand so these children could get the attention they require, maybe we could expect the future to be brighter.

Attitude Adjustment

One of the hardest things to ask people, if not *the* hardest, is to change. But if we care at all about the world around us, we have to take a serious look at the way we live. We have to learn some self-discipline, we have to learn to give a little more. One way of preserving some kind of decent future would be to limit the number of children we bring into the world; there are *too many people already!* As trends of the Quickening continue unaltered, ours is not really a world to bring children into anyway.

Another thing that humans could learn is to pay more attention to the needs of others; we have grown far too selfish and cold-hearted toward others. I don't mean the "touchy-feely, brotherly love" of New Age thinking. I speak of common decency, of civility, and both are in diminishing supply these days.

Those of us who are financially comfortable should be careful not to let our avarice overwhelm us. Usually, this means we are committed to material gain and less committed to the families we have. This means our priorities can be gravely confused, and it also affects the way we treat others. Discipline in other areas of life, such as the preoccupation with drugs, poor eating habits and other destructive behavior would help greatly.

And if America is to continue to be a superpower, we as individuals must learn to save more of our earnings. Someday, perhaps America will no longer be a debtor nation. It could help if we learned to do with less, instead of persisting in our unending consumer-minded mentality of use once and throw away forever. We could learn to participate in matters that do indeed affect our existence on this planet, like water conservation, rather than just thinking that if it doesn't affect us as individuals, we shouldn't bother.

The fact is, to continue to live as we do will yield people—our children and their children—who will not know how to adequately take care of themselves, to take care of each other and to care for the world upon which they must depend for resources. Our standard of living will decline, the world will become increasingly unstable and our very existence as a species will be in great jeopardy.

Hope for the World

Of course, man can take responsibility for some things, but certain parts of the world are beyond repair and we will probably not be able to change them. For example, how could we hope to reconcile ethnic hatred that has existed for centuries between certain peoples? How can we resolve the disparity between the rich and the poor? How do we reduce the likelihood that a nuclear war could occur in any number of "hot spots" throughout the world? We cannot undo the severe environmental destruction we brought on by the use of toxic chemicals and automobiles and their emissions. By forging ahead, by simply trying to survive, man has created many problems related to the way in which we co-exist with nature that we cannot undo.

My hope is that we as humans will come to our senses. Despite the things we cannot change, I hope that we will make some effort to make changes on an individual level. Where is the Quickening taking us? Will there be a global government with a "benevolent" dictator, overseeing global law, global police and a global judiciary in an attempt to make the world cleaner, peaceful and prosperous? If that is what it takes to achieve these ends, so be it. Right now, the world is only getting progressively more chaotic and dangerous.

At the very least, let us all hope and try to change what we can. We are at a crossroads in human history, and it is clear that unless we take some drastic measures to improve our plight, the road less traveled will not necessarily be the brightest one. Just wanting to believe that everything is "not really that bad" is not the solution. What we do in the Quickening of today will determine tomorrow's world.

References

CHAPTER ONE: TECHNOLOGY

1. Feis, Herbert. *The Atomic Bomb and the End of World War II*, 1966.

2. Bern, Daniel P., "Under Construction: Information Superhighway," *Home Office Computing*, August 1993, p. 36.

3. Ibid.

4. Naisbitt, John. *Megatrends 2000*, Avon Books, 1990, pp. 5-6.

5. Autonoff, Michael, "Living in a Virtual World," *Popular Science*, June 1993, pp. 85-86.

6. Roslin Institute, "Scientists at the Roslin Institute Publish Scientific Breakthrough," press release, February 25, 1997; CNN, "Scientists Defend Cloning of Sheep," February 25, 1997.

CHAPTER TWO: ECONOMY

1.   Corey, Lewis. *The House of Morgan,* G. Howard West, 1930, pp. 176-77.

2.   Frum, David, "Bearing Down of Milken," *National Review,* March 19, 1990.

3.   *Fortune Magazine,* "A New Revolution in the US Class Structure and Labor Force," April, 1985.

4.   *Los Angeles Times,* "How Milken Machine Financed Companies, Takeover Raids," March 30, 1989.

5.   Naisbitt, John. *Global Paradox,* Avon Books, 1990.

6.   Sheridan, John H., "Motorola's Team Bandit," *Industry Week,* December 5, 1988.

7.   Naisbitt, John. *Global Paradox,* Avon Books, 1990.

8.   "The Opening of Asia," *The Economist,* November 12, 1994, p. 23.

9.   Ibid.

CHAPTER THREE: GOVERNMENT

1.   from *McAlvaney Intelligence Advisor,* January 1994, p. 1.

2.   Kemp, Jack, *National Review,* August 15, 1994, p. 6.

3.   Jeffrey, Grant. *Final Warning,* Harvest House, 1996, pp. 171-72.

4.   Hawkins, William, "GATT May Be More Trouble Than Treaty," *Insights On News*, August 22, 1994, p. 20.

5.   Caufield, Catherine. *Masters of Illusion: The World Bank and the Poverty of Nations*, Holt/Wood, 1997.

6.   Driscoll, David D., "The IMF and the World Bank: How Do They Differ?" External Relations, IMF report, 1996, pp. 1-9.

7.   Knoke, William. *Bold New World*, Kodansha International, 1996, pp. 274-78.

8.   Ghali, Boutros-Boutros, "An Agenda For Peace," United Nations Report, 1992.

CHAPTER FOUR: SOCIETY

1.   *Washington Post*, "TV Opens Up Remote Villager's World," March 10, 1988.

2.   International Civil Aviation Organization, Montreal, Canada.

3.   *International Management*, February, 1988, p. 59.

4.   *U.S. News & World Report*, February, 1985, p. 49.

5.   Ibid.

6.   Demographics & Family Composition: Youth Indicators report, 1993.

7.   Ibid.

8.   Ibid.

9.   The National College Board.

10.   Youth Development Information Center.

11.   March of Dimes, "Teenage Pregnancy: Facts You Should Know," May 19, 1994.

12.   Dr. Neil Rosenberg, Medical Director, International Institute of Inhalant Abuse.

13.   University of Michigan Survey Research Center.

14.   US Department of Justice, "Prison and Jail Inmates, 1995 Statistics Bulletin," August 1996.

15.   Senator Joseph Biden, Jr., "Kids and Guns," press release, June 10, 1996.

16.   Ibid.

17.   D.N. Jones. *Understanding Child Abuse*, Macmillan, 1987.

18.   UNICEF, "UNICEF Proposals to Curb Ongoing Social Crisis in Eastern Europe," press release, November 14, 1995.

19.   *The Irish Times*, "Irish Abortion Rate is now 9% of Live Births," April 23, 1996.

20.   *U.S. News & World Report*, "I'm Okay, You're Not: Why Americans Think Their Lives Are Good, But The Nation Is In Peril," Dec. 16, 1996.

21.   Ibid.

22.   *Christian Science Monitor*, "The Rise of the Militias," May 1995.

23.   Interview with Art Bell, May 23, 1996.

24.   Mitchell, Chris, Christian Broadcasting News, March 6, 1996.

25. Lindsey, Hal. *The Final Battle*, Western Front Publishing, 1995, p. 38.

26. Ibid., pp. 10-11.

27. Brown, Lester, WorldWatch, "The State of the World," 1996.

28. US Census Bureau, 1996.

29. United Nations, *World Population Prospects: The 1992 Revision*.

30. based on World Health Organization Report, 1995.

31. Jeffrey, Grant, *Final Warning*, Harvest House, 1996, p. 157.

32. *Newsweek*, "A World Awash in Refugees," December 23, 1989, pp. 17-19.

33. *Christian Science Monitor*, "Migration to US Expected To Break Record in '90s," November 1991, p. 8.

34. *Los Angeles Times*, "The Labor Brokers: For A Price, There's A Job Abroad—Maybe," October 1, 1991, p. H-5.

CHAPTER FIVE: RELIGION & SPIRITUALITY

1. Monroe, Charles. *World Religions*, Prometheus Books, 1995, p. 287.

2. Ibid., p. 108.

3. Lindsey, Hal. *The Final Battle*, Western Front Publishing, 1995, p. 11.

4. Martin, Malachi. *The Keys of This Blood*, Harper Collins, p. 632.

5. Stopler, Pinchad. Union of Orthodox Jewish Congregations.

6. survey data derived from sociologist Jeffrey Hayden, 1982.

7. Monroe, Charles. *World Religions*, Prometheus Books, 1995, p. 108.

8. Cumby, Constance. *The Hidden Dangers of the Rainbow: The New Age Movement and Our Coming Age of Barbarism*, Huntington House, 1983, p. 43.

9. Peale, Norman Vincent. *Positive Imaging*, Fawcett-Crest, 1982, p. 1.

10. Galyean, Beverly, "Guided Imagery in Education," *Journal of Humanistic Psychology*, Fall 1981, p. 58, 61.

11. Monroe, Charles. *World Religions*, Prometheus Books, 1995, p. 108.

12. Schuller, Robert. "Possibility Thinking: Goals," Amway corporation audio tape.

13. Hill, Napoleon. *Think and Grow Rich,* Fawcett-Crest, 1979, pp. 215-220.

14. Peale, Norman Vincent. *Positive Imaging*, Fawcett-Crest, 1982, p. 77.

15. Jastrow, Robert, "The Case For UFOs," *Science Digest*, Nov/Dec 1980, pp. 83-85.

16. Gross, Martin. *The Psychological Society*, Random House, 1978, pp. 43-44.

17. MUFON, "A Short Introduction to Ufology," brief, 1996.

18. from Jeffrey, Kent, "Time for the Truth About Roswell," International Roswell Initiative, 1996.

19. CSICOP, "'Alien Autopsy' Film a Hoax Concludes Scientific Organization," report, August 25, 1995.

20. as quoted in Lindsey, Hal. *The Final Battle*, Western Front Publishing, 1995.

21. Berkeley Psychic Institute, "Introductory Document," 1996.

22. Constantine, Alex. *Virtual Government: CIA Mind Control Operations In America.*

23. Vickers, Roderic, "The Mostly Frequently Asked Questions About Psychic Ability," Star Concepts, Ltd., 1995.

24. *The Movement Newspaper*, January 1983.

25. *The Bible*, NIV version, 2 Thessalonians 2:11; Revelation 13:3, 4, 7, 8.

CHAPTER SIX: ENVIRONMENT

1. Toffler, Alvin. *PowerShift*, Bantam, 1990, pp. 370-371.

2. Knoke, William. *Bold New World*, Kodansha International, 1996, pp. 104-105.

3. World Resources Institute, "New Report Documents World Urbanization Trends and Impacts," press release, April 18, 1996.

4.   AQMD, "Health Effects of Southland Smog," report, July 1, 1996.

5.   O'Leary, Philip, Walsh, Patrick, *Waste Age,* Solid Hazardous Waste Education Center, University of Washington, January 1991, March 1992.

6.   Knoke, William. *Bold New World*, Kodansha International, 1996, p. 105.

7.   O'Leary, Philip, Walsh, Patrick, *Waste Age,* Solid Hazardous Waste Education Center, University of Washington, January 1991, March 1992.

8.   The Green Group. *101 Ways To Save Money & Save Our Planet*, Paper Chase Press, 1992, p. 11.

9.   Agency For Toxic Substances & Disease Registry, 1996 report.

10.   Environmental Protection Agency, "Questions & Answers About Lead & Submersible Well Pumps," report, April, 1994.

11.   Ronning, Audrey, "The Three Gorges Controversy," *Earth Times*, 1997.

12.   McRae, Hamish. *The World In 2020*, Harvard Business School Press, 1994, pp. 124-125.

13.   Ibid.

14.   Ibid.

15.   British Petroleum, "Statistical Review of World Energy," report, 1987.

16.   World Resources Institute, "New Report Documents World Urbanization Trends and Impacts," press release, April 18, 1996.

17. United Nations Environmental Programme (UNEP), "Environmental Effects of Ozone Depletion," report, November, 1991.

18. Knoke, William. *Bold New World*, Kodansha International, 1996, p. 108.

19. UNEP, "Scientific Assessment of Ozone Depletion, 1994, Executive Summary," August, 1994.

20. Ibid.

21. Nuclear Energy Agency, "Chernobyl Ten Years On: Radiological and Health Impact," report, November 1995.

CHAPTER SEVEN: DISEASE & FAMINE

1. Ziegler, P. *The Black Death*, Penguin, 1969.

2. Garrett, Laurie. *The Coming Plague*, Penguin, 1995, p. 36.

3. Ryan, Frank. *Virus X: Tracking the Killer Plagues*, Little, Brown, 1996, p. 6.

4. Jeffrey, Grant, *Final Warning*, Harvest House, 1996, p. 155.

5. Gear, J.S.S., "Outbreak of Marburg Virus Disease in Johannesburg," *British Medical Journal*, pp. 489-93.

6. RM Krause, in the foreword to Morse, S.S. *Emerging Viruses*.

7. Crosby, A.W., "The Influenza Pandemic of 1918," in Osborn, J.E., ed. *Influenza In America, 1918-1976*, Prodist, pp. 5-13.

8.   DeLuc, J.W., et al, *Journal of Infectious Diseases*, 162, 1990, pp. 1182-84.

9.   DeLuc, J.W., et al, *Annual Review of Public Health*, 13, 1992, pp. 79-98.

10.   Centers for Disease Control.

11.   Mertens, T.E., et al, *AIDS 1995*, 9, supplement A, pp. 5259-72; Piot, P., et al, "AIDS: An International Perpective," *Science*, 239, 1988, pp. 573-79.

12.   Reuters, "AIDS report," November 29, 1996.

13.   Ryan, Frank. *Virus X: Tracking the Killer Plagues*, Little, Brown, 1996, pp. 125-27.

14.   Garrett, Laurie. *The Coming Plague*, Penguin, 1995, pp. 264-67.

15.   Abramowicz, Mark for Microsoft Encarta 1994; American Liver Foundation, "Viral Hepatitis: Everybody's Problem?" 1995.

16.   Cole, Leonard, "The Specter of Biological Weapons," *Scientific American*, December, 1996, vol.275, no.6, pp. 60-65.

17.   Ibid.

18.   US Department of Defense, "Comprehensive Clinical Evaluation Program for Gulf War Veterans," report, August, 1995.

19.   World Resources Institute, "New Report Documents World Urbanization Trends and Impacts," press release, April 18, 1996.

20.   Pearce, Fred. *The Dammed: Rivers, Dams and the Coming World Water Crises*, The Bodley Head, 1992.

21.   CNN, "Obesity Rising in US Children," October 2, 1995.

22.   World Bank, "Rural Development" report, 1997.

23.   Freedom From Hunger, "Hunger Myths & Realities" report, 1997.

24.   CNN, "Summit Seeks World Without Hunger," November 11, 1996.

CHAPTER EIGHT: EARTH CHANGES

1.   *Los Angeles Herald Examiner*, May 22, 1984.

2.   Van Effen, Richard, "An Old Volcano Awakens on Montserrat," private source.

3.   US Geological Survey, "Cascade Volcanoes," file 94-585, 1997.

4.   Reuters, October 11, 1996.

5.   USGS, "Earthquakes," general interest publication, 1996.

6.   Ibid.; personal interview, Glen Reagor, USGS.

7.   USGS, National Earthquake Information Center, report, 1996.

8.   Advanced Geologic Exploration/Seismo Watch, Brief Earthquake Alert Bulletin, No. 96-267.

9.   National Weather Service, "Monthly Tropical Weather Summary," November 29, 1996.

10.   National Climatic Data Center, "Billion Dollar US Weather Disasters, 1980-1997," January 27, 1997.

11. Northeast Regional Climate Center, "Northeast Sets Snowfall Records As Blizzard of 1996 Dissipates," December, 1996.

12. National Climatic Data Center, "Billion Dollar US Weather Disasters, 1980-1997," January 27, 1997.

13. EQE, "Hurricane Andrew and Iniki 1992," Summary Report, 1992.

14. from "Tsunami! WWW Information Resource," January 1997.

15. *New York Times,* "Global Warming," January 4, 1996.

16. World Meteorological Organization, "Status of the Global Climate in 1995," Document 838.

17. EQE International, "The Southern California Wildfires of 1993," report, 1997.

18. *Weatherwise,* "Tornadoes Hit New Heights," February 1993, p. 29.

19. Roanoke Valley Governor's School for Science and Technology, "Asteroids: An Introduction and Study," November 6, 1995.

Acknowledgments

Writing a book is no easy task, and it takes a lot of time away from others and other things. I wish to thank my wife, Ramona for her patience and support in this and all my life's endeavors.

I would like to thank Alan Corbeth, president of Chancellor Broadcasting, whose vision and confidence has given me the opportunity to speak my mind on the airwaves.

Special thanks go to my editor, Jennifer Osborn, who has been insightful and knowledgeable during the writing of this book.

I wish to thank the Paper Chase Press staff, including editors Patricia Friedmann, Broeck Oder, Perry Morgan and Loren Werner, as well as the research assistants and other able members who worked hard and frenetically. I also want to thank my publisher, Werner Riefling, who took on this project with characteristic enthusiasm and energy.

Index

About the Author

Art Bell is America's voice in the night. With more than 20 million people listening to his radio shows, *Coast to Coast AM* and *Dreamland*, Art covers topics far and wide, from gun control to near death experiences, from politics to UFOs—nothing is beyond Art's realm. His first book, *The Art of Talk* (Paper Chase Press, 1995), is an autobiography. He lives in Pahrump, Nevada with his wife, Ramona, and three cats.

Art Bell is also the author of his autobiography, *The Art of Talk*.

For the first time, you can learn about the man behind the microphone. *The Art of Talk* reveals a life which is as diverse and interesting as his radio programs. With his dry humor and sensitivity, Art shares everything from where he grew up, his turbulent family life, his marriages, and how he got into radio, to the behind-the-scenes story of how his popular radio programs got started and have continued to succeed.

The Art of Talk is available as a hardcover book and as an audiobook, based on the book and performed by Art Bell.

The Art of Talk
Hardcover, color photos, 180 pages
$24.95 + $5.00 S&H
The Art of Talk audiobook
3 Cassettes, approx. 4 hrs., 30 mins.
$23.95 + $5.00 S&H

To order or to ask for <u>free</u> PAPER CHASE PRESS catalog, call: **1-800/864-7991**, or fill out form:

ORDER FORM

Please send me ___copy(ies) of The Art of Talk, book

Please send me ___copy(ies) of The Art of Talk, audiobook

NAME: _____

ADDRESS: _____

_____

_____

SIGNATURE (for credit card purchases)

Please indicate credit card: VISA ☐ MC ☐

Credit card #: _____   Expires: _____

Fill out form and send check or money order in U.S. funds only. All payments made to: PAPER CHASE PRESS. Send to: PAPER CHASE PRESS, 5721 Magazine St., Suite 152, New Orleans LA 70115. Add $5.00 S&H for each book ordered in the U.S. (call for outside of U.S.). Allow up to 4 weeks for delivery.